scc

God and the Founders

Madison, Washington, and Jefferson

Did the Founding Fathers intend to build a "wall of separation" between church and state? Are public displays of the Ten Commandments or the phrase "under God" in the Pledge of Allegiance consistent with the Founders' understandings of religious freedom? In *God and the Founders*, Dr. Vincent Phillip Muñoz answers these questions by providing new, comprehensive interpretations of James Madison, George Washington, and Thomas Jefferson. By analyzing Madison's, Washington's, and Jefferson's public documents, private writings, and political actions, Muñoz explains the Founders' competing church-state political philosophies. Muñoz explores how Madison, Washington, and Jefferson agreed and disagreed by showing how their different principles of religious freedom would decide the Supreme Court's most important First Amendment religion cases. *God and the Founders* answers the question, "What would the Founders do?" for the most pressing church-state issues of our time, including prayer in public schools, government support of religion, and legal burdens on individuals' religious consciences.

Dr. Vincent Phillip Muñoz is the Tocqueville Associate Professor of Religion and Public Life in the Department of Political Science at the University of Notre Dame. He has held appointments at Princeton University, Tufts University, Seattle University School of Law, and North Carolina State University.

God and the Founders

Madison, Washington, and Jefferson

VINCENT PHILLIP MUÑOZ

University of Notre Dame

CAMBRIDGE
UNIVERSITY PRESS

CAMBRIDGE UNIVERSITY PRESS
Cambridge, New York, Melbourne, Madrid, Cape Town, Singapore, São Paulo, Delhi

Cambridge University Press
32 Avenue of the Americas, New York, NY 10013-2473, USA

www.cambridge.org
Information on this title: www.cambridge.org/9780521735797

First published 2009

Printed in the United States of America

A catalog record for this publication is available from the British Library.

Library of Congress Cataloging in Publication Data

Muñoz, Vincent Phillip.
God and the founders : Madison, Washington, and Jefferson / Vincent Phillip Muñoz.
  p. cm.
Includes bibliographical references and index.
ISBN 978-0-521-51515-3 (hardback) – ISBN 978-0-521-73579-7 (pbk.)
1. Church and state – United States – History – 18th century. 2. Christianity and politics –
United States – History – 18th century. 3. Founding Fathers of the United States – Religious life.
4. Constitutional history – United States. 5. United States – Religion – To 1800. I. Title.
BR516.M86 2009
322'.10973–dc22   2008044199

ISBN 978-0-521-51515-3 hardback
ISBN 978-0-521-73579-7 paperback

For my parents
Vicente Serapio Muñoz, Jr., and
Mary Emma Muñoz

I must admit moreover that it may not be easy, in every possible case, to trace the line of separation between the rights of religion and the Civil authority with such distinctness as to avoid collisions & doubts on unessential points.

James Madison to Rev. Jasper Adams, 1833

Contents

Acknowledgments

I have been blessed by the assistance of many friends while completing this book. The initial drafts of Chapters 1 and 2 were written while I was a student at The Claremont Graduate School. An aspiring scholar could not have asked for a better or more supportive assembly of mentors than I had at Claremont. Charles R. Kesler, my dissertation chairman, is a model of a gentleman scholar. Mark Blitz contributed his reflective insight and thoughtful criticisms while contributing countless hours toward the improvement of my work. Ralph Rossum and Michael Uhlmann imparted their extensive knowledge of the American Constitution, not to mention gentle guidance and professional excellence. I am fortunate to be one of the last undergraduates to have studied with Harry V. Jaffa, who also was generous enough to read a part of an early version of the present manuscript.

Several friends and colleagues commented on drafts of various chapters as I completed them. Special thanks are owed to Jeremy Bailey, Meredith Brenholdt, Benjamin Carp, Paul Carrese, Daniel Dreisbach, Yannis Evrigenis, Mark Hall, Sandy Kessler, Thomas Kidd, Bryan McGraw, Fr. Richard John Neuhaus, Robert Scigliano, Kathryn Sensen, Vickie Sullivan, and Brad Wilson. Paul Rahe and Michael Zuckert generously commented on the entire manuscript. Thank you to all for your time and thoughtfulness. I completed this book while I was on leave from Tufts University, serving as the William E. Simon Visiting Fellow of Religion and Public Life at Princeton University. I owe a special debt of gratitude to those who made that leave possible, including Rob Devigne, Andrew McClellan, and Robert Sternberg at Tufts University and Robby George and Brad Wilson at Princeton's James Madison Program. I would also like to thank those who provided forums for me to develop and test my ideas, especially Michael Andrews, Bruce Chapman, Jack Miller, Michael Novak, Keith Pavlischek, Michael Ratliff, George Weigel, John G. West, and Stephen M. Wrinn. Several of my former students (often my fiercest critics) helped in the editing process. I want to thank in particular Lauren Haertlein, Elizabeth Herman, Matthew Kenny, Nicholas May, Kathryn Mims, Kate Rick, Matthew Shapanka, and Graedon Zorzi. Lewis Bateman at Cambridge University Press made this book possible through his insight and expertise. Thank you to all.

Two chapters of the book are based on previously published material. I would like to acknowledge my gratitude for the permission granted to draw material from these earlier publications: "James Madison's Principle of Religious Liberty," *American Political Science Review* 97, no. 1 (2003): 17–32; "Religion in the Life, Thought, and Presidency of James Madison," in *Religion and the American Presidency*, eds. Mark J. Rozell and Gleaves Whitney (New York: Palgrave Macmillan, 2007); "George Washington and Religious Liberty," *The Review of Politics* 65, no. 1 (2003): 11–33. The careful reader will notice a few notable revisions from my earlier work.

Introduction

The Founders, Religious Freedom, and the First Amendment's Religion Clauses

First Amendment religion jurisprudence may have reached the height of its incomprehensibility on the last day of the Supreme Court's 2004 term. Faced with two separate cases involving public displays of the Ten Commandments, the Court found postings of the Commandments in Kentucky courthouses unconstitutional but ruled a Ten Commandments monument on the grounds of the Texas state capitol constitutional. In the two cases, the nine justices issued ten separate opinions totaling 140 pages to explain their different positions. With one exception, every opinion included significant claims about the intentions of the Founding Fathers, and Justice Stephen Breyer's opinion – the only one that did not discuss the Founders – cited Tocqueville. Despite their common reliance on history, the ten opinions invoked at least four different tests to determine the outcomes of the cases – the "Lemon" test, prevention of "civic divisiveness" along religious lines, no "endorsement," and no "legal coercion" – a disagreement that reflected the justices' divergent interpretations of the Founders. David Souter, who wrote the majority opinion in the case that struck down the courthouse displays, claimed that the Founders' intentions made state-sponsored postings of the Ten Commandments unconstitutional. Looking at the same history, Antonin Scalia and Clarence Thomas reached the opposite conclusion.

The Court's confusing decisions regarding the Ten Commandments are emblematic of its church-state jurisprudence. For more than sixty years, the Constitution's protection of religious liberty has vexed the judiciary, spawning case law mired in bad history, unpersuasive precedents, and incongruous rulings. The Court's inability to settle church-state questions decisively has led to confusion about the meaning of the First Amendment and has made church-state relations an enduring theater in the nation's culture war, a battle that flares up with almost every Supreme Court religious liberty decision.

One might have expected that by now the Founders' views would be well understood and the meaning of the Constitution's religion clauses would be decided. The Supreme Court first turned to Jefferson to elucidate the Free Exercise Clause in 1878, and since the landmark Establishment Clause case *Everson v. Board of Education* in 1947, both liberal and conservative jurists have repeatedly appealed to the Founding Fathers to guide church-state jurisprudence.[1] The last three generations of scholarship and constitutional argument, however, have failed to resolve the historical record. If anything, the opposite has happened. Scholars and judges are more divided now than ever on how the Founders intended to protect religious liberty and what they meant by the separation of church and state. Those on the left often claim that the Founders were skeptical deists who sought to erect an impenetrable wall of separation. Their counterparts on the right regularly contend that the Founders were religious men who expected a Christian spirit to infuse American political and public life.

Previous studies have failed because they have been too focused on utilizing the Founders and insufficiently interested in understanding them. In an effort to influence constitutional decision-making, most interpreters have accepted a paradigm established by the Supreme Court's twentieth-century Establishment Clause jurisprudence and, accordingly, have tried to categorize the Founders as either "strict separationists," who would not allow government support of religion, or "nonpreferentialists," who would allow such support on a nondiscriminatory basis. This approach has failed because the leading Founders did not address questions of church and state through the separationist/nonpreferentialist dichotomy. Grafting twentieth-century legal categories onto eighteenth-century texts has led to distortions of the Founders' positions. A methodological assumption of originalist jurisprudence, moreover, has led historical studies astray. Originalism presumes that each provision of the Constitution has one definitive original meaning and that that meaning should govern contemporary constitutional disputes. Its use in church-state jurisprudence has led to the assumption that because each of the religion clauses of the First Amendment must have one original

---

[1] According to Mark David Hall, between 1878 and 2005, Supreme Court justices made more than 200 different appeals to the Founders in First Amendment religious liberty judicial opinions. See Mark David Hall, "Jeffersonian Walls and Madisonian Lines: The Supreme Court's Use of History in Religious Clause Cases," *Oregon Law Review* 85, no. 2 (2006): 568.

meaning, the Founders more generally shared a uniform understanding of the proper relationship between church and state. But as this book attempts to demonstrate, the leading Founders disagreed about the meaning of religious freedom and how church and state ought to be separated. Ironically, the use of the Founders in modern legal disputes has created categories of thought and an approach to history that does not and cannot understand the Founders correctly.

This book attempts to set the historical record straight for three of America's leading Founding Fathers: James Madison, George Washington, and Thomas Jefferson. I argue that none of these Founders embraced strict separationism or nonpreferentialism as those positions are typically understood. Moreover, I contend that Madison, Washington, and Jefferson disagreed about the separation of church and state and embraced different understandings of the right to religious liberty. When we let go of the strict separationist/nonpreferentialist dichotomy and abandon the assumption that the Founders shared a uniform understanding of church-state separation, we can start to understand individual Founders more precisely and with greater accuracy.

Before proceeding, let me anticipate two objections to the focus of this study, which may help to clarify this book's scope and purposes. Readers who are primarily concerned with consulting history to adjudicate constitutional jurisprudence – we can call them "originalists" – might discount the importance of Madison, Washington, and Jefferson as individual political thinkers. For most originalists what matters is the original meaning of the Constitution's text, not the political thought of individual Founders.[2] Other readers – let us call them "progressives" – might contend that a concern with the Founders is misguided, especially if the Founders themselves disagreed about church-state matters. Progressives are more interested in settling contemporary disagreements in light of contemporary values. Why attempt to understand admittedly difficult historical records, progressives might ask, if the end result is only to discover that the Founders, too, disagreed about church-state matters?

In partial response to the originalists, let me make clear that this book does not attempt to uncover the original meaning of the First Amendment's

---

[2] For a discussion of the history and varieties of originalism, see Vasan Kesavan and Michael Stokes Paulsen, "The Interpretive Force of the Constitution's Secret Drafting History," *Georgetown Law Journal* 91 (2003): 1134–48; Keith E. Whittington, "The New Originalism," *Georgetown Journal of Law and Public Policy* 2 (2004): 599–613; Jonathan O'Neill, *Originalism in American Law and Politics: A Constitutional History* (Baltimore: The Johns Hopkins University Press, 2005).

religion clauses. By articulating Madison's, Washington's, and Jefferson's understandings of religious freedom, I am not claiming that any one of these Founders' individual positions represents the original meaning of the First Amendment. I will address the First Amendment's original meaning in a sequel to this volume.[3] This book does, however, have implications for originalist constitutional arguments. Madison, Washington, and Jefferson have been used by originalists in their attempts to articulate the original meaning of the religion clauses. To the extent that they misinterpret the leading Founders as individuals, originalist legal arguments lie on erroneous historical grounds. And, as already mentioned, originalist scholarship and jurisprudence tend to assume that the leading Founders shared a uniform understanding of the separation of church and state. This book attempts to show that that assumption is mistaken. Because the leading Founders disagreed, no one Founder can be cited to represent "the Founders' position."

A more complete response to the originalists also contains my response to the progressives. Somewhat ironically from the progressive point of view, it involves identifying what I believe to be a deep philosophical problem with the usual defense of originalism. A review of recent books on the subject states the problem succinctly:

At the end of the day, words in a legal text, without more, cannot carry the philosophical weight that originalists place upon them. It is one thing to point out, as originalists do most effectively, that such-and-such a phrase had, and was meant to have, a particular, relatively fixed meaning at the time of its adoption. Persuading others that the identified meaning has, or should have, binding effect in our own day is another argument altogether. Ultimately, that argument must rest on the reaffirmation of the enduring, self-evident truths that must undergird the case for limited government, that is, on premises that are not explicitly identified in the constitutional text itself. A true originalism, in short, must look beyond the Constitution to justify the ground of its intellectual authority.[4]

One of the most well-known justifications for originalism was set forth by Attorney General Edwin Meese, who, in 1985 in a series of speeches explaining the Reagan White House's judicial philosophy, defended originalism in

---

[3] For initial statements of my interpretations of the original meanings of the First Amendment's religion clauses, see: Vincent Phillip Muñoz, "The Original Meaning of the Establishment Clause and the Impossibility of its Incorporation," *University of Pennsylvania Journal of Constitutional Law* 8, no. 4 (2006): 585–639; Vincent Phillip Muñoz, "The Original Meaning of the Free Exercise Clause: The Evidence From the First Congress," *Harvard Journal of Law and Public Policy* 31, no. 3 (2008): 1083–1120.

[4] Michael Uhlmann, "The Supreme Court v. the Constitution of the United States of America," *Claremont Review of Books* 6, no. 3 (Summer 2006): 37.

terms of democratic willfulness. "[B]elief in a Jurisprudence of Original Intention," Meese said, reflects "a deeply rooted commitment to the idea of democracy. . . . The Constitution is the fundamental will of the people; that is why it is the fundamental law."[5] In Meese's view, what justifies originalism and the use of the Founders' political theory for constitutional jurisprudence is the historical fact that the Constitution and Bill of Rights were willed by the American people. But, of course, only a fraction of the American people actually voted to ratify those documents, and no American living today has cast such a vote. If the will of the American people is the primary basis for constitutional authority, then it would seem that the will of contemporary democratic majorities ought to govern our fundamental law. In the name of democracy, Meese's position binds the living by the votes of the dead, which is an odd understanding of democracy to say the least.[6]

Whatever its merits, Meese's view is insufficient. The Constitution may have legal authority because it was originally willed by the people, but its contemporary moral authority cannot rest on those grounds alone. If the Founders' constitutionalism is worthy of respect today, it is because the rules it establishes and the rights it protects embody fundamental principles of justice, not because a powerful elite voted for the Constitution more than 200 years ago. The Founders' ideas should govern us today only to the extent that they are persuasive. To determine the extent to which their political theories are rationally defensible, we must attempt to understand them and the arguments that the Founders set forth in their defense.

Progressives discount such efforts because they believe history itself is progressive, making old ideas obsolete. The progressive position concludes the inquiry without having made it. The Founders may, in fact, be outdated, but to reach that conclusion we have to understand their arguments and explain why they are wrong or why they are no longer relevant. My response to the progressives is thus the same as my response to the originalists: Whether we are to follow the Founders (as originalists assume we should) or to dismiss them (as progressives assume we should), we have to

---

[5] Edwin Meese, speech before the American Bar Association, July 9, 1985, in *The Great Debate: Interpreting Our Written Constitution* (Washington, DC: The Federalist Society, 1986), 9.

[6] For different criticisms of Meese's position, see: William J. Brennan, Jr., "The Constitution of the United States: Contemporary Ratification," in *Interpreting the Constitution: The Debate Over Original Intent*, ed. Jack Rakove (Boston: Northeastern University Press, 1990), 23–34; Harry V. Jaffa, *Original Intent and the Framers of the Constitution* (Washington, DC: Regnery Gateway, 1994), 55–73. For a more recent defense of originalism, see Keith E. Whittington, *Constitutional Interpretation: Textual Meaning, Original Intent, and Judicial Review* (Lawrence: University Press of Kansas, 1999).

understand the Founders and judge the merits of their ideas. This book attempts to undertake that project for the church-state political philosophies of James Madison, George Washington, and Thomas Jefferson.

On the topic of religious liberty, the leading Founders also deserve our attention for another related reason. Around the same time that Thomas Jefferson wrote the "self-evident" truths of the Declaration of Independence, a young James Madison rewrote the religious freedom provision of the Virginia Declaration of Rights. George Mason's initial draft of the Virginia bill of rights had declared, "all Men should enjoy the fullest Toleration in the Exercise of Religion." Madison thought the language of "toleration" was inappropriate for citizens, who possessed rights by nature. He proposed instead, "all men are equally entitled to the full and free exercise of [religion]." In amended form, Madison's language would eventually appear in Article XVI of the 1776 Virginia Declaration of Rights and in the First Amendment of the United States Constitution. Perhaps thinking of Madison's revision of Mason's draft, George Washington wrote to a Jewish congregation a decade later, "It is now no more that toleration is spoken of as if it were the indulgence of one class of people that another enjoyed the exercise of their inherent natural rights...."[7]

Jefferson, Madison, and Washington did not believe that individuals possessed the right to religious liberty because it was willed by a democratic majority. Whatever their differences about church and state, all three Founders understood religious liberty to involve natural rights and, therefore, necessarily to limit the will of any just majority. We still use the language of rights today, but the idea of "natural rights" no longer holds much currency in America's law schools or among most contemporary political theorists. Whether the right to religious liberty can be defended persuasively without recurring to natural rights, however, is at least an open question and perhaps doubtful.

That partisans of liberal democracy need to articulate a defense of religious liberty is not in question or doubtful. In the first days of the twenty-first century, the world witnessed unspeakable acts of violence committed in the name of religion. As I write this, the United States is engaged in a costly war to bring freedom, including some forms of religious freedom, to a part of the world that has never embraced it. It would be naïve to think that arguments alone can win wars or deter those who would kill in the

---

[7] George Washington to the Hebrew Congregation in Newport, Rhode Island, August 18, 1790, *Papers of George Washington*, Presidential Series, ed. Mark A. Mastromarino (Charlottesville: University Press of Virginia, 1996), 6:285.

name of God. But if we wish to distinguish waging war in the name of freedom from terrorist acts committed out of religious fanaticism, we must be able to give an account of the freedoms that liberal democracies cherish and seek to spread. We must be able to explain why religious freedom is good and why it involves rights that belong to all individuals. Merely holding it as one of "our fundamental values" will never be persuasive to those who hold different values than we do, nor will it sustain the type of commitment and sacrifice needed to preserve freedom for ourselves or to secure it for others.

When the American Founders attempted to defend religious freedom, they turned to natural rights arguments.[8] Even if it is intellectually unfashionable, that path remains open to us today. We might consider traveling it not only because individuals actually may possess rights to religious freedom by nature but also because the idea of natural rights has profoundly aided the cause of human freedom. It is said that ideas have consequences, but for any idea to have consequences it must be articulated and understood. In American history, no three men did more to articulate and to constitutionally protect the natural right to religious freedom than Madison, Washington, and Jefferson. Their individual political thoughts and deeds may not reflect the original meaning of the First Amendment's religion clauses, but they help to illuminate the meaning of the right that the First Amendment seeks to protect. This study turns to Madison, Washington, and Jefferson because in coming to understand what they thought, what they did, and how they disagreed, we can think more clearly and more deeply about what it might mean for individuals to possess a natural right to religious liberty and how that right can be constitutionally protected.

PLAN OF THE WORK

This book contends that if any of the Founders are to be consulted to guide contemporary church-state questions, it should be because of the profundity of their thought, not because of their status as the Constitution's authors. The book argues that Madison, Washington, and Jefferson disagreed about the proper relationship between church and state. While each of these Founders believed that religious freedom included natural rights, they

---

[8] For a general discussion of the place of natural rights in the Founders' political theory, including the relationship between the Founders' political theory and Protestantism, see Michael P. Zuckert, *The Natural Rights Republic* (Notre Dame, IN: University of Notre Dame Press, 1996).

disagreed about what those rights consisted of and how they ought to be protected constitutionally. Part I consists of three chapters that explore, respectively, James Madison's, George Washington's, and Thomas Jefferson's different understandings of the right to religious freedom. Madison and Jefferson are selected for study because of their Herculean efforts to establish religious freedom in Virginia and in America. Washington is considered because he embodies the leading alternative to Madison and Jefferson. Others might have been discussed to reflect this alternative position – John Adams, for example – but as the first president, Washington established many of the constitutional precedents that individuals like Adams followed. Since Madison, Washington, and Jefferson understood the meaning of religious freedom differently, Chapters 1, 2, and 3 place particular emphasis on how each Founder defended religious freedom as a natural right. These chapters also attempt to explain how the Founders' different understandings of the right lead to their different positions on the proper relationship between church and state.

Part II of this work applies the Founders' positions to leading church-state constitutional issues. Chapter 4 attempts to extrapolate legal doctrines from the church-state philosophies of each Founder. Chapters 5 and 6 then apply those doctrines to modern church-state constitutional law. Rather than use hypothetical issues or facts, I attempt to explain how the Founders' different positions would have adjudicated actual cases that have come before the Supreme Court. Chapter 5 applies the Founders' doctrines to nineteen different Establishment Clause cases. Chapter 6 applies the Founders' doctrines to sixteen different Free Exercise Clause cases. The use of actual case law helps to clarify the Founders' different positions and reveals how and when Madison, Washington, and Jefferson agreed and disagreed.

The book concludes by comparing the Founders' different jurisprudential results with those reached by the Supreme Court and with the votes of a select group of Supreme Court justices who have been particularly influential on church-state questions. The concluding chapter also contains my evaluation of the strengths and weaknesses of each Founder's doctrine and a brief proposal as to how the Founders might best be employed to help guide contemporary church-state jurisprudence.

PART I

THE FOUNDERS' CHURCH-STATE POLITICAL PHILOSOPHIES

I

James Madison's Principle of State Noncognizance of Religion

> We maintain therefore that in matters of Religion, no man's right is abridged by the institution of Civil Society, and that Religion is wholly exempt from its cognizance.
>
> James Madison, "Memorial and Remonstrance" (1785)

No man is more responsible for the Constitution than James Madison. Leading delegate at the Philadelphia Convention, advocate and expositor as Publius, author and sponsor of the Bill of Rights: Madison rightfully earned his title "Father of the Constitution." Along with Thomas Jefferson, he also played the leading role in Virginia's battle for religious freedom, authoring in the process his landmark statement on religious liberty, "Memorial and Remonstrance Against Religious Assessments." It should be no surprise, then, that along with Thomas Jefferson, Madison has been considered an authoritative guide to the meaning of the First Amendment's religion clauses. The meaning of the "Memorial," however, is a matter of significant dispute. Strict separationist judges and scholars claim that Madison partnered with Jefferson to erect a "wall of separation" between church and state, thereby prohibiting all governmental support for religion. Nonpreferentialists challenge this interpretation, contending that, regardless of Jefferson's aims, Madison meant only to prevent the state from favoring one religious sect over others. The state may support religion, they claim, so long as it supports all religions equally. For Free Exercise cases, Madison has been invoked to defend the right to religious exemptions from facially neutral but burdensome laws. Justice Antonin Scalia, the Court's most articulate defender of originalism, has rejected that position, but, as we shall discuss, his opinions have failed to respond to his opponents' Madisonian arguments. Thus, although Madison's authority for First Amendment religion jurisprudence has been widely accepted, what he says on these matters remains sharply contested. Did Madison think state support of religion violates constitutional principles? If so, did he also intend to protect the free exercise of religion by granting religious citizens exemptions from oppressive laws?

This chapter attempts to answer these questions by articulating Madison's principle of religious liberty. It begins by reviewing the leading interpretations and constitutional applications of Madison's thought on religious liberty, all of which, I suggest, have failed to grasp Madison's position. I then offer my alternative interpretation. By focusing on the "Memorial's" social compact framework, I argue that Madison championed a "religion blind" constitution, a constitution that prohibits the state from taking cognizance of religion. In Madison's view, the state may not classify citizens on the basis of religious beliefs or religious affiliation, which means that government actors may neither privilege nor penalize religious institutions, religious citizens, or religiously motivated conduct as such. Unlike Jefferson, Madison's politics followed his public philosophy fairly consistently. The principle of religious noncognizance accounts for Madison's political actions, statements, and writings made as a state legislator, congressman, president, and elder statesman.

THE USE AND ABUSE OF MADISON

Around 200 Supreme Court opinions have appealed to Madison to help adjudicate religious liberty questions.[1] In judicial decisions and scholarship on the Establishment Clause, Madison has been identified both as a strict separationist who stood against any and all public support of religion and as a nonpreferentialist who proscribed only aid that favored some religions over others. For the Free Exercise Clause, Madison has been invoked as a defender of the right to religious exemptions from laws that burden religious exercise.

The Use of Madison in Establishment Clause Jurisprudence

The strict separationist interpretation of Madison began in the Supreme Court's landmark incorporation decision *Everson v. Board of Education* (1947). *Everson* was decided five to four, but all nine justices agreed that

---

[1] Mark David Hall, "Jeffersonian Walls and Madisonian Lines: The Supreme Court's Use of History in Religious Clause Cases," *Oregon Law Review* 85, no. 2 (2006): 563–614.

the meaning of the Establishment Clause was to be found in Jefferson's and Madison's writings establishing religious freedom in Virginia, and that these writings indicated that the Founders intended "to erect a wall of separation between church and state."[2] Justice Wiley Rutledge, writing in dissent, paid particular attention to Madison. His historical research led him to conclude that "Madison opposed every form and degree of official relation between religion and civil authority," and, therefore, that the Establishment Clause "forbids any appropriation, large or small, from public funds to aid or support any and all religious exercises."[3]

This strict separationist interpretation of Madison received scholarly confirmation four years later by Irving Brant, the distinguished biographer of the fourth president. According to Brant, freedom of religion was, for Madison, "the fundamental item upon which all other forms of civil liberty depended," and the fundamental requirement for religious freedom "was the total separation between government and religion."[4] Brant canvassed all of Madison's major writings on religious liberty, but he employed most forcefully the then newly rediscovered "Essay on Monopolies."[5] In that essay, Madison called the appointment of taxpayer-funded legislative chaplains by the First Congress a "palpable violation" of constitutional principles. Religious proclamations by the president were "shoots from the same root." Madison went so far as to identify a prohibition on taxpayer-funded chaplains for navy crewmen insulated at sea as "the consequence of a right principle."[6] Brant took the date and the dispassionate, retrospective tone of the "Essay on Monopolies" as conclusive proof that Madison "regarded any compulsory contribution to religion, through taxes, as a violation of the individual taxpayer's religious liberty."[7]

---

[2] *Everson v. Board of Education,* 330 U.S. 1, 19 (1947). The justices disagreed only on where the wall stood in the case at hand. The majority ruled that the New Jersey program in question, which reimbursed the transportation costs incurred by parents sending their children to Catholic schools, did not breach the wall.

[3] *Everson v. Board of Education,* 330 U.S. 1, 39, 41 (1947).

[4] Irving Brant, "Madison: On the Separation of Church and State," *William and Mary Quarterly,* 3rd Series, no. 8 (1951): 3.

[5] Madison's "Essay on Monopolies" had been published in *Harper's Magazine* in 1914 but was lost and forgotten until rediscovered and republished by Elizabeth Fleet in 1946 as "Madison's 'Detached Memoranda,'" *William and Mary Quarterly,* 3rd Series, no. 3 (1946): 558–62. The exact date of its composition is unknown, but it is thought that Madison drafted it between 1817 and 1832.

[6] Fleet, "Madison's 'Detached Memoranda,'" 558–62; Brant, "Madison: On the Separation of Church and State," 21–24.

[7] Brant, "Madison: On the Separation of Church and State," 11.

As the Supreme Court continued to hear Establishment Clause cases in the 1950s and 1960s, the prolific and influential jurist Leo Pfeffer augmented Brant's interpretation with a strict separationist reading of Madison's "Memorial and Remonstrance."[8] Pfeffer focused on the "Memorial's" political context, pointing out that Madison wrote it with a specific legislative intention, to defeat Patrick Henry's pending "Bill Establishing a Provision for Teachers of the Christian Religion." Henry's measure, according to Pfeffer, aimed to aid religion in a nonpreferential manner. Madison's opposition to it, Pfeffer thus concluded, demonstrated that Madison opposed all government aid to religion, including nonpreferential aid.[9]

In 1985, then–Associate Justice William Rehnquist challenged *Everson*'s strict separationist wall in a dissenting opinion in the public school "moment of silence" case *Wallace v. Jaffree* (1985). Building on the scholarship of Robert Cord, Rehnquist denied that the Founders in general or Madison in particular intended to erect a wall separating church and state or to require state neutrality between religion and irreligion.[10] The Founders, Justice Rehnquist claimed, intended only to prohibit government support that was sectarian. The Establishment Clause, accordingly, should be read only to prohibit preferential aid to some religions over others.

To make his case, Justice Rehnquist turned to the drafting of the Establishment Clause in the First Congress. There he found, contrary to the Court's ruling in *Everson*, that Madison was not trying to constitutionalize Jefferson's Virginia Statute for Religious Liberty. Madison, rather, was "an advocate for sensible legislative compromise."[11] Justice Rehnquist focused

---

[8] According to Gregg Ivers, it is "impossible to overestimate the impact that Leo Pfeffer, as an individual and as a public interest lawyer, had on the constitutional development of church-state law during the latter half of this [20th] century. . . . [F]or no lawyer has exercised such complete intellectual dominance over a chosen area of law for so extensive a period. . . ." Gregg Ivers, *To Build A Wall: American Jews and the Separation of Church and State* (Charlottesville: University of Virginia Press, 1995), 222. Cushing Strout reports that out of some fifty adversarial cases between 1951 and 1971 involving the Establishment Clause, Pfeffer was active in twenty of them at the trial stage and in fourteen at the appellate stage. Cushing Strout, "Jeffersonian Religious Liberty and American Pluralism," in *The Virginia Statute for Religious Freedom: Its Evolution and Consequence in American History*, ed. Merrill D. Peterson and Robert C. Vaughn (Cambridge: Cambridge University Press, 1988), 225.

[9] Leo Pfeffer, "The Case for Separation," in *Religion in America: Original Essays on Religion in a Free Society*, ed. John Cogley (New York: Meridian Books, 1958), 66.

[10] Justice Rehnquist cites Robert Cord only once in his opinion (p. 104), but his entire opinion seems to follow closely Cord's *Separation of Church and State: Historical Reality and Current Fiction* (New York: Lambeth Press, 1982).

[11] *Wallace v. Jaffree*, 472 U.S. 38, 97 (1985).

on the text of Madison's original draft amendment, "nor shall any national religion be established," and on his subsequent explanation on the House floor that it meant "that congress should not establish a religion, and enforce the legal observation of it by law." These statements indicated to Justice Rehnquist that Madison

saw the [First] Amendment as designed to prohibit the establishment of a national religion, and perhaps to prevent discrimination among sects. He [Madison] did not see it as requiring neutrality on the part of government between religion and irreligion.[12]

Everson and the strict separationist jurisprudence built on it, Justice Rehnquist concluded, were constructed on a "mistaken understanding of constitutional history. . . ."[13] Nonpreferentialism, not a "wall of separation," best reflects Madison's and the Founding Fathers' original intentions.[14]

Justice Rehnquist's reinterpretation brought forth a wave of separationist scholarship, the influence of which would appear in Justice David Souter's opinions.[15] In two nonmajority opinions in the 1990s, Justice Souter established himself as the leading originalist, strict separationist member of the Rehnquist Court. In *Lee v. Weisman* (1992), the public school graduation prayer case, Justice Souter pored over the same historical materials that Justice Rehnquist did in his *Wallace* dissent. Like Justice

---

[12] Ibid., 98. In his dissent in the released-time-for-religious-instruction case, Justice Stanley Reed also cited Madison's explanatory statement on the House floor as evidence that the Establishment Clause aimed only to proscribe an official state church. See, *McCollum v. Board of Education*, 333 U.S. 203, 244 (1948).

[13] *Wallace v. Jaffree*, 472 U.S. 38, 92 (1985).

[14] Ibid., 92. Both Cord and Rehnquist also introduce as evidence numerous instances in which the Founding Fathers endorsed and supported religion, including the reenactment of the Northwest Ordinance by the First Congress, which proclaimed, "Religion, morality, and knowledge, being necessary to good government and the happiness of mankind, school and the means of education shall forever be encouraged"; calls for national days of prayer and thanksgiving by Presidents Washington, Adams, and Madison; and Jefferson's authorization of direct payments by the federal government to a Catholic priest ministering to Native Americans. The deficiency in Cord's nonpreferentialist interpretation of Madison is that he cannot square it with Madison's seemingly separationist "Detached Memoranda." As such, Cord is forced to say that Madison was inconsistent or that he changed his mind as "an old man" in his "declining years," both highly dubious propositions. See Cord, *Separation of Church and State*, 35–36; and Robert Cord, "Original Intent Jurisprudence and Madison's 'Detached Memoranda,'" *Benchmark* 3 (1987): 79–85.

[15] The scholarship cited by Justice Souter includes Leonard Levy, *The Establishment Clause: Religion and the First Amendment* (New York: Macmillan, 1986), and Douglas Laycock, "'Nonpreferential' Aid to Religion: A False Claim About Original Intent," *William and Mary Law Review* 27 (Summer 1986): 875–923.

Rehnquist, Justice Souter focused on Madison's original draft amendment, but Justice Souter pointed out that Madison's initial draft was not adopted. A comparison of rejected drafts of the Establishment Clause with the actual adopted text, he argued, reveals that the Framers considered but ultimately rejected prohibiting only nonpreferential aid to religion.[16] When the Court ruled three years later that a University of Virginia Christian student newspaper could receive student activity funds in *Rosenberger v. University of Virginia* (1995), Justice Souter further developed his position with a strict separationist reading of Madison's "Memorial and Remonstrance." His dissenting opinion in that case emphasized Article 3, where Madison states, "Who does not see that . . . the same authority which can force a citizen to contribute three pence only of his property for the support of any one establishment, may force him to conform to any other establishment in all cases whatsoever?"[17] This statement, in addition to the fact that the "Memorial" was written against a general assessment, demonstrated to Justice Souter that Madison objected to any government subsidization of religion.

Justice Souter wrote his *Rosenberger* dissent in response to Justice Clarence Thomas' nonpreferentialist concurring opinion in the same case. Justice Thomas picked up Chief Justice Rehnquist's argument that the entire edifice of Establishment Clause jurisprudence had been built on a mistaken understanding of history. In addition to focusing on the records of the First Federal Congress, Justice Thomas also returned to the "Memorial and Remonstrance," specifically Article 4, which argues that Henry's proposed assessment "violates that equality which ought to be the basis of every law." According to Justice Thomas, Madison opposed Henry's assessment bill "not because it allowed religious groups to participate in generally available benefits, but because the bill singled out religious entities for special benefits."[18] A proper interpretation of the "Memorial," and thus the Establishment Clause, he concluded, prohibits government only from favoring some religious faiths over others.

Although Justice Thomas employed the "Memorial" to defend nonpreferentialism, his opinion betrayed a leery suspicion of Madison. Justice

---

[16] *Lee v. Weisman*, 505 U.S. 577, 615 (1992). Souter (pp. 622–26) also trumpeted Madison's "Detached Memoranda," employing the same evidence and reaching the same conclusion that Irving Brant did nearly fifty years prior.

[17] *Rosenberger v. University of Virginia*, 515 U.S. 819, 868 (1995).

[18] Ibid., 854–55.

Thomas conceded that others had interpreted the "Memorial" differently than he did,[19] and perhaps because the strict separationist interpretation of Madison looks so strong, he suggested that "the views of one man do not establish the original understanding of the First Amendment."[20] Is Madison, then, a strict separationist? Did he think that any and all aid to religion violates constitutional principles? If so, why did he not say so clearly in either his initial proposed constitutional amendment or in his later clarifying remarks made during the Constitutional Convention? And if Madison did intend strictly to separate religion and politics through the Establishment Clause, did he also, as some claim, intend vigorously to protect religion from politics with the Free Exercise Clause?

Madison and the Free Exercise Clause

WITHDRAWN

Until 1997, Madison was not invoked for Free Exercise jurisprudence nearly to the extent that he was for Establishment Clause cases. This was partially because when the Supreme Court first addressed the meaning of free exercise in the Mormon polygamy case *Reynolds v. United States* (1878), it turned to Jefferson.[21] When the Court later incorporated the Free Exercise Clause in *Cantwell v. Connecticut* (1940), and then expanded its reach to grant religious exemptions from generally applicable regulations and laws in *Sherbert v. Verner* (1963), it did so again without invoking Madison.[22] Chief Justice Burger did invoke Madison in the 1978 case *McDaniel v. Paty*, but the Court overlooked him in its controversial 1990 *Smith* decision.[23] A strong reaction to the latter case and the Court's denial of a constitutional right to religious exemptions from most generally applicable laws, however, led to a vigorous application of Madison's thought to the Free Exercise Clause.

The leading scholar to apply Madison to the Free Exercise Clause is Michael McConnell. In his widely cited *Harvard Law Review* article, "The Origins and Historical Understanding of Free Exercise of Religion," McConnell meticulously defends the case for religious exemptions from

---

[19] Ibid., citing Douglas Laycock, "'Nonpreferential' Aid to Religion."
[20] *Rosenberger v. University of Virginia*, 515 U.S. 819, 856 (1995).
[21] *Reynolds v. United States*, 98 U.S. 145, 164 (1878).
[22] *Cantwell v. Connecticut*, 310 U.S. 296, 303 (1940); *Sherbert v. Verner*, 374 U.S. 398 (1963).
[23] *McDaniel v. Paty*, 435 U.S. 618, 623–24, 626 (1978); *Employment Division, Department of Human Resources of Oregon v. Smith*, 485 U.S. 660 (1990).

laws that burden religious exercise.[24] At the center of his argument stands Madison's "Memorial and Remonstrance." In Article 1 of the "Memorial," Madison derives the right of religious liberty from "the duty of every man to render to the Creator such homage, and such only, as he believes to be acceptable to him." "This duty," Madison continues, "is precedent both in order of time and degree of obligation, to the claims of Civil Society." McConnell reasons,

> If the scope of religious liberty is defined by religious duty (man must render to God "such . . . homage as he believes acceptable to him"), and if the claims of civil society are subordinate to the claims of religious freedom, it would seem to follow that the dictates of religious faith must take precedence over the laws of the state, even if they are secular and generally applicable. This is the central point on which Madison differs from Locke, Jefferson, and other Enlightenment advocates of religious freedom.[25]

If religious duties conflict with civic regulations, civic regulations must give way. Although McConnell admits that the "Memorial" does not call for judicial exemptions explicitly, he claims that it "suggests an approach toward religious liberty consonant with them."[26]

To support this reading of the "Memorial," McConnell also introduces into evidence Madison's proposed revisions of the "free exercise provision" of the Virginia Declaration of Rights. He reports that, as drafted by George Mason, Article XVI stated:

> that all men should enjoy the fullest toleration in the exercise of religion, according to the dictates of conscience, unpunished and unrestrained by the magistrate, unless under color of religion any man disturb the peace, the happiness or safety of society.[27]

Madison, McConnell claims, objected on two grounds. First, Madison criticized the use of the word "toleration," because religious liberty is a right derived from duties more sovereign than civic obligations. He moved, accordingly, to strike Mason's language of toleration and substitute instead "all men are equally entitled to the full and free exercise of religion according to the dictates of conscience." Second, Mason and Madison clearly

---

[24] Michael W. McConnell, "The Origins and Historical Understanding of Free Exercise of Religion," *Harvard Law Review* 103 (1990): 1409–1517.

[25] Ibid., 1453.

[26] Ibid., see also Michael W. McConnell, "Believers As Equal Citizens," in *Obligations of Citizenship and Demands of Faith*, ed. Nancy L. Rosenblum (Princeton, NJ: Princeton University Press, 2000), 90–110.

[27] McConnell, "Origins and Historical Understanding," 1462.

anticipated exemptions from generally applicable laws, which is why they included balancing test standards at the ends of their drafts. Mason would have extended exemptions only to religious actions that did not disturb the "peace, happiness, or safety of society," a standard, McConnell suggests, "that would encompass virtually all legitimate forms of legislation."[28] Madison, according to McConnell, aimed to create a test much more favorable to religious citizens. He proposed to narrow the compelling state interest in denying religious exemptions only to cases manifestly endangering "the preservation of equal liberty and the existence of the state." This standard, McConnell concludes, "only the most critical acts of government can satisfy."[29]

McConnell's arguments have found a voice on the Supreme Court in Justice Sandra Day O'Connor. In her dissenting opinion in *City of Boerne v. Flores* (1997), Justice O'Connor called for a reversal of *Smith* and a restoration of the *Sherbert* balancing test because "The historical evidence casts doubt on the Court's current [non-exemption-granting] interpretation of the Free Exercise Clause."[30] For her historical evidence, she relied heavily on McConnell's interpretation of Madison.[31]

McConnell's and O'Connor's arguments have been criticized sharply both on and off the bench by those who deny that the First Amendment secures a right to religious exemptions from generally applicable laws. These critics have failed, however, to address adequately the McConnell/O'Connor interpretation of Madison. Philip Hamburger, the most thorough and persuasive critic of religious exemptions on historical grounds, has countered McConnell's historical research point-by-point. When it

---

[28] Ibid., 1463.

[29] Ibid., 1462–63. McConnell's history on this point suffers from his reliance on Sanford Cobb's *The Rise of Religious Liberty in America* (New York: Macmillan, 1902), 491–92, which offers an incomplete account of Madison's proposed revisions to Mason's text. What McConnell presents as Mason's original proposal is actually a slightly amended committee version of Mason's initial draft. Madison then offered two different sets of revisions on two different dates. What McConnell reports as Madison's proposed revisions is actually the second set of revisions he offered – Madison's initial revisions were rejected. McConnell appears to be unaware of Madison's first proposed revisions and thus fails to consider them. Unfortunately for McConnell, these revisions most clearly reveal Madison's intentions. For a complete account of the drafting of Article XVI of the Virginia Declaration of Rights, see Daniel L. Dreisbach, "George Mason's Pursuit of Religious Liberty in Revolutionary Virginia," *The Virginia Magazine of History and Biography* 108 (2000): 9–18.

[30] *City of Boerne v. Flores*, 521 U.S. 507, 549 (1997).

[31] For a discussion of how Justice O'Connor follows McConnell, see Vincent Phillip Muñoz, "The Original Meaning of the Free Exercise Clause: The Evidence from the First Congress," *Harvard Journal of Law & Public Policy* 31 (2008): 1087–95.

comes to McConnell's reading of Madison's "Memorial and Remonstrance," however, Hamburger is noticeably silent.[32] The same omission also can be attributed to Justice Antonin Scalia, the Court's leading critic of exemptions. In both his *Smith* majority opinion, in which he originally overturned the Court's exemption-granting balancing test, and then his defense of *Smith* in response to O'Connor in *Boerne*, Justice Scalia failed to address McConnell's and O'Connor's strongest argument: that James Madison, architect of the First Amendment, grounds the right to religious liberty on the premise that religious obligations are precedent in time and significance to civil obligations. Those who defend a constitutional right to religious exemptions from burdensome laws seem to have Madison on their side.

First appearances, however, can be deceiving. The pro-exemption interpretation of Madison is incorrect. Both the strict separationist and non-preferentialist interpretations also fail to accurately reflect Madison's position. Madison has been misinterpreted regarding the Establishment Clause and the Free Exercise Clause because scholars and judges have failed to see the social compact framework of the "Memorial and Remonstrance." Prior interpreters thus have failed to see Madison's clearly stated principle of religious liberty, that the state must remain noncognizant of religion.

MADISON'S PRINCIPLE OF NONCOGNIZANCE

Madison's most mature and philosophical defense of religious liberty is his "Memorial and Remonstrance against Religious Assessments."[33] He drafted the "Memorial and Remonstrance" in the spring of 1785 in the midst of a fierce debate over Patrick Henry's proposed "Bill Establishing a Provision for Teachers of the Christian Religion." Before discussing the "Memorial's" argument, it is important to note what exactly Madison was arguing against. Henry's proposed assessment bill, according to Leo Pfeffer,

represents the closest approximation in American history to absolutely non-preferential government aid to religion. It is difficult to conceive of any measure which adheres more closely to the requirements of non-discrimination and equality among sects.[34]

---

[32] Philip A. Hamburger, "A Constitutional Right of Religious Exemptions: An Historical Perspective," *George Washington Law Review* 60 (April 1992): 915–48. See especially pp. 926–29, which discuss McConnell's use of Madison.

[33] For the text of the "Memorial and Remonstrance," see Appendix A.

[34] Pfeffer, "The Case for Separation," 66.

Pfeffer is simply wrong. Though more accommodating than the pre-revolutionary establishment or the proposed establishment of 1779, it is incorrect to claim that Henry's bill was nondiscriminatory or established equality among all religious sects. The title alone, "A Bill Establishing a Provision for Teachers of the Christian Religion," belies Pfeffer's interpretation. Only ministers of recognized Christian sects were eligible for state funding. In December 1784, an amendment was passed to drop the word "Christian" in order to open up the assessment to any religious society, but Benjamin Harrison, the former governor, managed to have the change reversed.[35] Instead, in the final text there appeared a statement of the bill's liberality that more clearly reveals its limits:

[I]t is judged that such a provision may be made by the Legislature, without counteracting the liberal principle heretofore adopted and intended to be preserved by abolishing all distinctions of preeminence amongst the different societies or communities of Christians.[36]

Henry's bill may have erased distinctions among Protestants, but it was not nonsectarian.

What it constituted was a property tax to fund some religious ministers. Under the bill's provisions, each property owner was to specify the Christian denomination to which he wished his tax directed. The sheriffs of the several counties would then distribute the taxes accordingly, minus 5 percent for administration. If a taxpayer failed or refused to specify a Christian society, his tax would go to the public treasury "to be disposed of under the direction of the General Assembly, for the encouragement of seminaries of learning . . . and to no other use or purpose whatsoever." Similarly, the taxes received by the various denominations were to be "appropriated to a provision for a Minister or Teacher of the Gospel, or the providing of places of divine worship, and to none other use whatsoever." An exception to this rule was made for Quakers and Mennonites, who were allowed to place their distributions in their general funds because they lacked the requisite clergy.

The restrictions on how funds were to be distributed, with the noted exceptions, were due to the bill's stated educational purpose. The bill began,

WHEREAS the general diffusion of Christian knowledge hath a tendency to correct the morals of men, restrain their vices, and preserve the peace of society, which cannot be effected without a competent provision for learned teachers . . .

---

[35] Thomas Buckley, *Church and State in Revolutionary Virginia* (Charlottesville: University of Virginia Press, 1977), 108.
[36] The text of Henry's assessment bill can be found in Appendix B.

This educational facade was not present in the bill's original version, which was designed to support Christian ministers, churches, and worship. A drafting committee added it, probably to increase the bill's appeal.[37] Even with these changes, however, everyone knew that the purpose of the bill was to keep the Christian ministry, particularly Episcopalian clergy, active and solvent.[38] And even with the educational preamble, ministers who received appropriations were not required to use them for educational purposes. In its effect, the bill granted a direct subsidy to Christian clergymen.

Madison revealed his perception of the measure and what he thought was at stake in a letter to Thomas Jefferson on January 9, 1785. "Should the bill ever pass into law in its present form," he wrote, "it may and will be easily eluded." Madison probably had in mind the assessment's provision that allowed citizens not to name their denomination and thereby steer their taxes to a state general education fund. "It is chiefly obnoxious," he continued, "on account of its dishonorable principle and dangerous tendency."[39] For Madison, defeating Henry's assessment was primarily a matter of principle. This understanding is reflected in the nature of the "Memorial's" argument. It addresses specifics of Henry's bill and its immediate political consequences, but its true force is its theory of religious freedom. While not ignoring immediate politics – indeed, while intending directly to influence them – Madison's "Memorial" offers a philosophical understanding of the proper relationship between church and state.

The "Memorial's" Argument

The "Memorial and Remonstrance" consists of fifteen articles. Each article is written as if to stand alone, but a clear sequence exists. Articles 1 through 4 argue from principle; 5 through 14 offer pragmatic reasons for defeating Henry's proposed assessment. Article 15 returns to the principle articulated in Article 1. Madison sets forth his doctrine of religious liberty in the first

---

[37] Buckley, *Church and State in Revolutionary Virginia*, 105. Cf. Eva Brann, "Madison's 'Memorial and Remonstrance,'" in *The Past Present: Selected Writings of Eva Brann*, ed. Pamela Kraus (Annapolis, MD: St. John's College Press, 1997), 210.

[38] Buckley, *Church and State in Revolutionary Virginia*, 109.

[39] James Madison, *Letters and Other Writings of James Madison* (New York: R. Worthington, 1884), 1:131.

article. Although almost all commentators focus on it, its exact meaning has been missed.

The structure of Article 1's argument follows Lockean social compact theory. In the *Second Treatise on Government*, John Locke teaches that men are originally born into the state of nature, a condition in which every man possesses the rights to life, liberty, and property and the right to execute the law of nature. Because of the tendency of each man to execute the law of nature to his own advantage, no effective common law exists among men and the state of nature tends to break down into a state of war. To escape this situation of war and poverty that ill secures man's rights, men enter into a social compact with one another. They consent equally to give up their full natural right to execute the law of nature in exchange for governance under the rule of law as expressed by the majority. Rights such as property, which in the state of nature are left to each individual to secure for himself, are protected by a common civil law that is executed by a government whose ultimate authority derives from the consent of the governed.

Following Locke, the "Memorial" begins with a statement of natural rights: Men have a natural right to exercise religion according to conviction and conscience. Madison derives this right from the "fundamental and undeniable truth" that had been set forth previously in Article XVI of the Virginia Declaration of Rights:

Religion or the duty which we owe to our Creator and the Manner of discharging it, can be directed only by reason and conviction, not by force or violence.

The "Memorial" presupposes this "truth" as its fundamental starting point. As is discussed in the next section, it does not attempt to demonstrate how or why religion can be directed only by reason and conviction; it takes this theological point as given.

Because the exercise of religion must follow one's own conscience and conviction, it is a particular kind of natural right, an inalienable natural right. Madison gives two reasons why. First:

because the opinions of men, depending only on the evidence contemplated by their own minds, cannot follow the dictates of other men. . . .

Since religion is a matter of conviction and conscience, the essence of religion is opinions – namely, opinions about the duties man owes to the Creator and how those duties ought to be discharged. Opinions, Madison says, depend only on the evidence contemplated by the mind. Similarly to Jefferson in the

Virginia Statute, Madison here follows the argument of Locke's *A Letter Concerning Toleration*. Every man, Locke claims, comes to his opinions and beliefs individually by virtue of the evidence he sees and finds persuasive. Since opinions and beliefs can be shaped by evidence alone, no man can impose his opinions on any other man; all that can be proffered is persuasive evidence and argument. Similarly, no man can simply accept the opinions of another, even if he wishes to, if he is not truly persuaded.[40] Opinions, then, are very different from other types of property such as land and money. Whereas a man can freely give away his money or have it stolen from him, no man can cede or lose his opinions unless he loses his mind. The right to one's opinions, accordingly, is different from one's right to other forms of property. Whereas men transform their natural right to possessions into a civil right to property upon entering into the social compact, men do not similarly transform the right to their opinions. Opinions by their nature cannot be alienated, and therefore religion, which is essentially opinion, is an inalienable natural right.[41]

The second reason Madison gives for the inalienable character of man's natural religious right is that:

what is here a right towards men, is a duty towards the Creator. It is the duty of every man to render to the Creator such homage, and such only, as he believes to be acceptable to him. This duty is precedent both in order of time and degree of obligation, to the claims of Civil Society.

Here, again, Madison relies on a distinction made by Locke in *A Letter Concerning Toleration*. Civil society, Locke maintains, arises in order to

---

[40] John Locke, *A Letter Concerning Toleration*, ed. James H. Tully (Indianapolis: Hackett, 1983 (originally published in 1689)), 27.

[41] Madison also makes the distinction between alienable (e.g., money) and inalienable (e.g., opinions) types of property in his essay, "Property," which originally appeared on March 29, 1792, in the *National Gazette*:

> In its larger and juster meaning, it [property] embraces everything to which a man may attach a value and have a right, and *which leaves to every one else the like advantage.* In the former sense, a man's land, or merchandise, or money, is called his property. In the latter sense, a man has a property in his opinions and the free communication of them. He has a property of peculiar value in his religious opinions, and in the profession and practice dictated by them .... In a word, as a man is said to have a right to his property, he may be equally said to have a property in his rights. ... Conscience is the most sacred of all property; other property depending in part on the positive law, the exercise of that being a natural and unalienable right.

> Madison's emphasis. James Madison, "Property," in *The Mind of the Founder: Sources of the Political Thought of James Madison*, ed. Marvin Meyers, rev. edition (Hanover, NH: Brandeis University Press, 1981), 186–87.

overcome war and poverty. At the most basic level, the social compact aims at the protection of life and to secure the conditions that allow for material comfort.[42] Religion, in contrast, is concerned with the good of the soul, which means, ultimately, either eternal salvation or damnation.[43] Madison assumes Locke's separation of religion from civic obligations and, from this, concludes that religious duties take precedence over the claims of civil society. Religious duties are precedent in time because a man's relationship with God exists prior to his citizenship. More importantly, religious duties are precedent in degree of authority because man's eternal soul is of higher status than his temporal body. Just as no rational man would ever sacrifice his eternal soul for the temporary good of his body, a man could never rationally forsake his duties to God in order to fulfill his duties as a citizen. Duties of citizenship – that is, the obligations one agrees to upon entering the social compact – cannot trespass upon duties to God. It would be irrational and contrary to the gravity and nature of man's religious obligations for men to agree to a social compact that includes religious obligations or precepts. Religion, thus, is an inalienable natural right.

Having established the inalienable nature of man's natural religious right, Madison's argument reaches its pinnacle:

We maintain therefore that in matters of Religion, no man's right is abridged by the institution of Civil Society, and that Religion is wholly exempt from its cognizance.

For Madison, the inalienable character of man's natural right to religion has a precise meaning and implication.[44] Because man's religious right is inalienable, it does not become part of the social compact. Literally, it is not alienated; men retain what they possessed in the state of nature. The status of man's religious right, then, is different from property rights such as land and money within the social compact. Whereas the right to land or money is limited equally within civil society (and thereby better

---

[42] Locke, *Letter Concerning Toleration*, 26.
[43] Ibid., 28.
[44] For a discussion of the Founders' understanding of the difference and relationship between natural rights and civil rights, see Philip A. Hamburger, "Equality and Diversity: The Eighteenth-Century Debate About Equal Protection and Equal Civil Rights," in *1992 The Supreme Court Review*, eds. Dennis J. Hutchinson, David A. Strauss, and Geoffrey R. Stone (Chicago: University of Chicago Press, 1993), 295–392.

•

secured), religion, Madison says, "is wholly exempt from its [civil society's] cognizance."

Used in a legal sense, the word "cognizance," then as now, means "the action of taking judicial or authoritative notice," or "jurisdiction." More generally, it means "knowledge," "perception," or "the state of being aware of."[45] A state noncognizant of religion lacks jurisdiction over religion. It may not take authoritative notice of or perceive religion or the religious affiliation of its citizens. A government noncognizant of religion, in other words, must be blind to religion. It cannot use religion or religious preference as a basis for classifying citizens. This is the doctrinal teaching of the "Memorial and Remonstrance." The state, which is a product of the social compact between men originally born in the state of nature, must remain noncognizant of religion because religion is not a part of the social compact. Religion cannot be part of the social compact because of the inalienable character of man's right to direct his religion according to conviction and conscience.

Insofar as Henry's bill is cognizant of religion, then, it usurps power. It violates the fundamental principles of the social compact. This is why Madison uses the language of tyranny and slavery in Article 2 of the "Memorial." The preservation of free government, he says, requires, first, the separation of powers, but also, and more importantly, that no branch of government "overleap the great Barrier which defends the rights of people." This great barrier is the social compact through which the people grant legitimate authority to those who govern. Rulers guilty of an encroachment on the social compact "exceed the commission from which they derive their authority, and are Tyrants." It may seem hyperbolic and demagogic to characterize the Virginia House of Delegates as tyrannical for considering a bill favored by many citizens, but Madison's point is that every encroachment of the social compact, even a popular one, usurps power. It is to rule without legitimate consent, which is tyranny. "The People who submit to it," Madison continues, "are governed by laws made neither by themselves, nor by an authority derived from them. . . ." No free people could approve legislation that classifies citizens and grants them benefits on account of their religious affiliation

[45] *Oxford English Dictionary*, 2nd ed., *s.v.* "cognizance." See also the entry under "cognition" in Samuel Johnson, *A Dictionary of the English Language* (London: W. Strahan, 1755) and "cognizance" in John Ash, *The New and Complete Dictionary of the English Language* (London: 1775).

because religion lies outside the jurisdiction of any social compact that respects and secures natural rights.

In the "Memorial's" fourth article, Madison derives the implications of noncognizance with regard to equality. "If all men are by nature equally free and independent," Madison reasons,

all men are to be considered as entering into Society on equal conditions; as relinquishing no more, and therefore retaining no less, one than another, of their natural rights. Above all they are to be considered as retaining an *equal* title to the free exercise of Religion according to the dictates of conscience . . . . As the Bill violates equality by subjecting some to peculiar burdens; so it violates the same principle, by granting to others peculiar exemptions.[46]

Madison does not identify who Henry's proposed bill burdens but presumably he means non-Christians and, perhaps, Catholics. Like everyone else, they had to pay the tax, but their ministers were not eligible for funding under the bill. The "extraordinary" privilege Madison rails against is that Quakers and Mennonites (or "Menonists," as both the bill and Madison called them) would receive their appropriations with no restrictions attached. On its face, this exception does not seem like a distinct privilege but rather a realistic accommodation for denominations that lacked ministers of the gospel – in order to use the funds appropriated to them for Christian education, Quakers and Mennonites would have to fall under a different set of rules. A corollary to the doctrine of noncognizance, however, is formal equality. Members of different religions may not be treated differently on account of their religion because any legal exemption or exception based on religious affiliation by definition takes religion into the state's cognizance. To grant exemptions or exceptions on the basis of religious affiliation requires the recognition of religion. All exemptions and exceptions, therefore, no matter how miniscule or convenient, violate the principle of religious liberty.[47]

---

[46] Emphasis in the original.

[47] I disagree with Steven D. Smith's criticism of the "Memorial" regarding its treatment of Quakers and Mennonites. Smith writes, "the fudginess in Madison's treatment of Quakers and Mennonites points to a larger problem that afflicted Madison's 'Memorial and Remonstrance' at all levels"; namely, that Madison begged the question of the meaning of religious liberty by appealing to "equality." See Steven D. Smith, "Blooming Confusion: Madison's Mixed Legacy," *Indiana Law Journal* 75 (Winter 2000): 66–68. I believe that Smith fails to recognize that Madison's appeal to "equality" in Article 4 derives from his social compact argument in Article 1. Smith thus does not see the basis on which Madison derives his principle.

The principle of formal equality follows from the principle of noncognizance.[48]

Articles 5 through 14 of the "Memorial" offer prudential arguments. Henry's proposed assessment should be rejected, Madison contends, because it: implies either that the civil magistrate is a competent judge of religious truth or that he may employ religion as an engine of civil policy (Article 5); is not needed for the support of the Christian religion (Article 6); will corrupt the purity and efficacy of religion (Article 7); is unnecessary for the support of civil government (Article 8); is a signal of persecution and

---

[48] Although I agree with most of Paul Weber's interpretation of Madison in "James Madison and Religious Equality: The Perfect Separation," *Review of Politics* 44 (April 1982): 163–86, I disagree with his contention that equality is the fundamental teaching of the "Memorial and Remonstrance." The "Memorial's" argument from equality, Weber correctly points out, reveals Madison's understanding that a proper church-state relationship requires the state to treat all religions and religious citizens equally to one another and equally to nonreligious citizens. Equality does not exhaust the principle of noncognizance, however. The demand for equal treatment could be met while still using religion as a basis for classification (the 1790 census, discussed in this chapter, is an example of such a case). To say the same thing differently, equality relates only to the application of a law to different classes of citizens; it says nothing about the authority of the state to make those classifications in the first place. In the assessment case, equality demands that all citizens be treated equally regardless of religion. But equality alone does not consider whether the state has the authority to pass an assessment for religion. The "Memorial's" fundamental teaching, with which it both begins and ends, is jurisdictional – namely, that states lack jurisdiction to enact a law that takes cognizance of religion. This is why Madison concludes in Article 15 by calling Henry's bill a dangerous "usurpation" by the legislature violating "the trust committed to them." While the assessment does violate the equality "which ought to be the basis of every law," its most egregious offense is its "dangerous abuse of power," which will allow the legislature to act tyrannically, thus enslaving the people.

The shortcoming in Weber's interpretation is that he overemphasizes Article 4 of the "Memorial" at the expense of recognizing Madison's social compact argument in Article 1. This leads him to misinterpret Article 15, which begins, "Because, finally, 'the equal right of every citizen to the free exercise of his Religion according to the dictates of conscience' is held by the same tenure with all our other rights." Weber takes this statement to mean that individuals' religious rights are protected just like other natural rights. For Madison, Weber contends, "religion is an inalienable right on a par with other natural rights such as life and property" (p. 185). Madison's point in Article 15 is actually that religious rights, like other rights, are secure only if the legislature respects the terms of the social compact. Both inalienable natural rights (religion) and natural rights limited and protected as equal civil rights (property) are secured by the maintenance of the social compact. Madison's point is not that they have the same status under that compact, but that they are both protected by respecting the limits of the compact. Nonetheless, I agree with Weber's conclusion that "Madison's principle [of religious liberty] was that religious individuals had the same rights and privileges – and no other – as any other individuals and associations" (p. 185). It is precisely because religion is an inalienable natural right, different from other natural rights, that this conclusion is true.

thus will discourage immigration (Article 9); encourages emigration (Article 10); will encourage rivalry between sects to control the government (Article 11); is adverse to the diffusion of the light of Christianity (Article 12); is obnoxious to a great proportion of the citizens, who will not follow the law, thus enervating the authority of the law in general (Article 13); and because a matter of such importance should not be imposed without the clearest evidence of a support of the majority, which is not secured (Article 14).[49] Article 15, as mentioned, concludes the "Memorial" by returning to its social compact foundations. The principal and principled argument of the "Memorial," to repeat, is that the exercise of religion is an inalienable natural right and therefore that religion is not part of the social compact. The state, accordingly, must remain noncognizant of religion, which means that it can neither privilege nor punish citizens on account of religion or religious affiliation.

Although the "Memorial and Remonstrance" adopts Locke's basic social contract framework, Madison's derivation of the principle of non-cognizance represents a significant break from Locke. In *A Letter Concerning Toleration*, Locke does not speak of religion as an "inalienable" right, nor does he claim that the state must remain noncognizant of religion. Locke explicitly says that civil magistrates are not obliged to tolerate "opinions contrary to human society, or to those moral rules which are necessary to the preservation of civil society."[50] In this context, Locke famously teaches that civil magistrates need not tolerate atheists or "that church [whose members] ... *ipso facto* deliver themselves up to the protection and service of another prince," that is, the Catholic Church.[51] Locke clearly allows the state to be cognizant of a citizen's religious belief or lack thereof. Madison breaks from Locke on this point; his principle of noncognizance is uniquely his own.

The "Memorial's" Implicit Theology

We noted in the previous section that the "Memorial" begins with the premise "that Religion or the duty which we owe to our Creator and

---

[49] For a helpful restatement of the bare bones of the "Memorial's" argument, see Eva Brann, "Madison's 'Memorial and Remonstrance,'" in *The Past Present: Selected Writings of Eva Brann*, ed. Pamela Kraus (Annapolis, MD: St. John's College Press, 1997), 245.

[50] Locke, *Letter Concerning Toleration*, 49.

[51] Ibid., 50.

the Manner of discharging it, can be directed only by reason and conviction, not by force or violence," language Madison borrowed from Article XVI of the Virginia Declaration of Rights. The "Memorial" then states, "The Religion then of every man must be left to the conviction and conscience of every man; and it is the right of every man to exercise it as these may dictate." Madison does not defend this particular under-standing of religious obligation. He does not explain why religion can be directed only by reason and conviction. He takes these theological premises as given.

The "Memorial's" argument assumes that a "Creator" exists and that it is attentive to an individual's conviction and conscience. The argument also assumes that men owe this providential deity a particular sort of "homage" – our religious duties must be "directed by reason and convic-tion" in accordance with our "conviction and conscience." The Creator presumed by the "Memorial and Remonstrance" favors only free and voluntary worship that reflects the individual's interior conviction; it does not recognize religious duties discharged on account of force or violence. The "Memorial" does not specify the particular forms of worship that the Creator requires (if such forms exist), but it does claim that whatever they may be, the individual himself must believe that they are acceptable to God. It assumes that if God requires specific rituals or actions, they must be performed with sincere belief to be salutary. In the "Memorial's" theology, faith is primary; an individual conceivably could achieve salvation with faith alone, but he could not with acts absent faith.[52]

The "Memorial's" focus on the individual's conscience suggests that salvation is granted to individuals as such and that the individual's rela-tionship with God is separate from national citizenship. The argument assumes that God does not save nations, communities, or territories, and that He does not reward particular peoples or traditions as such. The "Memorial's" Creator must grant salvation to individuals as such because it posits that the sincerity of an individual's beliefs is essential

---

[52] I disagree with Thomas Lindsay, who, in interpreting the "Memorial and Remonstrance," claims, "Madison's project for religious liberty is theoretically grounded in the denial of human capacity to know the nature of and existence of the commands of – and thus the duties toward – revelation's God." The opposite seems to be true. The "Memorial" appears to be premised on the theological insight that the "Creator" requires sincere and authentic worship. See Lindsay, "James Madison on Religion and Politics: Rhetoric and Reality," *American Political Science Review* 85, no. 4 (1991): 1326.

in the economy of salvation. Madison's God, moreover, does not allow one individual to meet the religious obligations of another. Proselytizing can only take the form of persuasion. Insofar as law fails to speak to interior conviction, the coercive force of law cannot lead men to salvation. Lawgivers, accordingly, are all but impotent in such matters. Because "it is the duty of every man to render to the Creator such homage, and only such, as he believes to be acceptable to him," citizens cannot have a duty to render homage deemed appropriate by those who possess political power. The New Testament might say, "Let every person be subject to the government authorities; for there is no authority except from God, and those authorities that exist have been instituted by God,"[53] but according to the "Memorial," political rulers possess no special authority to determine religious obligations.

The "Memorial," in fact, denies that God establishes specific political authorities. Article 2 declares that political authorities "are but the creatures and vicegerents" of society at large. Article 4 states that if men abuse their freedom and fail to meet their religious duties, "it is an offence against God, not against man." The failure to perform one's religious obligations cannot offend political authorities, according to Madison's argument, because God has given no man legal authority to enforce the religious obligations of another.

Given this theology, one might easily agree with historian Lance Banning that "the 'Memorial' was obviously written from a Christian point of view."[54] Precision demands, however, that all we say with certainty is that Madison's argument for religious freedom adopts a theology compatible with many forms of Christianity. This reservation accounts for the possibility that Madison may have believed his argument was grounded on natural theology alone. We must also remember that Madison wrote the "Memorial" in the midst of the fierce battle over Patrick Henry's proposed general religious establishment bill. His immediate (though certainly not his only) intention was to persuade a largely Protestant audience. Although the political context is not decisive in itself, it should not surprise

---

[53] Rom. 13:1 (New Revised Standard Version).

[54] Lance Banning, *The Sacred Fire of Liberty: James Madison and the Founding of the Federal Republic* (Ithaca, NY: Cornell University Press, 1995), 436n.68. Gary Rosen makes a similar point, referring to "the obvious Protestant subtext" of the "Memorial." Rosen then draws out the following theological implications: "Religious truth becomes a particular sort of experience rather than a doctrine. In this view, sincerity takes the place of right-thinking and -acting." Gary Rosen, *American Compact: James Madison and the Problem of Founding* (Lawrence: University Press of Kansas, 1999), 23.

us that Madison employed arguments that appealed to his immediate audience.[55]

MADISON'S POLITICAL EFFORTS TO ESTABLISH RELIGIOUS LIBERTY

The "Memorial and Remonstrance" offers Madison's most comprehensive philosophical statement on the fundamental political principles excluding religion as such from civil jurisdiction. It stands as the pinnacle of his theoretical reflections on the subject of church and state. We must not overlook, though, that Madison was a man of political practice as well as political philosophy. He labored for the cause of religious liberty throughout his political career, from his first year in the Virginia House of Delegates to his final station as the nation's foremost retired statesman. These efforts offer ample material to test any hypothesized interpretation of Madison's principle of religious liberty. A careful consideration of these events reveals that the principle of noncognizance explains many of Madison's political actions. Aside from two exceptional instances, Madison maintained a sustained commitment to the maxim that the state may neither privilege nor penalize citizens on account of their religion.

Madison's Revision of the Virginia Declaration of Rights

Madison's first political contribution to the cause of religious liberty was a proposed amendment to the religion article of the Virginia Declaration of Rights. In the late spring of 1776, Virginia's Revolutionary Convention moved to adopt a declaration of rights. George Mason's slightly revised initial draft stated:

That religion or the duty which we owe to our CREATOR, and the manner of discharging it, can be governed only by reason and conviction, not by force or

---

[55] Regarding this point, Lance Banning states,

> Admittedly, this [the "Memorial's" Christian point of view] may have been a tactical consideration, but it was not a *necessary* tactic in this situation. I am convinced that Madison consistently adopted tactics that did not dissemble his private views, that there was a very little of the propagandist in his makeup. The Memorial is thus my major reason for concluding that his thinking still had room for the authority of revelation at least as late as 1785.

Banning's emphasis, *Sacred Fire of Liberty*, 436n.68. Thomas Lindsay, on the contrary, argues that Madison's theology in the "Memorial" was merely rhetorical and disconnected from his private views. See Lindsay, "James Madison on Religion and Politics," 1321.

violence; and therefore, that all men should enjoy the fullest toleration in the exercise of religion, according to the dictates of conscience, unpublished and unrestrained by the magistrate, unless, under colour of religion, any man disturb the peace, the happiness, or safety of society. And that it is the mutual duty of all to practice Christian forbearance, love and charity, towards each other.[56]

Dissatisfied with Mason's text, Madison initially proposed the following revision (Madison's additions are in bold type):

That **R**eligion or the duty we owe to our Creator, and the manner of discharging it, **being under the direction of** reason and conviction only, not violence or **compulsion**, all men **are equally entitled to** the full and **free exercise** of it accord[in]g to the dictates of Conscience; **and therefore that no man or class of men ought, on account of religion to be invested with peculiar emoluments or privileges, nor subjected to any penalties or disabilities** unless under &c.[57]

Most commentators highlight Madison's replacement of Mason's language of toleration with the language of rights.[58] More important, however, is Madison's clarification of what the right of free exercise means. Men are equally entitled to the full and free exercise of religion according to conscience; therefore, Madison explains, no man or class of men is to be invested with particular privileges or subject to particular penalties on account of religion. The full and free exercise of religion and freedom of conscience means no privileges or penalties on account of religion.[59] Madison says here exactly the same thing he would declare a decade later in the "Memorial and Remonstrance": Religious citizens are to be treated the same

---

56 James Madison, *The Papers of James Madison*, Congressional Series, ed. William T. Hutchinson et al. (Chicago: University of Chicago Press, 1962–91), 1:173.

57 Ibid., 174.

58 See, e.g., Gaillard Hunt, "James Madison and Religious Liberty," in *Annual Report of the American Historical Association for the Year 1901* (Washington, DC: Government Printing Office, 1901), 1:166; Buckley, *Church and State in Revolutionary Virginia*, 18; Dreisbach, "George Mason's Pursuit of Religious Liberty in Revolutionary Virginia," 14. For a discussion of the difference between religious "toleration" and religious "liberty," see Daniel Palm, "Religious Toleration and Religious Liberty at the Founding," in *On Faith and Free Government*, ed. Daniel Palm (Lanham, MD: Rowman & Littlefield, 1997), 29–42.

59 Cf. Aviam Soifer, "The Fullness of Time," in *Obligations of Citizenship*, ed. Nancy Rosenblum (Princeton, NJ: Princeton University Press, 2000), 245–79. In "The Origins and Historical Understanding of Free Exercise of Religion," Michael McConnell fails to address the meaning of Madison's proposed language – "therefore that no man or class of men ought, on account of religion to be invested with peculiar emoluments or privileges, nor subjected to any penalties or disabilities" – because he relies on Sanford Cobb's incomplete historical record. See note 29.

as all other citizens, with no distinctions made on the basis of religious affiliation. Civil government is to be blind to religion as such.

The Virginia Convention quickly rejected Madison's proposed amendment because his language seemed incompatible with the existing Anglican establishment.[60] If no class of men was eligible for peculiar emoluments on account of their religion, then Anglican clergy could not be employed by the state. Instead, Virginia adopted an amendment that declared that "all men are equally entitled to the free exercise of religion, according to the dictates of conscience" without clarification.[61] The exact parameters of "free exercise of religion" were left unstated, and debate over the Anglican establishment was left for another day. Madison, however, had already arrived at his understanding of the principle of religious liberty. A decade later, when political circumstances had changed, he would bring Virginia's law of religious freedom more in accordance with his understanding of the right to religious freedom.

Madison and the Drafting of the Bill of Rights

By 1789 Madison had left the Virginia House of Delegates to represent his state in the U.S. House of Representatives. One of his first legislative aims was to secure the adoption of a bill of rights. The drafting of the First Amendment, however, offers little guidance for understanding Madison's principle of religious liberty. Along with nearly every member of the Constitutional Convention, Madison initially did not think a bill of rights essential.[62] Political liberty

---

[60] Buckley, *Church and State in Revolutionary Virginia*, 19.

[61] The following was adopted as Article XVI of the Virginia Declaration of Rights:

> That religion, or the duty to which we owe to our CREATOR, and the manner of discharging it, can be directed only by reason and conviction, not by force or violence; and therefore, all men are equally entitled to the free exercise of religion, according to the dictates of conscience; and that it is the mutual duty of all to practice Christian forbearance, love, and charity, towards each other.

> Reprinted in *The Founders' Constitution*, eds. Philip B. Kurland and Ralph Lerner (Chicago: University of Chicago Press, 1987), 5:70.

[62] The Constitutional Convention spent almost no time considering whether to include a bill of rights in the Constitution. When adopting a bill of rights was proposed on September 12, no state delegation voted in favor of the motion. See Max Farrand, *The Records of the Federal Convention of 1787*, revised edition (New Haven, CT: Yale University Press, 1966), 2:588. See also James Wilson's recollection during the Pennsylvania Ratifying Convention of the Constitutional Convention's near-unanimous opinion of the lack of necessity of a bill of rights in Farrand, *The Records of the Federal Convention of 1787*, 3:143–44.

required a carefully designed system of representation; the separation of powers; and the cultivation of republican character in an extended, diverse, commercial republic – elements that were provided by the unamended Constitution. Bills of rights, Madison said, were "parchment barriers" and, therefore, not to be relied on to protect rights.[63]

Madison's view of the necessity of adopting a bill of rights would change, but his leadership to secure amendments remained primarily defensive.[64] By pushing Congress to adopt amendments, Madison aimed to fulfill the promise made to those states that ratified the Constitution with the expectation of alterations. At the same time, he sought to silence the Constitution's critics and to prevent a second meddlesome and potentially damaging constitutional convention.[65] Last in his priorities was to make changes that might do some good.[66] For Madison, the adoption of the Bill of Rights was more pragmatic than principled. This is one of the reasons why he identified the battle for disestablishment in Virginia and the Virginia Statute, and not the debates in the First Congress and the First Amendment, as "where religious liberty is placed on its true foundation and is defined in its full latitude."[67]

Compounding this difficulty is also the fact that the final text of the First Amendment was the product of debate and compromise within and among legislative committees. The religion clauses went through several changes offered by numerous congressmen.[68] Although Madison certainly had influence, he was not the sole author and, hence, not solely responsible for the adopted text.[69]

---

[63] For Publius' (Hamilton) statement against a bill of rights, see *Federalist* 84.

[64] Robert A. Goldwin, *From Parchment to Power: How James Madison Used the Bill of Rights to Save the Constitution* (Washington, DC: AEI Press, 1997), esp. Chapters 4 and 5. For a somewhat different view, see Michael P. Zuckert's review of Goldwin's book in *Interpretation* 26, no. 3 (1999): 418.

[65] For Madison's view of the possible danger of a second constitutional convention, see his letter to Edmund Randolph, April 10, 1788, in *Letters and Other Writings of James Madison*, 1:386.

[66] See Madison's letter to George Eve, January 2, 1789, in *Letters and Other Writings of James Madison*, 1:446–48.

[67] Fleet, "Madison's 'Detached Memoranda,'" 554.

[68] For a discussion of the drafting of the Establishment Clause, see Vincent Phillip Muñoz, "The Original Meaning of the Establishment Clause and the Impossibility of Its Incorporation," *University of Pennsylvania Journal of Constitutional Law* 8 (2006): 623–31. For a discussion of the drafting of the Free Exercise Clause, see Vincent Phillip Muñoz, "The Original Meaning of the Free Exercise Clause," 1100–09.

[69] For a discussion of the degree to which Madison is responsible for the final text of the First Amendment's religion clauses, see Donald L. Drakeman, "Religion and the Republic: James Madison and the First Amendment," *Journal of Church and State* 25 (1983): 427–45.

What we know for certain is that Madison drafted the initial text proposed and that he made a few comments on subsequent proposals on the House floor. For the national government, Madison proposed,

The civil rights of none shall be abridged on account of religious belief or worship, nor shall any national religion be established, nor shall the full and equal rights of conscience be in any manner or in any pretext, infringed.[70]

He also proposed an amendment to apply against the states:

No state shall violate the equal rights of conscience.[71]

Madison clearly sought to prevent the federal government from penalizing citizens because of their religious affiliation or practices, as can be seen in his proposed text, "The civil rights of none shall be abridged on account of religion or worship." During the House debates, Madison also associated immunities from legal penalties with the prohibition against an establishment and the protection of the rights of conscience. On August 15, 1789 – when the House was considering the text "No religion shall be established by Law, nor shall the equal rights of conscience be infringed" – Madison was recorded as making the following statement:

Mr. MADISON said he apprehended the meaning of the words to be, that congress should not establish a religion, and enforce the legal observation of it by law, nor compel men to worship God in any manner contrary to their conscience; whether the words were necessary or not he did not mean to say, but that had been required by some of the state conventions, who seemed to entertain an opinion that under the clause of the constitution, which gave power to congress to make all laws necessary and proper to carry into execution the constitution, and the laws made under it, enabled them to make laws of such a nature as might infringe the rights of conscience or establish a national religion. To prevent these effects he presumed the amendment was intended, and he thought it as well expressed as the nature of language would admit.[72]

As explained by Madison here, the text prohibiting an establishment and recognizing the rights of conscience is meant to prohibit the creation of laws that penalize individuals on account of their religious practices or lack thereof. We also note that Madison's comment reveals a degree of indifference toward the precise language used because, he intimates, an amendment

---

[70] *Annals of the Congress of the United States, 1789–1834* (Washington, DC: Gales and Seaton, 1789), 1st Cong., 1st sess., 1:451; Madison, *Papers of James Madison*, 12:201.
[71] Ibid.
[72] *Annals of Congress*, 1st Cong., 1st sess., 758.

is not really necessary. The underlying purpose of the amendment, he says, is to satisfy those who ratified the Constitution with reservations, not to remedy defects in the Constitution.[73]

Whereas the no-penalty aspect of Madison's approach to religious liberty appears in his draft of the First Amendment, no evidence exists to suggest that Madison sought to impose the rule of no privileges for religion as such. If Madison believed the prohibition of an establishment or the rights of conscience meant no privileges, he never said so directly. In the First Congress, Madison may have been reticent about what he was willing to say given his experience in Virginia in 1776, where his advocacy of no privileges was defeated. We also know that Madison doubted the efficacy of adopting a bill of rights, in part because he feared that any attempt to do so would fail to define the rights of the people in the requisite latitude. "I am sure that the rights of conscience in particular," he wrote to Jefferson in 1788, "if submitted to public definition, would be narrowed much more than they are likely ever to be by an assumed [federal] power."[74]

Madison also likely did not push the no-privileges rule because it would have contradicted one of his other proposed amendments. Madison's original proposal for what became the Second Amendment read:

The right of the people to keep and bear arms shall not be infringed; a well armed and well regulated militia being the best security of a free country: but no person religiously scrupulous of bearing arms shall be compelled to render military service in person.[75]

When Madison proposed this text, the states of Virginia and North Carolina had already proposed to Congress a constitutional amendment to exempt conscientious objectors from military service. Additionally, anti-Federalist

---

[73] All familiar with Madison's politics would have known that one year earlier he had vehemently argued that such an amendment was unnecessary. At the Virginia Ratifying Convention on June 12, 1788, Madison had declared that "there is not a shadow of a right in the general government to intermeddle with religion" and that the national government's "least interference with it [religion] would be a most flagrant usurpation." *Debates in the Several State Conventions on the Adoption of the Federal Constitution*, ed. Jonathan Elliot (Washington, DC, 1836), 3:330. Madison's reasoning, which was stated by many Federalists, was that the national legislature's powers were enumerated and no power over religion was granted to Congress; therefore, with or without an amendment, Congress lacked authority over religion. Given this lack of authority, Federalists such as Madison likely thought that the exact language used to restrict Congress's power over religion did not much matter.

[74] James Madison to Thomas Jefferson, October 17, 1788, *Letters and Other Writings of James Madison*, 1:424.

[75] *Annals of Congress*, 1st Cong., 1st sess., 451.

minorities from Pennsylvania and Maryland also had called for a conscientious exemption amendment.[76] Given this context, Madison's proposal can be understood as an attempt to address a concern the Constitution's critics had repeatedly articulated.

Nonetheless, his proposed conscientious objector provision facially violated his principle of noncognizance by granting a legal privilege on account of religious belief. The proposed text, moreover, explicitly used the phrase "religiously scrupulous." Madison did not try to minimize the state's cognizance of religion by using a nonreligious standard for exemption eligibility. Unfortunately, the records of the First Congress lack any statements by Madison commenting on this proposal, which was ultimately defeated in the Senate. Perhaps Madison thought it had to be proposed to satisfy the Constitution's critics and, therefore, that it was a political necessity. But even if it was necessary, the proposal to exempt "religiously scrupulous" conscientious objectors from military service contradicts the principle of noncognizance articulated in the "Memorial and Remonstrance."

Given Madison's expressly stated political intention in securing a bill of rights and the paucity and unreliability of the congressional record, the records of the drafting of the Bill of Rights are a relatively poor source for information about Madison's doctrine of religious liberty. It is clear, however, that Madison did not propose the rule of noncognizance for what would become the First Amendment. His proposed language preventing the national government from abridging the civil rights of citizens on account of their religion approximates noncognizance's no-penalty provision. Madison also associated his proposed prohibition of establishments and the rights of conscience with immunity from legal penalties on account of religion. But Madison's proposal for what became the Second

---

[76] Rhode Island would later submit the same text that Virginia and North Carolina had proposed, which read, "That any person religiously scrupulous of bearing arms ought to be exempted, upon payment of an equivalent to employ another in his stead." *The Founders Constitution*, 5:16 (Virginia), 5:18 (North Carolina); *The Debates in the Several State Conventions*, 1:335 (Rhode Island). During the Pennsylvania ratification debates, opponents of the Constitution had argued, "[t]he rights of conscience may be violated, as there is no exemption of those persons who are conscientiously scrupulous of bearing arms." *The Debates on the Constitution: Federalist and Antifederalist Speeches, Articles, and Letters During the Struggle Over Ratification*, ed. Bernard Bailyn (New York: The Library of America Press, 1993), 1:532. During the Maryland ratification debates, the anti-Federalist minority proposed the following constitutional amendment: "That no person, conscientiously scrupulous of bearing arms in any case, shall be compelled personally to serve as a soldier." *The Complete Anti-Federalist*, ed. Herbert J. Storing (Chicago: University of Chicago Press, 1981), 5:97.

Amendment departed from the principle of noncognizance by extending exemptions from militia service to those who were "religiously scrupulous."

Madison on Government Classifications Based on Religious Affiliation

When Madison first had the opportunity to interpret the First Amendment a few months later, however, he returned to his strict noncognizance doctrine. In early 1790, following Article I, section 2, of the Constitution, the House of Representatives made preparations to conduct the first national census. Madison suggested that, in addition to obtaining an enumeration of the population, the census include questions that might provide information useful to Congress, such as the relative proportions of citizens engaged in agriculture, manufacturing, and commerce.[77] There was a limit, however, to what questions Congress could ask. The census, he said, should ascertain information "only so far as to be extremely useful, when we come to pass laws, affecting any particular description of people." It could not ask, therefore, whether a citizen was a religious minister:

> As to those who are employed in teaching and inculcating the duties of religion, there may be some indelicacy in singling them out, as the General Government is proscribed from interfering, in any manner whatever, in matters respecting religion; and it may be thought to do this, in ascertaining who, and who are not ministers of the Gospel.[78]

Madison's comments suggested two problems with asking citizens if they are religious ministers. First, knowing the relative number of ministers would in no way be useful to Congress. Ministers as such could never properly be the subject of legislation because the Constitution proscribes the federal government from intermeddling with religion. Second, the very act of ascertaining who is and who is not a minister itself violates constitutional principles. To identify ministers as ministers is to classify citizens on account of their religion. Even in something as innocuous as a census, Madison stood firm on the principle of noncognizance.[79]

---

[77] *Annals of Congress*, 1st Cong., 2nd sess., 1115.

[78] Ibid., 1146.

[79] Brant, "Madison: On the Separation of Church and State," 17–18, interprets Madison's remarks on the census to support his larger contention that Madison sought to prohibit all federal aid to religion. While it is true that Madison would prohibit aid to religion as such, Brant fails to recognize that this conclusion is derivative from Madison's principle of noncognizance, not Madison's principle itself. Because of privacy concerns (see Mr. Livermore's objections in *Annals of Congress*, 1st Cong., 2nd sess., 1145), the 1790 census asked only the names and numbers of persons in every household.

Madison had taken exactly the same position on a different issue two years earlier. In 1788 he had received a letter from John Brown, a leading politician from Kentucky, asking his opinions about Thomas Jefferson's draft of a constitution. Jefferson had published his proposed constitution for Virginia as an appendix to *Notes on the State of Virginia*, and it was being read with attention because Kentucky was drafting its own constitution in preparation for statehood. Jefferson's proposed constitution included a provision excluding "ministers of the gospel" from the legislative assembly, a practice that was common at the time, especially in the South.[80] In his response to Brown, Madison singled out this exclusion for particular disparagement:

EXCLUSIONS. Does not the exclusion of Ministers of the Gospel as such violate a fundamental principle of liberty by punishing a religious profession with the privation of a civil right? does it [not] violate another article of the plan itself which exempts religion from the cognizance of Civil power? does it not violate justice by at once taking away a right and prohibiting compensation for it? does it not in fine violate impartiality by shutting the door against the Ministers of Religion and leaving it open for those of every other.[81]

To single out ministers for exclusion from political office penalizes them on account of religion. It is to act on the basis of religion, which is what the principle of religious liberty forbids. Here again Madison requires the law to be blind to the religious affiliation of citizens.

Madison on Government Support to Religion as Such

As president, Madison employed the principle of noncognizance to veto two congressional statutes. In February 1811, Congress passed a bill incorporating the Protestant Episcopal Church of Alexandria, DC. In addition to recognizing the church as a corporate body, the bill specified rules for

---

[80] About half the states belonging to the Union in the first half-century after independence, including Virginia, had constitutional provisions excluding clergymen and ministers of the gospel from serving in their state legislatures. See Anson Phelps Stokes, *Church and State in the United States* (New York: Harper & Brothers, 1950), 1:622–28.

[81] James Madison, *The Writings of James Madison,* ed. Gaillard Hunt (New York: G. P. Putnam's Sons, 1900–10), 5:288. Madison's reference "to another article of the plan" refers to text just three paragraphs below the provision excluding clergymen from public office, which stated, "The general assembly shall not have power to infringe this constitution, to abridge the civil rights of any person on account of his religious belief, to restrain him from professing and supporting that belief. . . ." The relevant passages of Jefferson's draft of a constitution can be found in *The Writings of Thomas Jefferson,* ed. Andrew A. Lipscomb (Washington, DC: Thomas Jefferson Memorial Association, 1904), 2:286–87.

electing and removing the church's ministers. This, Madison said, would make the church a religious establishment by law. It would subject sundry rules and proceedings pertaining purely to the church's internal organization to enforcement by the state. A government blind to religion could not make or enforce laws for the internal governance of a church. Madison also objected to Section 8 of the bill, which stated, "That it shall and may be lawful for the said vestry to make such provisions for the support of the poor of the said church as shall by them be thought proper. . . ."[82] This provision, Madison claimed, "would be a precedent for giving to religious Societies as such, a legal agency in carrying into effect a public and civil duty."[83] Madison's words "as such" indicate that his objection was not that the bill would allow a religious society to participate in the carrying out of public duties, but rather that it could be interpreted to imply that the church had legal mandate to help the poor because it was a church. Madison objected to the state granting a religious group special privileges because it was religious. It was the singling out of religion – the treating of religious groups as religious groups as such – that he said violated the Constitution.[84]

For the same reason, Madison vetoed a second bill concerning religion one week later. Congress passed a bill resolving the land claims of five individuals in the Mississippi territory.[85] The sixth section of the bill

---

[82] James Madison, *The Papers of James Madison,* Presidential Series, eds. J. C. A. Stagg et al. (Charlottesville: University of Virginia Press, 1984), 3:176.

[83] Ibid. Congress first passed the bill on February 8, 1811. Following Madison's veto, the House of Representatives debated the constitutionality of the bill and the means of reconsidering it before voting against its passage on February 23, 1811. See *Annals of Congress,* 11th Cong., 3rd sess., 129, 453, 828, 983–85, 995–98.

[84] James Hutson claims that the veto represents Madison's effort undertaken later in life to limit the political influence of ecclesiastical institutions, i.e., that Madison targeted religious institutions for unfavorable treatment. See James Hutson, "James Madison and the Social Utility of Religion: Risks vs. Rewards" (paper presented at the symposium "James Madison: Philosopher and Practitioner of Liberal Democracy," Library of Congress, Washington, DC, March 2001), 16–17. In his "Detached Memoranda," Madison did warn that "there is an evil which ought be guarded agst [sic] in the indefinite accumulation of property from the capacity of holding in perpetuity by ecclesiastical corporations." But Madison also said that "the power of *all corporations,* ought to be limited in this respect" (emphasis added). See Fleet, "Madison's 'Detached Memoranda,'" 556. Madison's concern about the accumulation and concentration of property was not exclusively about the property of religious institutions, as Hutson seems to suggest.

[85] "An Act for the relief of Richard Tervin, William Coleman, Edwin Lewis, Samuel Mims, Joseph Wilson, and the Baptist church at Salem meeting house, in the Mississippi Territory," passed by Congress on February 20, 1811, *American State Papers: Miscellaneous* (Washington, DC: Gales and Seaton, 1834), 2:154.

granted five acres to the Baptist church, which had erected a meeting house on the land. Madison vetoed the bill on the straightforward grounds that

reserving a certain parcel of land of the United States for the use of said Baptist Church, comprizes [sic] a principle and precedent for the appropriation of funds of the United States, for the use and support of Religious Societies . . . .[86]

Both vetoes reflected Madison's understanding that the rights of conscience and the functions of religion are, as he stated in his first Inaugural Address, "wisely exempted from civil jurisdiction."[87]

It would seem that Madison violated his principle of noncognizance in 1812 when he issued the first of his four presidential proclamations declaring national days of prayer and thanksgiving. The practice of issuing religious proclamations had been started by George Washington and continued by John Adams. Jefferson refused to issue them and Madison sought to follow Jefferson's example. During the War of 1812, however, Congress requested that President Madison revive the tradition. A perusal of the text of Madison's proclamations reveals his ambivalence in issuing them.[88] Each one begins with a statement that Congress had requested that a proclamation be issued. Madison's first proclamation, which is typical of all four, begins: "Whereas the Congress of the United States, by a joint resolution of the two Houses, have signified a request that a day may be recommended to be observed by the people. . . ."[89] Madison never takes personal responsibility for initiating the proclamations. He is careful, moreover, to emphasize their advisory character. He "recommends" "to all those who shall be piously disposed to" pray to do so.[90] Madison also uses nonsectarian language. He recommends that citizens render homage to the "Sovereign of the

---

[86] Madison, *Papers of James Madison*, Presidential Series, 3:193. On March 2, 1811, both Houses of Congress reconsidered the bill. The House failed to override Madison's veto, then passed the bill after removing the sixth section. The Senate concurred on March 3, 1811. See *Annals of Congress*, 11th Cong., 3rd sess., 125, 127, 150–51, 329, 508, 900, 1098, 1103, 1105, 1106. See also Madison's discussion of his veto in his letter dated June 3, 1811, to the Baptist Churches on Neal's Creek and on Black Creek, North Carolina, in *Letters and Other Writings of James Madison*, 2:511–12.

[87] Madison, *Papers of James Madison*, Presidential Series, 1:17.

[88] Madison's four proclamations requesting days of prayer and thanksgiving can be found in James D. Richardson, *A Compilation of the Messages and the Papers of the Presidents, 1789–1897* (Washington, DC: Government Printing Office, 1899), 1:513, 532–33, 558, 560–61.

[89] James Madison, Thanksgiving Proclamation of July 9, 1812, in Richardson, *A Compilation of the Messages and the Papers of the Presidents*, 513.

[90] James Madison, Proclamation of July 23, 1813, in Richardson, *A Compilation of the Messages and the Papers of the Presidents*, 532.

Universe" and "the Benefactor of Mankind" and celebrate "the goodness of the Great Disposer of Events."[91] In his "Detached Memoranda," Madison said that he issued the proclamations because he thought "it was not proper to refuse a compliance [to Congress] all together."[92] Removed from the exigencies of war and politics, however, Madison forthrightly revealed that his true position was that religious proclamations by the president violated the Constitution.

This revelation has been interpreted as conclusive proof that Madison stood for the strict separationist wall between church and state.[93] Madison's own explanation is more nuanced, however. First, Madison explicitly permits public leaders to make religious proclamations as private individuals, a point that is often overlooked:

In their individual capacities, as distinct from their official station, they [government officials] might unite in recommendations of any sort whatever, in the same manner as any other individuals might do. But then their recommendations ought to express the true character from which they emanate.[94]

What violates the Constitution are religious proclamations made by a government official acting in his official capacity. Even though proclamations alone are only advisory, "they imply a religious agency, making no part of the trust delegated to political rulers."[95] For the president acting in his official capacity to advise citizens to pray and give thanksgiving to God suggests that prayer is a legitimate subject for government action. But prayer, like every other aspect of religious worship, is not a part of the social compact. To issue an official religious proclamation implies that the state has authority over religion, which indicates a lack of understanding of the legitimate authority of the state and the nature of man's inalienable religious right.

In his "Detached Memoranda," Madison also writes that congressional and military chaplains violate the First Amendment for the same reason. The purpose of chaplains is to facilitate religious worship, and although "it [may] be proper that public functionaries, as well as their Constituents shd [sic] discharge their religious duties," such is not a proper object for

---

[91] James Madison, Thanksgiving Proclamation of March 4, 1815, in Richardson, *A Compilation of the Messages and the Papers of the Presidents*, 561.

[92] Fleet, "Madison's 'Detached Memoranda,'" 562.

[93] Brant, "Madison: On the Separation of Church and State," 23.

[94] Fleet, "Madison's 'Detached Memoranda,'" 560. Locke makes this same point in *A Letter Concerning Toleration*, 27.

[95] Fleet, "Madison's 'Detached Memoranda,'" 560.

the law.[96] It would have been much better proof of their pious feelings, Madison later wrote to Edward Livingston, if individual congressmen would have maintained a chaplain with contributions from their own pockets. The same would go for the military.[97]

MADISON'S PRUDENTIAL CONSIDERATIONS IN SUPPORT OF NONCOGNIZANT SEPARATION

Madison's discussion of legislative chaplains nicely summarizes his doctrine of noncognizance and how, in his judgment, that principle leads to better, safer politics. The selection of a legislative chaplain necessarily requires favoring one religion over others unless a chaplain of every denomination is employed. With such a selection before them, legislators are encouraged to think of themselves along sectarian lines; one sect's benefit is necessarily another sect's loss. Noncognizance tends to moderate sectarian politics by preventing the government from either privileging or punishing religion as such. Sectarian political aspirations are frustrated because religious affiliation is not allowed as grounds for government action. Legislators and citizens are thus encouraged to see themselves not as sectarian partisans but as fellow citizens who mutually respect one another's rights. The multiplicity of sects further encourages this by giving every religion an interest in mutual toleration and respect. The intractable problem of religious faction and oppression that follows from a multiplicity of religious interests is thus submerged within a republic dedicated to respecting individuals' natural rights.

Madison also argued that noncognizance of religion would benefit religion itself. As we shall discuss in the next chapter, Founders such as George Washington thought that religion was indispensable in nurturing the moral qualities necessary for republican citizenship and, therefore, that the government ought to endorse and promote religion. Madison rejected this teaching. He did not deny that virtue was an important aid to republican government or that religion helped to nourish virtue. Madison himself wrote in a private letter that,

the belief in a God All Powerful wise & good, is so essential to the moral order of the World & to the happiness of man, that arguments which enforce it cannot be drawn from too many sources nor adapted with too much solicitude to the different characters & capacities to be impressed with it.[98]

---

[96] Ibid.
[97] James Madison to Edward Livingston, July 10, 1822, in *Writings of James Madison*, 9:100.
[98] James Madison to Fredrick Beasley, November 20, 1825, in *Writings of James Madison*, 9:230.

But Madison vehemently disagreed that religion required the support of government. He articulated his position most forcefully in Article 6 of his "Memorial and Remonstrance":

Because the establishment proposed by the Bill is not requisite for the support of the Christian Religion. To say that it is, is a contradiction to the Christian Religion itself; for every page of it disavows a dependence on the powers of this world: it is a contradiction to fact; for it is known that this Religion both existed and flourished, not only without the support of human laws, but in spite of every opposition from them; and not only during the period of miraculous aid, but long after it had been left to its own evidence, and the ordinary care of Providence: Nay it is a contradiction in terms; for a religion not invented by human policy, must have pre-existed and been supported, before it was established by human policy.[99]

After he left the presidency, Madison made this same point repeatedly in his private correspondence. In an 1819 letter to Robert Walsh touting the increase of religious instruction since the American Revolution, Madison wrote:

It was the Universal opinion of the Century preceding the last, that Civil Govt. could not stand without the prop of a Religious establishment, & that the X^n. religion itself would perish if not supported by a legal provision for its clergy. The experience of Virginia conspicuously corroborates the disproof of both opinions. . . . [T]he number, the industry, and the morality of the Priesthood, & the devotion of the people, have been manifestly increased by the total separation of the Church from the State.[100]

In response to receiving a sermon sent by New York clergyman F. L. Schaeffer, Madison stated,

The experience of the United States is a happy disproof of the error so long rooted in the unenlightened minds of well-meaning Christians, as well as in the corrupt hearts

---

[99] Even as a young man, Madison expressed doubts regarding whether religion needed the support of government. In 1773, he posed the following questions to his good friend, William Bradford:

Here allow me to propose the following Queries. Is an Ecclesiastical Establishment absolutely necessary to support civil society in a supreme Government? and [sic] how far is it hurtful to a dependent State? I do not ask for an immediate answer but mention them as worth attending to in the course of your reading and consulting experienced Lawyers and Politicians upon. When you have satisfied yourself in these points I should listen with pleasure to the Result of your researches.

James Madison to William Bradford, December 1, 1773, in Robert S. Alley, *James Madison on Religious Liberty* (Buffalo, NY: Prometheus Books, 1985), 46–47.

[100] James Madison to Robert Walsh, March 2, 1819, in Alley, *James Madison on Religious Liberty*, 81.

of persecuting usurpers, that without legal incorporation of religious and civil polity, neither could be supported. A mutual independence is found most friendly to practical religion, to social harmony, and to political prosperity.[101]

Madison sounded the same theme the following year in a letter to Edward Livingston:

We are teaching the world a great truth that Governments do better without kings and nobles than with them. The merit will be doubled by the other lesson: that Religion flourishes in greater purity without, than with the aid of government.[102]

Madison's position that religion did not need the support of government – nay, that it would better flourish without the support of government – reflected two prior suppositions. He believed that religion contained within itself the prerequisites for its own perpetuation. "[T]here are causes in the human breast, which ensure the perpetuity of religion without the aid of the law. . . . ," Madison wrote to Edward Everett.[103] In a letter to Reverend Jasper Adams written at the end of his life, Madison stated similarly,

There appears to be in the nature of man what ensures his belief in an invisible cause of his present existence, and anticipation of his future existence. Hence the propensities & susceptibilities in that case of religion which with a few doubtful or individual exceptions have prevailed throughout the world.[104]

Madison did not elaborate or explain what these "causes in the human breast" are, but whatever they are, he thought men were naturally disposed to seek a power beyond themselves, and thus were naturally inclined toward religious belief. This fact, he claimed, comported with the history of early Christianity itself, which demonstrated that government did not need to support religion for religion to flourish.

Madison also argued against government support of religion because he believed that such support tended to corrupt religion and to encourage religious persecution. Madison identified two types of corruption in particular. First, dependence on government corrupted religious clergy by freeing

---

[101] James Madison to F. L. Schaeffer, December 3, 1821, in Alley, *James Madison on Religious Liberty*, 82.

[102] James Madison to Edward Livingston, July 10, 1822, in *Writings of James Madison*, 9:102–03. See also James Madison to Edward Everett, March 19, 1823, in *Writings of James Madison*, 9:127.

[103] James Madison to Edward Everett, March 19, 1823, in *Writings of James Madison*, 9:126–27.

[104] James Madison to Jasper Adams, Spring 1833, in Alley, *James Madison on Religious Liberty*, 87.

them from accountability to the laity. "Experience witnesseth [sic]," Madison wrote in Article 7 of the "Memorial and Remonstrance,"

that ecclesiastical establishments, instead of maintaining the purity and efficacy of Religion, have had a contrary operation. During almost fifteen centuries, has the legal establishment of Christianity been on trial. What have been its fruits? More or less in all places, pride and indolence in the Clergy; ignorance and servility in the laity; in both superstition, bigotry and persecution. Enquire of the Teachers of Christianity for the ages in which it appeared in its greatest lustre; those of every sect, point to the ages prior to its incorporation with Civil policy. Propose a restoration of this primitive state in which its Teachers depended on the voluntary rewards of their flocks; many of them predict its downfall. On which side ought their testimony to have greatest weight, when it is for or against their interest?[105]

Madison suggests that when clergy are dependent on the voluntary contributions of church members for their income, they will better serve the laity. Excessively prideful and indolent ministers will likely be unpopular and, hence, unsupported. Without state support, moreover, the laity themselves are less likely to be passive because they must actively choose to contribute to those who minister to them. Government support of clergy thus lessens responsibility in both the clergy and the laity, causing the spiritual harm to both.

Madison thought that state support corrupted religion, secondly, by introducing incentives to religious persecution. Madison understood that in a religiously pluralistic society, competition among clergy for followers and contributors was inevitable. That competition, which could help secure religious freedom if properly channelled, would more likely threaten freedom if the state funded religion. Writing to his good friend William Bradford, Madison said that state-funded clergy

will naturally employ all their art and interest to depress their rising adversaries; for such they must consider dissenters who rob them of the good will of the people, and may, in time, endanger their livings and security.[106]

---

[105] Madison's reproachful view of the established Anglican clergy in colonial Virginia likely decisively shaped his thinking on ecclesiastical establishments. As early as 1774 he wrote to William Bradford,

If the Church of England had been the established and general religion in all the northern colonies as it has been among us here [in Virginia], and uninterrupted tranquillity had prevailed throughout the continent, it is clear to me that slavery and subjection might and would have been gradually insinuated among us.

James Madison to William Bradford, January 24, 1774, in *The Mind of the Founder*, 2.

[106] Ibid., 3.

Instead of better serving the laity to secure voluntary contributions, state-supported clergy could protect their position through governmental regulations or even legal constraints on competing sects. Connection with and dependence on the state introduces incentives to use the power of government to limit the religious activities and freedom of non-state-privileged religions. In this way, Madison thought state funding of religion inevitably introduced the "diabolical, hell-conceived principle of persecution."[107]

CONCLUSION

James Madison's church-state politics closely, although not perfectly, reflected his principle of state noncognizance of religion. He grounded that principle on man's inalienable natural right to religious freedom. Because religion did not become part of the social contract, he concluded that government must remain blind to religion as such. He also thought noncognizance led to a prudentially sound politics of church-state separation. As we shall discuss in Chapters 4, 5, and 6, a Madisonian approach to the First Amendment would require the government to neither privilege religion nor punish citizens on account of their religion. With the exceptions of his proposed "religiously scrupulous" conscientious objector amendment and his religious proclamations as president, Madison held fast to this position throughout his entire political life, from his first year in the Virginia legislature, when he proposed amendments to the Virginia Declaration of Rights, to his last reflections as the "father of the Constitution" in his "Detached Memoranda."

[107] Ibid.

George Washington on Church and State

Religion and the Civic Good

Individuals entering into society, must give up a share of liberty to preserve the rest. The magnitude of the sacrifice must depend as well on situation and circumstance, as on the object to be obtained. It is at all times difficult to draw with precision the line between those rights which must be surrendered, and those which may be reserved. . . .

> G. Washington, Letter submitting the proposed constitution to the President of Congress, September 17, 1787[1]

Compared with Thomas Jefferson and James Madison, George Washington's political thought regarding church and state has long been overlooked. It is commonly assumed that on matters of religious liberty Jefferson and Madison speak for the founding generation. The near-exclusive concern with Jefferson and Madison can be traced to *Everson* v. *Board of Education* (1947), in which the Supreme Court presumed, first, that the Founding Fathers shared a uniform understanding of religious freedom and, second, that Jefferson and Madison represented the Founders' view.[2] Ever since, most historically minded constitutional scholars and judges have uncritically accepted *Everson's* presumptions.[3] George Washington, however, was no less dedicated to securing religious freedom than were his second and third presidential successors. In a 1783 letter he testified that "the establishment

---

[1] *The Records of the Federal Convention of 1787*, ed. Max Farrand (New Haven, CT: Yale University Press, 1966), 2:666.

[2] *Everson v. Board of Education*, 330 U.S. 1, 13 (1947).

[3] For further discussion of this point, see Daniel L. Dreisbach, "A Lively and Fair Experiment: Religion and the American Constitutional Tradition," *Emory Law Journal*, 49 (Winter 2000): 228–38.

of Civil and Religious Liberty was the Motive which induced me to the field [of battle]."[4] Washington, moreover, offers a different understanding of the right to religious freedom than either Jefferson or Madison – who, we will attempt to show, themselves disagreed. Anticipating themes that would later appear in Tocqueville's *Democracy in America*,[5] Washington believed a pious citizenry was indispensable to republican government. Unlike Madison and in a different way than Jefferson, he thought that the state could and should nurture citizens' religious beliefs and encourage religious practices. He also thought that the right to religious liberty was limited by the legitimate duties of republican citizenship. Washington's understanding of the right of religious freedom reveals the diversity of thought within the founding generation and it reflects the leading contemporaneous alternative to Jefferson's and Madison's positions.

WASHINGTON'S POLITICAL DIFFERENCES WITH MADISON

Deducing Washington's church-state philosophy is not an easy task. Unlike Jefferson and Madison, Washington did not compose a singular document on religious liberty. His political theory, accordingly, must be extrapolated from his political practice, including the letters and writings that belong to it.

When one turns to Washington's practical politics regarding religion, one cannot help but be struck by how different they were from Madison's. While Madison attempted to make government noncognizant of religion, Washington consistently sought to use governmental authority to encourage religion and to foster the religious character of the American people. Washington, for example, initially was not opposed to Patrick Henry's general assessment bill, the proposed statute that sparked Madison to write the "Memorial and Remonstrance." Writing to George Mason, a leading assessment foe, Washington explained,

Altho [sic], no man's sentiments are more opposed to *any kind* of restraint upon religious principles than mine are; yet I must confess, that I am not amongst the number

---

[4] George Washington to the Reformed German Congregation in the City of New York, November 27, 1783, in *The Writings of George Washington*, ed. John C. Fitzpatrick (Washington, DC: United States Government Printing Office, 1938), 27:249.

[5] For an excellent discussion of Tocqueville's view of the relationship between religion and American democracy, see Sanford Kessler, *Tocqueville's Civil Religion: American Christianity and the Prospects for Freedom* (Albany: State University of New York Press, 1994).

of those who are so much alarmed at the thoughts of making people pay towards the support of that which they profess, if of the denominations of Christians; or declare themselves Jews, Mahomitans or otherwise, and thereby obtain proper relief.[6]

In the same letter, Washington further explains,

As the matter now stands, I wish an assessment had never been agitated and as it has gone so far, that the Bill could die an easy death; because I think it will be productive of more quiet to the State, than by enacting it into a Law. . . .[7]

Washington opposed Henry's measure not because he thought it violated a proper understanding of religious liberty, Madison's principal argument, but because he feared that it was causing unnecessary political turmoil.

Washington's opinion of the propriety of military chaplains reflects a second difference from Madison. Madison thought taxpayer-funded chaplains violated constitutional principles.[8] Such a thought probably never crossed Washington's mind. As commander-in-chief of the Continental Army, Washington sought not only to procure chaplains for his soldiers but also to ensure that the Continental Congress offered a salary generous enough to attract "men of abilities."[9] Chaplains, he believed, helped to improve discipline, raise morale, check vice, and to fortify courage and bravery, and at the same time they helped to secure respectful obedience and subordination to those in command.[10] Washington, moreover, did not make chaplains available only to those who wanted them. He repeatedly

---

[6] Washington's emphasis. George Washington to George Mason, October 3, 1785, *Writings of George Washington*, 28:285. Washington wrote to Mason on account of Mason's sending to Washington a copy of a memorial and remonstrance against Henry's bill. It is fair to assume that Mason sent Washington Madison's "Memorial and Remonstrance," although it is unclear from Washington's letter, which refers only to "a memorial and remonstrance." Madison published his "Memorial and Remonstrance" anonymously, and several other petitions against the bill were also circulating at that time.

[7] Ibid.

[8] Elizabeth Fleet, "Madison's 'Detached Memoranda,'" *William and Mary Quarterly*, 3rd series, 3 (1946): 559–60.

[9] George Washington to the President of Congress, December 31, 1775, *Writings of George Washington*, 4:197–98, requesting an increase in the salary of military chaplains to $33 a month. On July 29, 1775, the Continental Congress, in its first official act regarding army chaplains, passed a resolution providing for a salary of $20 a month, the same as captains. For a discussion of Washington's military requests and orders pertaining to religion, see Paul F. Boller, *George Washington & Religion* (Dallas: Southern Methodist University Press, 1963), 49–60.

[10] George Washington to Governor Jonathan Trumbull, December 15, 1775, *Writings of George Washington*, 4:162.

commanded his soldiers to attend Sunday services if the war effort permitted it. "The General," he declared in one such typical order,

requires and expects, of all Officers and Soldiers, not engaged in actual duty, a punctual attendance on divine Service to implore the blessings of heaven upon the means used of our safety and defence [sic].[11]

The "regularity and decorum" with which the Sabbath was observed, Washington explained following another such order,

will reflect great credit on the army in general, tend to improve the morals, and at the same time, to increase the happiness of the soldiery, and must afford the most pure and rational entertainment for every serious and well disposed mind.[12]

It would also reduce "profane cursing, swearing and drunkenness," he said on another occasion.[13]

General Washington also commanded his soldiers to observe special days of "Fasting, Humiliation and Prayer." Sometimes he issued orders to comply with resolutions passed by the Continental Congress, but on other occasions, in particular after key victories or successful strategic operations, Washington relied on his own authority. After receiving news of the conclusion of an alliance with France in 1778, he issued the following:

It having pleased the Almighty ruler of the Universe propitiously to defend the Cause of the United American-States and finally by raising us up a powerful Friend among the Princes of the Earth to establish our liberty and Independence up[on] lasting foundations, it becomes us to set apart a day for gratefully acknowledging the divine Goodness and celebrating the important Event which we owe to his benign Interposition.[14]

Washington brought to the presidency the practice of declaring special days of prayer and thanksgiving, which brings forth another sharp divergence with Madison. As discussed in the previous chapter, Madison issued four official religious proclamations during the War of 1812, but he later acknowledged that such measures violated the spirit of the Constitution. Washington took no such view. He issued two official presidential days of prayer and thanksgiving proclamations, the first on October 3, 1789, in response to a request by Congress, and the second on January 1, 1795, apparently under his

[11] General Orders, July 4, 1775, *Writings of George Washington*, 3:309.
[12] General Orders, March 22, 1783, *Writings of George Washington*, 26:250.
[13] General Orders, July 4, 1775, *Writings of George Washington*, 3:309.
[14] General Orders, May 5, 1778, *Writings of George Washington*, 11:354.

own initiative.[15] Nothing indicates that Washington hesitated in any way when issuing them.

The proclamations themselves, moreover, speak in defense of their own propriety. Both start with a statement of duty. Washington begins the first decree:

Whereas it is the duty of all nations to acknowledge the providence of Almighty God, to obey His will, to be grateful for His benefits, and humbly to implore His protection and favor ..."[16]

The first paragraph of his 1795 proclamation similarly maintains:

In such a state of things [exemption from foreign war and the existence of domestic tranquility] it is in an especial manner our duty as a people, with devout reverences and affectionate gratitude, to acknowledge our many and great obligations to Almighty God and to implore Him to continue and confirm the blessings we experience.[17]

Madison's proclamations, by comparison, all begin with the bland assertion that the Congress has called for a national proclamation, and they do not emphasize the propriety or duty of giving thanks to the Almighty. Since Washington thought that the American people had a duty to recognize and acknowledge God, he did not think it improper for the president to facilitate its performance.

Washington's official religious presidential proclamations reflect his deliberate intention to sanctify solemn public statements and occasions. All of Washington's most important public addresses include religious language. His 1783 "Circular to the States," the closest thing to a national or presidential speech in American history prior to 1789, ends with an "earnest prayer" for God's "holy protection."[18] His first Inaugural Address, similarly, begins and ends in prayer. Toward the beginning of that address, Washington proclaims:

[I]t would be peculiarly improper to omit, in this first official act, my fervent supplications to that Almighty Being who rules over the universe; who presides in the councils of nations; and whose providential aid can supply every human defect; that his benediction may consecrate to the liberties and happiness of the

---

[15] Both proclamations marked significant events, the former the ratification of the Constitution and the latter when the prospect of another foreign war had decreased.

[16] George Washington, "Proclamation. A National Thanksgiving," October 3, 1787, in James D. Richardson, *A Compilation of the Messages and Papers of the Presidents: 1789–1897* (Washington, DC: Government Printing Office, 1899), 1:64.

[17] George Washington, "A Proclamation," January 1, 1795, in Richardson, *A Compilation of the Messages and Papers of the Presidents*, 1:180.

[18] George Washington, "Circular to the States," June 14, 1783, *George Washington: A Collection*, ed. W. B. Allen (Indianapolis: Liberty Classics, 1988), 249.

People of the United States, a Government instituted by themselves for these essential purposes. . . . In tending this homage to the Great Author of every public and private good, I assure myself that it expresses your sentiments not less than my own; nor those of my fellow citizens at large less than either. No people can be bound to acknowledge and adore the invisible hand which conducts the affairs of men, more than the people of the United States.[19]

The use of taxes to support religion, the appointment of military chaplains, the propriety of issuing religious presidential proclamations, and the deliberate inclusion of sacred language in public ceremonies reflect the distance between Washington and Madison on the proper disposition of government toward religion. Washington did not think that state actors must or should be noncognizant of religion. He agreed that religious worship was a natural right and that the purpose of government was to secure the rights of man, but he did not translate those general principles into Madison's specific limitations on the powers of government.

WASHINGTON'S DEFENSE OF GOVERNMENT SUPPORT FOR RELIGION: THE FAREWELL ADDRESS

Washington's most definitive political statement regarding religion, in fact, pertains not to the limits of government power but rather to the propriety of governmental support. In his Farewell Address, Washington's valedictory statement to the American people, he explains why republican government must endorse religion:

Of all the dispositions and habits which lead to political prosperity, Religion and morality are indispensable supports. In vain would that man claim the tribute of Patriotism, who should labor to subvert these great pillars of human happiness, these firmest props of the duties of Man and citizens. The mere Politician, equally with the pious man ought to respect and to cherish them. A volume could not trace all their connections with private and public felicity.[20]

---

[19] George Washington, "First Inaugural Address," April 30, 1789, *Papers of George Washington*, Presidential Series, ed. Dorothy Twohig (Charlottesville: University Press of Virginia, 1987–), 2:174.

[20] George Washington, Farewell Address, September 19, 1796, *Writings of George Washington*, 35:229. Washington's Farewell Address was not a speech but a long letter addressed "To the PEOPLE of the United States," first published in the *American Daily Advisor*, Philadelphia's largest newspaper, on September 19, 1796. For a discussion of the drafting and publication of the Farewell Address, see Matthew Spalding and Patrick J. Garrity, *A Sacred Union of Citizens: George Washington's Farewell Address and the American Character*, Introduction by Daniel J. Boorstin (Lanham, MD: Rowman & Littlefield, 1996), 45–61; Felix Gilbert, *To The Farewell Address: Ideas of Early American Foreign Policy* (Princeton, NJ: Princeton University Press, 1961), Chapter V.

Religion and morality are indispensable because, Washington explains a few lines later, "'Tis substantially true, that virtue or morality is a necessary spring of popular government."[21] Washington's reference to virtue as the "spring" of popular government is Montesquieuian. In *The Spirit of the Laws*, Montesquieu taught that each form of government relies upon a "principle" or "spring," by which he meant the ruling passion that sets the regime in motion and perpetuates its existence.[22] The principle or spring of republican government, Montesquieu claimed, is virtue. By virtue Montesquieu did not mean the classical moral virtues or even human excellence more generally, but rather what he called political virtue, self-sacrifice for the common good.[23] In his Farewell Address, Washington uses virtue and morality in both their classical and their modern, Montesquieuian senses. Washington follows the classical teaching insofar as he explicitly connects individual virtue to human happiness. Yet his analysis is also distinctly modern and Montesquieuian insofar as he makes virtue and morality instrumental to political life, not the aim of politics. Virtue and morality are needed for public felicity because without them:

Let it simply be asked where is the security for property, for reputation, for life, if the sense of religious obligation *desert* the oaths, which are the instruments of investigation in Courts of Justice?[24]

Washington venerates virtue and morality because they prompt citizens to act in a decent, truthful, and law-abiding manner. Virtuous citizens govern themselves voluntarily and respect the rights of others, thereby reducing the need for government to secure rights through the coercive force of law. Virtue and morality are indispensable because they make self-government possible.

But Washington recognizes that for most men most of the time, virtue and morality are not choice-worthy in and of themselves. Republican government needs religion because virtue and morality depend on religious faith:

And let us with caution indulge the supposition, that morality can be maintained without religion. Whatever may be conceded to the influence of refined education on

[21] George Washington, Farewell Address, September 19, 1796, *Writings of George Washington*, 35:229.

[22] Montesquieu, *The Spirit of the Laws*, Book 3, Chapters 1 and 2.

[23] Ibid., Book 3, Chapter 2. For Montesquieu's clarification of what he means by virtue see *The Spirit of the Laws*, Book 3, Chapter 5, n.9, and Book 5, Chapter 2.

[24] Washington's emphasis. Farewell Address, September 19, 1796, *Writings of George Washington*, 35:229.

minds of peculiar structure, reason and experience both forbid us to expect that National morality can prevail in exclusion of religious principle.[25]

Washington concedes that a few may be good on account of their "refined education," but he implies that most men require the fear of eternal damnation and the prospect of eternal salvation to fortify their character. Washington possesses a sober view of human nature; he reaffirms Madison's portrait of human nature in *Federalist* 51 that men are not angels. Yet Washington's accommodation of man's lack of virtue goes beyond Madison's prescription. Whereas *The Federalist* seems to accept human nature as it is – and therefore emphasizes the separation of powers and checks and balances – Washington focuses explicitly on shaping the moral character of the American people. He endorses the use of religion for political purposes, something that Madison labeled "an unhallowed perversion of the means of salvation."[26] Washington thought the Madisonian position failed to respect reason and the lessons of experience, both of which taught that patriotic republicans ought to recognize and endorse religion because only a religious citizenry could sustain republican self-government.

GOVERNMENT SUPPORT OF RELIGION AND THE CIVIC GOOD

Washington's critique of Madison's position brings forth an obvious question, especially to modern sensibilities that have been colored by generations of strict separationist Supreme Court jurisprudence: Did Washington think that government support of religion was compatible with religious freedom? Does support not favor religion over irreligion, thus violating the neutrality that religious freedom guarantees? Washington's answer is relatively simple: Religious liberty does not require governmental neutrality toward religion. He believed that republican government ought to favor religion and discourage irreligion because religion favors republican government.

The more difficult question, which Washington was obviously aware of but never addressed theoretically, is, how can government support religion without inviting discord among competing religious sects? Government support of religion can invite irreconcilable theological differences to enter into the political arena. While one can speak of supporting religion in the abstract, it is difficult to do in practice; all religions are particular, and thus

---

[25] Ibid. Cf. Montesquieu, *The Spirit of the Laws*, Book 24, Chapters 1 and 6.

[26] James Madison, "A Memorial and Remonstrance Against Religious Assessments," Article 5, in *The Writings of James Madison*, ed. Gaillard Hunt (New York: G. P. Putnam's Sons, 1900–10), 2:187.

support of religion in general often results in the support of some sects and not others. Positive government action easily can trigger partisan politics along religious lines, pitting sects against one another for scarce political resources, thus inviting political strife among groups least able to reconcile their differences. Madison sought to avoid this dilemma by denying religion as such direct government support, thereby limiting sectarian politics.

From Washington's perspective, Madison's approach ignores the reality that republican government requires religion. Separating religious morality from state support unnecessarily destabilizes the very foundation on which republican government rests. Yet how Washington chose to support religion reflects his awareness of the problem that such support entails. In his public speeches and writings, Washington used only nonsectarian language. His first Inaugural Address includes fervent supplications to "that Almighty Being who rules over the universe," homage to "the Great Author of every public and private good," and humble supplications to "the benign Parent of the human race."[27] His presidential proclamations of days of prayer and thanksgiving recognize "that great and glorious Being who is the beneficent author of all the good that was, that is, or that will be,"[28] and render hearty thanks to "the Great Ruler of Nations."[29] Washington's support of military chaplains also reflects the delicate balance that he sought to maintain. He not only wanted chaplains, but chaplains of every denomination so that each soldier could attend his own religious services. When the Continental Congress sought to appoint chaplains by brigade rather than at the regiment level, Washington protested. Since brigades were larger than regiments, the likelihood of unanimity of religious sentiment was reduced. Washington feared that the reduced number of chaplains could have "a tendency to introduce religious disputes into the Army," that is, disputes over the denomination of the chaplain to be secured. Brigade chaplains, moreover, "in many instances would compel men to a mode of Worship which they do not profess." If employed incorrectly, military chaplains, whom Washington thought were absolutely necessary to the war effort, could have a deleterious effect by introducing "uneasiness and jealously among the Troops."[30]

[27] George Washington, First Inaugural Address, April 30, 1789, *Papers of George Washington*, 2:173–77.
[28] George Washington, "Proclamation. A National Thanksgiving," October 3, 1789, *A Compilation of the Messages and Papers of the Presidents*, 1:64.
[29] George Washington, "A Proclamation," January 1, 1795, *A Compilation of the Messages and Papers of the Presidents*, 1:180.
[30] George Washington to the President of Congress, June 8, 1777, *Writings of George Washington*, 8:203.

Washington recommended to Congress that chaplains remain assigned at the level where most soldiers would have a chaplain of their own religious persuasion, thereby minimizing religious discord.

Washington's efforts to maintain military chaplains at the regiment level exemplify how he thought government could and should support religion yet maintain respect for the individual's right of conscience. He included within the right of conscience the right not to be compelled to practice a mode of worship that one does not profess. He did not extend this to a more general right to abstain from worship, however, for he did command his soldiers to attend religious services. But if military superiors expected their soldiers to attend religious services, they ought to provide chaplains of the soldiers' denominations.

Washington also excluded from the rights of conscience a right not to be taxed for the support of religion. Military chaplains were legitimate because they supported the war effort, which itself was directed at the common good. Insofar as religion contributes to a civic good, it was a legitimate object of taxpayer dollars. Washington thus explicitly disagreed with Jefferson's doctrine in the Virginia Statute (as will be discussed in the following chapter) and Madison's assertion in the "Memorial" that compelling support for religion as such violated the principle of religious liberty.[31] Washington was always careful, however, to link public support of religion to a civic good. In the case at hand, Washington explicitly connected military chaplains to the discipline and morale of the armed forces. Washington's definition of the civic good was expansive – it included the formation of moral character – but, nonetheless, he did not promote support of religion as an end in and of itself.

Washington's position is most similar to those who have suggested the "secular purpose" rule for Establishment Clause jurisprudence – government may support religion so long as it puts forth a legitimate secular reason for doing so.[32] He probably would have disliked the term "secular purpose," as that term itself can seem unnecessarily hostile toward religion, and instead favored "civic policy" or "the civic good" – government may support religion insofar as it does so in a manner that supports a legitimate civic end. Washington would have disagreed with today's strict separationists, who claim that government may not favor religion over irreligion. He also would

---

[31] Madison, "Memorial and Remonstrance," Article 3, *The Writings of James Madison*, 2:185–86.

[32] See, for example, Justice Byron White's opinion in *Lemon v. Kurtzman*, 403 U.S. 602 (1971).

have disagreed, though less emphatically, with nonpreferentialists, who claim government may support religion if it supports all religions equally. Washington's position is more discriminating. Government should support religion because religion supports republican government. By implication, government ought not support those religions that maintain principles hostile toward republicanism or advocate behavior contrary to good citizenship.[33]

THE LIMITS OF THE RIGHT TO THE FREE EXERCISE OF RELIGION

Just as concern for the civic good sanctioned Washington's endorsement of governmental support of religion, the civic good also defined the legitimate limits that he thought government could impose on religion. Washington agreed with the structure of Madison's social contract framework in the "Memorial and Remonstrance"; he, too, believed that a limit on the realm of legitimate governmental action existed. He disagreed with Madison, however, on where the lines demarcating the right of free exercise should be drawn. Whereas Madison sought to establish the precise rule that government must not be cognizant of religion and, therefore, may not act in a manner that penalizes religion as such, Washington found the natural boundaries of the right to free exercise established by the reasonable demands of maintaining the social contract. To put the matter in more Washingtonian language, Washington held that the right to religious liberty must recognize the legitimate demands of good citizenship.

Washington addressed this theme most directly in a series of letters written soon after his assumption of the presidency. Upon his election, Washington received numerous congratulatory letters, including letters from churches of several religious denominations. Washington's response to these groups captures the truly revolutionary character of the American regime. As Harry Jaffa has written and as Washington sought to make clear, for the first time in human history political citizenship would no longer be based on religious affiliation.[34] In an act of the highest statesmanship, Washington staked his considerable personal prestige on the new nation's commitment

---

[33] Thomas G. West claims that the American Founders in general maintained this position. See Thomas G. West, "Religious Liberty: The View from the Founding," in *On Faith and Free Government*, ed. Daniel C. Palm, Foreword by Dan Quayle (Lanham, MD: Rowman & Littlefield, 1997), 3–27.

[34] Harry V. Jaffa, *The American Founding as the Best Regime: The Bonding of Civil and Religious Liberty* (Claremont, CA: The Claremont Institute for the Study of Statesmanship and Political Philosophy, 1990), 25.

to religious freedom. In doing so, he not only demonstrated his personal commitment to this right but pledged the nation to it as well.

These letters also make clear, however, that religious freedom does not supplant the duties of republican citizenship. Washington's epistle to the Baptists of Virginia captures the theme of his post-election letters. In their letter to Washington, the Baptists expressed concern that the Constitution did not sufficiently secure the liberty of conscience. In his response, Washington assured them that "I would have never placed my signature to it [the Constitution]" if the general government might render the liberty of conscience insecure. He continued, then, to explain and define the liberty of conscience:

For you, doubtless, remember that I have often expressed my sentiment, that every man, conducting himself as a good citizen, and being accountable to God alone for his religious opinions, ought to be protected in worshipping the Deity according to the dictates of his own conscience.[35]

Washington says that the right to liberty of conscience secures for the individual the freedom to worship the Deity according to the dictates of one's conscience, which means that government ought not impose a mode of worship on an individual that he or she finds objectionable.

But what about individual modes of worship that the government finds objectionable? To take an extreme but historical example, what about the Aztec religion, which ordained the sacrifice of human beings in supposed obedience to a divine command? If government prevents this, does it fail to protect the individual's right of conscience? And what if government commands the performance of acts that an individual believes violates his religion? May government legitimately prescribe such actions?

Washington's answer to these questions is clear: A condition of civil society, and thus of a government capable of protecting the rights of conscience, is that individuals must conduct themselves as good citizens. In his letter to the Baptists, the modifying clause, "conducting himself as a good citizen," defines the limits of liberty of conscience. The right to religious freedom does not include the right to perform actions contrary to the duties of citizenship. The state possesses no affirmative obligation to tolerate actions opposed to good citizenship, including religiously motivated actions. And the state may legitimately expect all citizens to perform the reasonable duties of citizenship, even those that religious citizens find objectionable.

[35] George Washington to the United Baptist Churches of Virginia, May 1789, *Papers of George Washington*, Presidential Series, 2:424.

Washington does not define here what the obligations of good citizenship include, but whatever they are, they stand as a precondition for one's rights to be secured.

Washington faced this difficult issue concretely in his dealings with the Quaker religion. Most Quakers at the time interpreted their religious precepts to forbid any kind of participation in the armed forces. Washington encountered Quaker pacifism as early as 1756, during the French and Indian War, when six Quakers were drafted into the Virginia militia and sent to serve under his command. In Washington's own words, they would "neither bear arms, work, receive pay, or do anything that tends, in any respect, to self-defence [sic]."[36] He faced similar resistance throughout the Revolutionary War, which we shall discuss later in this section. In 1789, the Quakers wrote to Washington to explain their principle of pacifism and "to assure thee [Washington], that we feel our Hearts affectionately drawn towards thee, and those in Authority over us. . . ."[37] Washington's response to the Quakers is a model of magnanimity and charity, especially considering that it comes from a life-long military commander. Nonetheless, it falls short of an absolute endorsement of the Quakers, and it delivers a stinging criticism. Washington writes:

The liberty enjoyed by the People of these States, of worshipping Almighty God agreeably to their Consciences, is not only among the choicest of their *Blessings*, but also of their *Rights* – While men perform their social duties faithfully, they do all that society or the state can with propriety demand or expect; and remain responsible only to their Maker for the Religion, or modes of faith, which they may prefer or profess.

Your principles & conduct are well known to me – and it is doing the People called Quakers no more than Justice to say, that (except their declining to share with others the burthen of the common defense) there is no Denomination among us who are more exemplary and useful Citizens.[38]

Washington recognizes the right of conscience as a liberty enjoyed by all Americans, and thus by the Quakers. At the same time, he refuses to recognize the political legitimacy of their refusal to take up arms. Society and the state can properly expect all citizens, even religious pacifists, to share in the burden of the common defense. To the extent that the Quakers refused to

[36] George Washington to Robert Dinwiddie, June 25, 1756, *Writings of George Washington*, 1:394. Washington refused to discharge the six Quakers on account of their religious beliefs.

[37] The Religious Society called Quakers, from their Yearly Meeting for Pennsylvania, New Jersey, and the western Parts of Virginia and Maryland, September 28–October 3, 1789, to George Washington, *Papers of George Washington*, Presidential Series, 4:267.

[38] George Washington to the Society of Quakers, October 1789, *Papers of George Washington*, Presidential Series, 4:266.

fight in defense of their country and of their rights, Washington implied that they are not exemplary or useful citizens.

Perhaps in anticipation of the Quakers' disappointment with his polite but stern rebuke, Washington concludes his letter charitably:

I assure you very explicitly that in my opinion the Conscientious scruples of all men should be treated with great delicacy & tenderness; and it is my wish and desire, that the Laws may always be as extensively accommodated to them, as due regard to the Protection and essential Interests of the Nation may Justify and permit.[39]

When perceived religious obligations conflict with fulfilling the duties of citizenship, Washington's "wish and desire" was that the laws may be accommodating. To "wish and desire" that such may be the case is to express a hopeful opinion of a particular outcome, but it by no means promises that outcome or in any way indicates that the state has an affirmative obligation to reach it. Washington, moreover, explicitly calls attention to limitations on making legal accommodations to religion. The protection of the legitimate interests of the nation must first be recognized and secured. Washington establishes a clear hierarchy when religious practices clash with legitimate obligations of citizenship: The political is higher than the religious. Religious individuals must accommodate their conscientious scruples to the essential interests of the nation in matters of reasonable social duties.[40]

We see this same formula in Washington's letters to the Roman Catholics of America and to the Hebrew Congregation in Newport.[41] In the latter, perhaps his most famous address to any religious society, Washington writes:

It is now no more that toleration is spoken of, as if it was by the indulgence of one class of people, that another enjoyed the exercise of their natural rights. For happily the Government of the United States, which gives to bigotry no sanction, to persecution no assistance requires only that they who live under its protection should demean themselves as good citizens, in giving it on all occasions their effectual support.[42]

---

[39] Ibid.

[40] Cf. John G. West, Jr., "George Washington and the Religious Impulse," in *Patriot Sage: George Washington and the American Political Tradition*, eds. Gary L. Gregg and Matthew Spaulding, Foreword by William J. Bennett (Wilmington, DE: ISI Books, 1999), 285.

[41] George Washington to the Roman Catholics in America, March 15, 1790, *Papers of George Washington*, Presidential Series, 5:299–300.

[42] George Washington to the Hebrew Congregation in Newport, Rhode Island, August 18, 1790, *Papers of George Washington*, Presidential Series, 6:285.

In two sentences, Washington recognizes the revolutionary character of the American regime. The rights and privileges of United States citizenship do not depend on religious affiliation. These rights, however, are conditioned by corresponding duties, the first of which is that every individual must "demean" himself a good citizen.

Washington's letters contain an approach to church-state matters that focuses on the ends or purposes of state action. He defended governmental actions that touched religion by their connection to a legitimate civic end. In the absence of a legitimate civic purpose, the state could not dictate the tenets of any religion or prescribe a particular mode of worship for the purpose of directing citizens toward the "true" religion. For the same reasons, Washington suggested that the state could not condition the rights and privileges of citizenship on the basis of religious affiliation. The most fundamental rights of republican citizens, the rights to property and to participate in rule through voting and holding office, could not depend on one's theological beliefs or lack thereof. On matters involving the legitimate civic interests of the state, however, the state had no obligation to recognize religious dissent. If it so chooses, the state could accommodate conscientious religious scruples – Washington expressed his wish and desire that it would – but it had no obligation to do so. On matters pertaining to the civic interests of the nation and the duties of good citizenship, religious individuals could only expect to be tolerated.

The manner in which Washington dealt with Quaker pacifism offers a revealing case study of the degree to which he understood religious liberty to include an element of toleration only, with "toleration" defined as a conditional willingness to bear that with which one disagrees. As mentioned previously, Washington first encountered Quaker pacifism in 1756, when six young Quakers were drafted into the Virginia militia and sent to serve under his command.[43] At the time, Washington was commanding Virginian forces with responsibility for frontier defense. Upon finding the Quakers completely unwilling to "do any thing that tends, in any respect, to self-defence," Washington confined them and then wrote to Virginia Governor Robert Dinwiddie asking how he should proceed.[44] In the same letter, he informed the governor that he had discharged three other draftees who were "unfit for service." Dinwiddie responded, "If the six Quakers will not fight

---

[43] Paul F. Boller reports that this was Washington's first important encounter with the Quakers. Paul F. Boller, "George Washington and the Quakers," *The Bulletin of Friends Historical Association* 49, no. 2 (1960): 69.

[44] George Washington to Robert Dinwiddie, June 25, 1756, *Writings of George Washington*, 1:394.

you must compel them to work on the forts, to carry timber, &c.; if this will not do confine them with a short allowance of bread and water, till you bring them to reason."[45] Washington had no success pressing the Quakers into service, writing back to the governor, "I could by no means bring the Quakers to any terms. They chose rather to be whipped to death than bear arms, or lend us any assistance whatever upon the fort, or any thing of self-defence."[46] Dinwiddie's final order, which Washington followed, was to "use them with lenity, but as they are at their own expense I would have them remain as long as the other Draughts."[47]

Although this episode occurred more than three decades before the adoption of the First Amendment, we do learn something of Washington's initial response toward the conflict between perceived religious obligations and civic duties. In his initial letter, as mentioned, Washington informed the governor that he had discharged three draftees who were "unfit for service." By implication, Washington did not believe the Quakers' conscientious objection to military service made them unfit for service. Despite knowing that the Quakers were resisting for religious reasons, Washington appears not to have believed that their religious objections exempted the Quakers from military service.

Washington exhibited more leniency toward the Quakers during the Revolutionary War. At times, General Washington sought to accommodate the Quakers' refusal to bear arms. When the war shifted to Pennsylvania in early 1777, for example, he wrote to the Pennsylvania Council of Safety that

it is absolutely necessary, that every Person able to bear arm (except such as are Conscientiously scrupulous against it in every Case), should give their personal Service, and whenever a part of the Militia is required only, either to join the Army or find a Man in their place.[48]

Washington did not mention the Quakers by name, but it is fair to assume that he anticipated their religious objection to military service. Later in that same year, he sent home several Virginia Quakers who had been drafted into the militia.[49]

At other times, however, Washington acted more harshly toward the Quakers, especially those in Pennsylvania whose neutrality was interpreted

---

[45] Dinwiddie to Washington, July 1, 1756, *Writings of George Washington*, 1:394n.76.

[46] George Washington to Robert Dinwiddie, August 4, 1756, *Writings of George Washington*, 1:420.

[47] Dinwiddie to Washington, August 19, 1756, *Writings of George Washington*, 1:420n.86.

[48] George Washington to the Pennsylvania Council of Safety, January 19, 1777, *Writings of George Washington*, 7:35. Also see Washington's letter to the same, dated January 29, 1777.

[49] Boller, "George Washington and the Quakers," 73.

by many to be, in effect, pro–British Toryism. In May 1777, he wrote to Pennsylvania Governor William Livingston:

I have been informed by Colo. Forman, that the Quakers and disaffected are doing all in their power to counteract your late Militia Law; but I hope, if your Officers are active and Spirited, that they will defeat their evil intentions and bring their Men into the Field.[50]

During the British occupation of Philadelphia, Washington's ire peaked. When giving orders to impress supplies from the countryside, Washington twice commanded his officers to "take care, that, the unfriendly Quakers and others notoriously disaffected to the cause of American liberty do not escape your Vigilance."[51] In March 1778, Washington went so far as to order his officers to prevent Quakers from entering Philadelphia so they could not attend their religious services, "an intercourse," Washington explained, "that we should by all means endeavour [sic] to interrupt, as the plans settled at these meetings are of the most pernicious tendency."[52]

The Quaker problem Washington faced anticipates the contemporary free exercise jurisprudential question of whether religious citizens possess a right to exemptions from generally applicable state actions that burden religious exercise. The Quakers of Washington's time made the same principled claim that Seventh Day Adventists, the Amish, and members of the Native American Church have made before the Supreme Court: Equal respect for religious freedom requires exemptions from neutral but burdensome laws.[53] A Washingtonian approach to religious free exercise would not admit a constitutional right to religious exemptions. Washington did not treat the Quakers' religious pacifism as a right. He was inclined to accommodate the Quakers' sincere religious exercises and at times he was willing to permit the Quakers not to fight. But he never acted under the presumption that the right to religious freedom entitled the Quakers to preferential treatment because of their religious beliefs. His orders to his officers to be vigilant in impressing Quaker property, moreover, reflect his belief that they failed to contribute their fair share to the war effort and that their refusal to fight, whatever the reason, was in some sense unjust to other more dutiful citizens. Furthermore, his command to prevent Quakers

---

[50] George Washington to Governor William Livingston, May 11, 1777, *Writings of George Washington*, 8:44–45.

[51] George Washington, Power to Officers to Collect Clothing, Etc., November 1777, *Writings of George Washington*, 10:124. See also Washington's commands to Colonel John Siegfried, October 6, 1777, *Writings of George Washington*, 9:318.

[52] George Washington to Brigadier General John Lacy, Junior, March 20, 1778, *Writings of George Washington*, 11:114.

[53] *Sherbert v. Verner*, 374 U.S. 398 (1963); *Wisconsin v. Yoder*, 406 U.S. 205 (1972); *Employment Division, Department of Human Resources of Oregon v. Smith*, 494 U.S. 872 (1990).

from attending religious services clearly evinces his belief that religiously motivated actions could be prevented if they were antithetical to the interests of the
nation. Washington permitted or constrained Quaker religious exercises as the
civic good dictated. His actions during the war perfectly match the theory
expressed in his presidential letters to the various religious denominations.
And thus, though Washington writes against mere "toleration" in his letter
to the Hebrew Congregation, his understanding of religious liberty, both as
espoused in his letters and reflected in his practice, recognizes the legitimacy of
it in cases where legitimate civic interests are involved.

For the most part, Washington did not force Quakers into combat. He
attempted to minimize the tension between the Quakers and the war effort
just as he sought to minimize religious disagreements within the army by
maintaining chaplains at the regiment level. Washington's consistent attempts
to reduce conflict between government and religious sentiment suggest that he
would support discretionary legislative or executive religious accommodations. But the right of religious free exercise for Washington did not mean
that religion could not be legitimately limited within civil society. Washington
thought that just as religion could be encouraged and accommodated because
it supported the moral foundations necessary for good government, religious
exercises could be limited when required for the civic good.

This brings forth a final question: If Washington respected individuals'
sincerely held religious beliefs, why, then, when these beliefs came into
conflict with the interests of the nation, did he favor the government over
the individual? Why not favor the individual's perception of his religious
duties over the government's interests?

Washington's papers, unfortunately, do not include a theoretical discussion or a carefully nuanced answer to this question. In a letter to the General
Assembly of the Presbyterian Church, however, he gives a brief indication of
how he thought the tension between an individual's religion and governmental interests could be resolved. The Presbyterians were the first religious group
to write to Washington after his election to the presidency. Their letter was
full of high praise. In particular, the Presbyterians testified:

[we] esteem it a peculiar happiness to behold in our chief Magistrate, a steady, uniform, avowed friend of the Christian religion, who has commenced his administration
in rational and exalted sentiments of Piety, and who in his private conduct adorns the
doctrines of the Gospel of Christ, and on the most public and solemn occasions
devoutly acknowledges the government of divine Providence.[54]

---

[54] General Assembly of the Presbyterian Church to George Washington, May 30, 1789, *Papers
of George Washington*, Presidential Series, 2:422.

Washington's response to the Presbyterians, like all of his responses to various congregations that wrote him at this time, mirrors their letter to him. The Presbyterians' letter began by announcing their adoration of God for giving to the United States a man of such talents and public virtue. Washington's response, in turn, begins by thanking the Presbyterians and reiterating his dependence on the "assistance of Heaven" for his arduous undertakings.[55] The Presbyterian letter then praises Washington for his Christian character. Washington's response at this point takes an interesting turn. Rather than reiterating his Christian beliefs, he offers a statement on the new nation's dedication to the principle of religious liberty, even though the Presbyterians' letter did not broach the subject. At the very point that the Presbyterians become sectarian, Washington becomes ecumenical. He indirectly instructs the Presbyterians on the nonsectarian character of the new American regime. While he affirms his reliance on providence and heaven, he does not invoke the name of Jesus Christ.[56]

Here we see a subtle yet instructive example of Washington's strategy for minimizing the conflict between the duties of citizenship and the sentiments

[55] George Washington to the General Assembly of the Presbyterian Church, May 1789, *Papers of George Washington*, Presidential Series, 2:420–21.

[56] The nature and content of Washington's religious beliefs lie beyond the scope of this chapter. For a recent study, see Michael and Jana Novak, *Washington's God: Religion, Liberty, and the Father of Our Country* (New York: Basic Books, 2006). Paul F. Boller's *George Washington & Religion* offers the most comprehensive account of Washington's beliefs. Boller concludes that Washington was a Deist. The numerous quotations he assembles, however, reveal that Washington espoused belief in the existence of a good and providential God. John G. West points out that Washington's belief in divine providence means, by definition, that he should not be labeled a Deist. See John G. West, Jr., "George Washington and the Religious Impulse," 269.

Washington clearly did not possess the anticlerical spirit that animates some Enlightenment figures like Jefferson, but less clear is the strength and depth of Washington's interior conviction. Washington rarely spoke about Christ, and he usually referred to the divine in only the most general terms. Toward the end of his life he wrote, ". . . in politics, as in religion, my tenets are few and simple. . . ." (George Washington to James Anderson, December 24, 1795, *Writings of George Washington*, 34:407). The simplicity of his faith is also captured in a short passage he wrote three months before his death: "I was the *first*, and am now the *last* of my fathers Children by the second marriage who remain. When I shall be called upon to follow them, is known only to the giver of life. When the summons comes I shall endeavour to obey it with a good grace" (Washington's emphasis. George Washington to Colonel Burgess Ball, September 22, 1799, *Writings of George Washington*, 37:372). Washington's religious practices reflect the same ambivalence captured in his written words. He was a lifelong member of the Anglican Church in Virginia, in which he was baptized, married, and served as a godfather for the children of various relatives and friends. Yet, according to Frank E. Gizzard, Jr., *George Washington: A Biographical Companion* (Denver: ABC-CLIO, 2002), 268, Washington attended church services only infrequently. We may say with confidence that Washington believed in a good and providential god, but other than these basic tenets, he kept his faith to himself.

of religion. The United States can avoid unnecessarily highlighting tensions between civic duties and religious sentiments if it avoids sectarian rhetoric and policy. Washington's letter then goes one step further. He writes,

While all men within our territories are protected in worshipping the Deity according to the dictates of their consciences; it is rationally to be expected from them in return, that they will be emulous of evincing the sanctity of their professions by the innocence of their lives and the beneficence of their actions; for no man, who is profligate in his morals, or a bad member of the civil community, can possibly be a true Christian, or a credit to his own religious society.[57]

Government can rationally expect that all religious citizens will be good citizens because no true religion would encourage its followers to be bad members of the American civil community. I highlight Washington's use of the term "rationally" because in it must lie the ultimate justification for the government's encroachment on an individual's religious sentiments. The American polity, founded on the self-evident truth that "all men are created equal," is in its founding principles and constitutional government a polity that respects reason. It accords with the transcendent principles of "nature and nature's God" as apprehended by man using his natural reason. And thus that which is essential to the civic good of the nation is itself reasonable, defensible, and just.

The religious sentiments of "bad members of the civil community," including those who fail to fulfill their civic duties for religious reasons, legitimately can be limited because these sentiments, Washington suggests, cannot possibly be true to Christianity or any rational religion. The precepts of true religion and good citizenship are not in tension in a regime grounded on the principles of "nature and nature's God." In demanding good citizenship and only sometimes tolerating religious actions that contravene good citizenship, Washington thought the state would offend neither true religion nor a rational understanding of justice.

CONCLUSION

Washington's civic good approach to religious free exercise – government noninterference grounded on natural rights for religious matters beyond the civic good, discretionary legislative and executive toleration for matters involving the interests of the nation and duties of citizenship – is perfectly

[57] George Washington to General Assembly of the Presbyterian Church, May 30, 1789, *Papers of George Washington*, Presidential Series, 2:420.

compatible with his approval of government support of religion. Both positions emerge from his belief that the state may permissibly take action to foster the civic good of the community. Washington thought religion not only a moral duty for the individual but also a potential public good for the polity. He thought it proper for the state to support and endorse those religious sentiments that supported the civic good. Washington also thought that the state could legitimately limit religious practices so long as those limitations were connected to the civic good.

George Washington did not participate in the drafting of the First Amendment. (Of course, neither did Thomas Jefferson.) One cannot and ought not claim that a Washingtonian understanding represents the original meaning of the drafters or the ratifiers of the First Amendment. An investigation of Washington's thought, however, reveals that significant differences existed among the leading Founding Fathers on the meaning and limitations of the right to religious liberty. Washington believed that the purpose of both government support of and limitations on religion must be defended in terms of the civic good. His writings and actions offer an alternative to Jefferson and Madison concerning how a religiously diverse people can think and act in ways that safeguard both the individual's religious freedom and the community's legitimate concern for the civic good.

3

Thomas Jefferson's Natural Rights Philosophy and Anticlerical Politics of Religious Liberty

> History, I believe furnishes no example of a priest-ridden people maintaining a free civil government.
>
> Thomas Jefferson to Alexander von Humboldt,[1] December 6, 1813

> Truth advances, and error recedes step by step only; and to do our fellow man the most good in our power, we must lead them where we can, follow where we cannot, and still go with them, watching always the favorable moment for helping them to another step.
>
> Thomas Jefferson to Thomas Cooper,[2] October 7, 1814

James Madison may be "the Father of the Constitution" and George Washington "the Father of our Country," but Thomas Jefferson is the Founding Father most often identified with America's commitment to religious freedom. When the Supreme Court issued its first significant interpretation of the Free Exercise Clause in *Reynolds v. United States* (1878) and its first significant interpretation of the Establishment Clause in *Everson v. Board of Education* (1947), it turned to Jefferson. This is not to say that Jefferson's views have been universally accepted or even commonly understood. Scholars who study him and judges who invoke him disagree about how Jefferson

---

[1] Thomas Jefferson to Alexander von Humboldt, December 6, 1813, in *Thomas Jefferson: Writings* (hereafter *Jefferson: Writings*), ed. Merrill D. Peterson (New York: The Library of America, 1984), 1311.

[2] Thomas Jefferson to Thomas Cooper, October 7, 1814, in *The Writings of Thomas Jefferson* (hereafter *Writings of Thomas Jefferson*), ed. H. A. Washington (Washington, DC: Taylor & Maury, 1854), 6:390.

sought to separate church from state.[3] That we disagree about Jefferson today should not be surprising. Even in his own lifetime, his ideas about religion and religious freedom were controversial and sharply contested. In his autobiography, Jefferson described the early battles to disestablish the Anglican Church in revolutionary Virginia as "the severest contests" in which he had ever been engaged.[4] During the election of 1800, his Federalist opponents charged that he was unfit for office because, in Alexander Hamilton's words, he was "an atheist in religion and a fanatic in politics."[5] Before the University of Virginia's opening in 1825, evangelical Christians attempted to derail Jefferson's plans, fearing that his choice of professors would lead to the corruption of Virginia's youth and the teaching of heterodox religious opinions.[6]

Jefferson's ideas were controversial in his day for the same reasons they remain contentious today: His thought is both explosive and elusive. A master rhetorician, Jefferson proclaimed political maxims in a manner that obfuscates as much as it elucidates: "Almighty God hath created the mind free"; the First Amendment builds a "wall of separation between church and state." Many Americans might agree with these statements, but what they actually mean is not self-evident. Jefferson, moreover, was involved in church-state controversies throughout his life. His work offers multiple episodes for the scholar to interpret and explain. Are we to find his true position on religious freedom in his 1777 draft of what became the Virginia Statute for Religious Freedom? In his 1802 letter to the Danbury Baptist Association? In his efforts to minimize clerical influence in the various plans for education he drafted throughout his life, culminating with the founding of the University of Virginia in 1825? And even if we can understand each of these episodes in its own context, what if Jefferson took different positions at different times? Where and when are we to find Jefferson's most definitive position on church and state?

---

[3] For an example of the scholarly debate over Jefferson's position on church and state, see the symposium on the subject in *William and Mary Quarterly*, 3rd Series, 56, no. 4 (October 1999).

[4] Thomas Jefferson, "Autobiography," in *Jefferson: Writings*, 34.

[5] Alexander Hamilton to Gov. John Gay, May 7, 1800 in *The Works of Alexander Hamilton*, ed. Henry Cabot Lodge (New York and London: G. P. Putnam's Sons, 1904), 10:372.

[6] For a discussion of the Presbyterian opposition to the university see Joseph Cabell's letter to Thomas Jefferson, December 29, 1817, in *Early History of the University of Virginia, as Contained in the Letters of Thomas Jefferson and Joseph C. Cabell*, ed. Nathaniel Francis Cabell (Richmond, 1856), 89–94. For a general discussion of the Christian opposition to the University of Virginia, see Cameron Addis, *Jefferson's Vision for Education, 1760–1845* (New York: Peter Lang, 2003), 68–87.

In 1878 and 1947, the Supreme Court presumed that Jefferson's letter to the Danbury Baptist Association and its "wall of separation" metaphor captured his essential and authoritative teaching. That presumption is only partially true and by no means exhaustive. Jefferson did seek to establish a wall of separation. He intended that wall, however, not to separate religion from government generally, but rather to impede a specific type of religious belief and to suppress a particular type of religious influence. Jefferson sought to subjugate the "church," by which he meant ecclesiastical clergy who preached traditional Christian dogmas, and to replace it with what he considered to be the "rational" religion of reason and enlightenment. He aspired to create a society in which what he considered to be "irrational" theological superstitions no longer guided human thinking. History, he said, "furnishes no example of a priest-ridden people maintaining a free civil government."[7] Jefferson believed both political and religious liberty required freedom from clerical religious influence and the mental tyranny he believed it imposed on individuals and society.

The anticlerical wall, however, was not his only position on church and state. Jefferson also said that religious freedom meant that individuals should not be punished for their religious beliefs and that civil rights should not be affected by individuals' religious opinions. He went so far as to say that "the opinions of men are not the object of civil government, nor under its jurisdiction."[8] This understanding of religious freedom, which Jefferson presented in terms of natural rights, appears in the philosophic preamble of the Virginia Statute for Religious Freedom.

The difficulty that envelops Jefferson's thought – and the difficulty with which this chapter wrestles – is that these two positions sometimes contradicted one another. Jefferson's attempt to overcome clerical influence required that he trespass some of the natural rights he identified. He said that individuals' civil rights should not be affected on account of their religion, but he sought to impose specific legal disabilities on clergy on account of religion. He declared that the opinions of men lie outside the jurisdiction of civil government, yet he aimed to use the state to cultivate the religious opinions he believed to be conducive to human freedom and to hinder the religious opinions he believed threatened religious and political liberty. As with other aspects of his political life, Jefferson's philosophical

---

[7] Thomas Jefferson to Alexander von Humboldt, December 6, 1813, in *Jefferson: Writings*, 1311.

[8] Jefferson's original draft of the Virginia Statute for Religious Freedom can be found in Appendix C.

ideals seem to be inconsistent with, if not outright contradicted by, his political practice.[9]

This chapter attempts to explain how some of the disparity between Jefferson's thought and practice might be explained. Jefferson seems to have believed that different levels of religious freedom were appropriate for different stages of political and societal development. He championed the idea that individuals possessed natural rights of religious freedom and that a just society should aspire to protect those rights. At the same time, he did not believe that society could extend all the rights of religious freedom to religious clergy as long as clergy threatened the rights and freedoms of others. The "establishment" of religious freedom, as Jefferson called it, first required freedom *from* clerical influence in American society and then, and only then, securing in practice the natural rights of religious liberty. Jefferson's developmental view of religious freedom meant that the degree to which religious liberty could be protected depended on the level of rational development society had achieved.

What makes Jefferson difficult to understand is that he did not call attention to the progressive nature of his project or, of course, to the contradictions between his professed philosophy and his actual political practice. In fact, he did the opposite. Jefferson publicly defended religious freedom in terms of a priori principles. In his public documents, he wrote as if a just polity always ought to secure individuals' natural rights to religious freedom. Moreover, the philosophical argument he offered suggested that any state abridgement of the natural rights to religious freedom was both tyrannical and irrational. However, when we take these arguments seriously and interpret them in light of their own internal logic, their philosophical shortcomings become apparent. Jefferson's public philosophy, moreover, does not explain his own efforts to establish religious liberty. Indeed, his political practice and his private writings reveal that Jefferson did not follow his publicly professed principles. Instead, he adopted a more pragmatic program to establish religious freedom in tandem with the rationalization of American society.

---

[9] For a general discussion of the tension between Jefferson's thought and practice, see Leonard W. Levy, *Jefferson & Civil Liberties: The Darker Side* (New York: Quadrangle, 1973 (first published by Harvard University Press, 1963)). Levy believes one exception existed in Jefferson's otherwise contradictory political philosophy. "Between his [Jefferson's] words and deeds on religious liberty," Levy claims, "there was an almost perfect congruence. . . ." (p. 15). Jefferson's apparent inconsistencies are more profound than Levy appreciates; in matters of religious liberty, too, Jefferson's actions deviate from his professed principles. On this point also consider John G. West, who argues that "Jefferson, the prudent realist, was never very consistent in translating his theory on church-state separation into action." John G. West, *The Politics of Revelation and Reason* (Lawrence: Kansas University Press, 1996), 57.

To understand Jefferson on church and state, we have to examine both what he said and what he did. We also have to evaluate when what he did cannot be explained by what he said. The points when Jefferson said one thing but did something else point toward the aspects of his church-state political philosophy that he did not publicly articulate. Nonetheless, the starting point for any investigation of Jefferson's position on church and state should be his publicly stated philosophical principles. Jefferson most thoroughly articulated these principles in the Virginia Statute for Religious Freedom. In his self-composed epitaph, moreover, he listed the Virginia Statute as one of his three greatest accomplishments – the other two being his authorship of the Declaration of Independence and his fatherhood of the University of Virginia. Following Jefferson's own identification of the statute's importance, the heart of this chapter consists of a careful examination of its argument. I conclude that some of the legal maxims that Jefferson claims belong to the natural rights of mankind cannot in fact be derived from the statute's philosophical starting point of the freedom of the human mind. More importantly, I contend that the Virginia Statute's philosophy does not actually explain Jefferson's efforts to establish religious freedom. The statute's boldest claim, that the opinions of men lie beyond the jurisdiction of government, is more rhetorical than real. His actions to establish religious freedom were not based on the statute's claim that "Almighty God hath created the mind free" but rather were part of his attempt to free the minds of men from what he believed to be irrational theological dogmas.

This conclusion is not meant to cast doubt on Jefferson's belief in religious freedom or to question his commitment to the legal maxims he sets forth in the statute. But it does suggest that if we want to understand Jefferson, we have to look beyond his stated philosophy in the Virginia Statute. I contend that Jefferson's project to establish religious freedom is most clearly revealed in his plans for public education. Through public education, he intended to strip clergy and traditional Christianity of their societal influence and to shape Americans' religious opinions. After discussing the Virginia Statute, this chapter explains the role of public education in Jefferson's project to establish religious freedom, an aspect of Jefferson's church-state politics that has not been well understood.

Before proceeding to the philosophy of the Virginia Statute and Jefferson's educational politics, the chapter briefly examines Jefferson's letter to the Danbury Baptist Association. Since *Everson v. Board of Education* (1947) and *McCollum v. Board of Education* (1948), the letter and its "wall of separation" metaphor have stood in the public mind as the Jeffersonian – and, according to some, the Founders' – position on the proper relationship between church and state. A careful reading of the Danbury Baptist letter reveals that it merely repeats doctrines more fully explained in the Virginia Statute. Even if we take the "wall" to stand for the Jeffersonian position, to understand what that wall separates requires that we go beyond the Danbury letter. I begin with the Danbury letter, nonetheless, because of the significant role it has played in constitutional jurisprudence and in scholarly interpretations of Jefferson's position on religious freedom.[10]

JEFFERSON'S "WALL OF SEPARATION" AND THE VIRGINIA STATUTE

Everson and the Building of the Strict-Separationist "Wall of Separation"

Jefferson's iconic status for "strict-separationist" First Amendment religion jurisprudence lies in the Supreme Court's first Establishment Clause incorporation cases, *Everson v. Board of Education* (1947) and *McCollum v. Board of Education* (1948). The *Everson* Court declared in grand and sweeping language:

The "establishment of religion" clause of the First Amendment means at least this: Neither a state nor the Federal Government can set up a church. Neither can pass laws which aid one religion, aid all religions, or prefer one religion over another. Neither can force nor influence a person to go to or remain away from a church against his will or force him to profess a belief or disbelief in any religion. No person can be punished for entertaining or professing religious beliefs or disbeliefs, for church attendance or non-attendance. No tax in any amount, large or small, can be levied to support any religious activities or institutions, whatever they may be called, or whatever form they may adopt to teach or practice religion. Neither a state nor the Federal Government can, openly or secretly, participate in the affairs of any religious organizations or groups and *vice versa*. In the words of Jefferson, the clause against establishment of religion by law was intended to "erect a wall of separation between church and state."[11]

Everson's bark was louder than its bite, as the Court actually upheld the state action under scrutiny, a New Jersey school district plan that reimbursed transportation costs for children attending Catholic and public schools. However, one year later in *McCollum*, the Court implemented *Everson's* "strict-

---

[10] Recent scholarship on the Danbury letter includes James Hutson, "Thomas Jefferson's Letter to the Danbury Baptists: A Controversy Rejoined," *William and Mary Quarterly*, 3rd series, 56, no. 4 (October 1999): 776; Daniel L. Dreisbach, *Thomas Jefferson and the Wall of Separation Between Church and State* (New York: New York University Press, 2003).

[11] *Everson v. Board of Education*, 330 U.S. 1, 15–16 (1947).

separationist" language. Citing the passage just quoted, an eight-member majority struck down an Illinois school district policy that allowed religious teachers to
offer voluntary religious instruction in public schools during the school day.
Rejecting the argument that the American Founders meant only to prohibit
government preference of one religion over all others, the Court said that the
First Amendment "has erected a wall between Church and State which must be
kept high and impregnable," and, therefore, that the government may not aid a
particular religion or all religions in the dissemination of religious doctrines or
ideals.[12] Using jurisprudential tests descending from the "wall," subsequent
Supreme Court decisions found unconstitutional directed nondenominational
prayer and Bible readings in public schools, state-funded teachers in religious
schools, moments of silence "for meditation or voluntary prayer" in public
schools, and nativity scenes and postings of the Ten Commandments in county
courthouses.[13] Once the Court built the "wall" in *Everson* and *McCollum*, it
never seriously examined Jefferson's thought again.[14] Even in *Everson*, the
Court did not explain how the "wall" followed from Jefferson's philosophical
arguments or how it fit into Jefferson's political philosophy more generally.[15]

---

[12] *McCollum v. Board of Education*, 333 U.S. 203, 211–12 (1948).

[13] *Engel v. Vitale*, 370 U.S. 421 (1962); *Abington School District v. Schempp*, 374 U.S. 203
(1963); *Lemon v. Kurtzman*, 403 U.S. 602 (1971); *Wallace v. Jaffree*, 472 U.S. 38 (1985);
Allegheny County v. Greater Pittsburgh ACLU, 497 U.S. 573 (1989); *McCreary County v.
American Civil Liberties Union of Kentucky*, 545 U.S. 844 (2005).

[14] In his challenge to the nonpreferentialist interpretation of the Establishment Clause, Justice
David Souter cited the Virginia Statute and Jefferson's refusal to issue official days of prayer
and thanksgiving as president. Justice Souter, however, did not engage in a comprehensive
examination of Jefferson's thought; instead, he cited secondary literature that advances the
strict-separationist interpretation of Jefferson. See Souter's concurring opinion in *Lee v.
Weisman*, 505 U.S. 577, 623–24 (1992), and his dissenting opinion in *Rosenberger v.
Rector and Visitors of University of Virginia*, 515 U.S. 819, 870–74, 891 (1995). Secondary
literature Souter cited includes Thomas Curry, *The First Freedoms: Church and State in
America to the Passage of the First Amendment* (New York: Oxford University Press, 1986);
Douglas Laycock, "'Nonpreferential' Aid to Religion: A False Claim About Original
Intent," *William & Mary Law Review* 27 (1986): 875–916.

[15] This is not to say that scholarly interpretations of Jefferson have not found him to support a
strict separation between church and state. See, for example, Merrill D. Peterson, *Thomas
Jefferson and the New Nation: A Biography* (New York: Oxford University Press, 1970),
133–45; John D. Whaley's contribution in Daniel L. Dreisbach and John D. Whaley, "What
the Wall Separates: A Debate on Thomas Jefferson's 'Wall of Separation' Metaphor,"
Constitutional Commentary 16 (Winter 1999): 635–49; Robert M. O'Neil, "The 'Wall
of Separation' and Thomas Jefferson's Views of Religious Liberty," *William and Mary
Quarterly*, 3rd Series, 56, no. 4 (October 1999): 791–94; William Lee Miller, *The First
Liberty: Religion and the American Republic* (New York: Knopf, 1986), 56–59, 69; David
N. Mayer, *The Constitutional Thought of Thomas Jefferson* (Charlottesville: University
Press of Virginia, 1994), 163–65; Isaac Kramnick and R. Laurence Moore, *The Godless
Constitution: The Case Against Religious Correctness* (New York: Norton, 1996), 97.

The Danbury Letter and the Virginia Statute

In its entirety, the second paragraph of the Danbury Baptist letter states:

Believing with you that religion is a matter which lies solely between man and his God, that he owes account to none other for his faith or his worship, that the legitimate powers of government reach actions only, and not opinions, I contemplate with sovereign reverence that act of the whole American people which declared that their legislature should "make no law respecting an establishment of religion, or prohibiting the free exercise thereof," thus building a wall of separation between Church and State. Adhering to this expression of the supreme will of the nation in behalf of the rights of conscience, I see with sincere satisfaction the progress of those sentiments which tend to restore to man all his natural rights, convinced he has no natural right in opposition to his social duties.[16]

Everson focused on Jefferson's assertion that the First Amendment builds a "wall of separation" between church and state, but it is actually earlier in the paragraph that Jefferson states what constitutes an individual's natural rights. He sets forth three interrelated principles: 1) "that religion is a matter which lies solely between man and his God," 2) "that he owes account to none other for his faith or his worship," and 3) "that the legitimate powers of government reach actions only, and not opinions." Jefferson used the introductory phrase "believing with you" because the Danbury Baptist Association had listed similar beliefs in their letter to him. The Danbury Baptists wrote:

Our sentiments are uniformly on the side of Religious Liberty – That Religion is at all times and places a Matter between God and Individuals – That no man ought to suffer in Name, person or effects on account of his religious Opinions – That the legitimate Power of civil Government extends no further than to punish the man who *works ill to his neighbor.*[17]

[16] Thomas Jefferson to Nehemiah Dodge and Others, A Committee of the Danbury Baptist Association, in the State of Connecticut, January 1, 1802, in *The Portable Thomas Jefferson*, ed. and Introduction by Merrill D. Peterson (New York: Penguin, 1975), 303–04. The letter reprinted in *The Portable Thomas Jefferson* contains a typographical error. In the second paragraph Jefferson writes, "that the legitimate powers of government reach actions only, and not opinions." In the Peterson collection and in other collections, the word *legislative* is mistakenly submitted for the word *legitimate*. For a discussion of this point, see Daniel L. Dreisbach, *Thomas Jefferson and the Wall of Separation Between Church and State* (New York: New York University Press, 2002), 48n.71.

[17] Emphasis in the original. Letter from a committee of the Danbury Baptist association to Thomas Jefferson, October 7, 1801, *The Papers of Thomas Jefferson* (Manuscript Division, Library of Congress), Series 1, Box 87, August 30, 1801–October 15, 1801; Presidential Papers Microfilm, Thomas Jefferson Papers (Manuscript Division, Library of Congress), Series 1, Reel 24, June 26, 1801–November 14, 1801. The full text of the Danbury Baptist letter to Jefferson is also in Dreisbach, "'Sowing Useful Truths and Principles,'" 460–61.

TABLE 1. *Danbury Baptists' Letter and Jefferson's Response*

Danbury Baptists' Letter	Jefferson's Response
1. That religion is at all times and places a matter between God and individuals	1. That religion is a matter which lies solely between man and his God
2. That no man ought to suffer in name, person or effects on account of his religious opinions	2. That he owes account to none other for his faith or his worship
3. That the legitimate power of civil government extends no further than to punish the man who works ill to his neighbor	3. That the legitimate powers of government reach actions only, and not opinions

The side-by-side comparison shown in Table 1 reveals how Jefferson's letter mirrors the Danbury Baptists' sentiments.

Jefferson reiterated the Danbury Baptists' tenets without substantively altering them. This is not surprising because the Danbury Baptists' letter itself reflects principles Jefferson articulated years earlier in the Virginia Statute for Religious Freedom (see Table 2).

The Danbury Baptists, no doubt, were familiar with the Virginia Statute when they composed their letter.[18] Jefferson's response merely reiterates principles he had previously stated. The primary difference between Jefferson's two documents is the ground in which he anchors his principles. In the Virginia Statute, Jefferson connects his principles to a broader philosophical argument. In the Danbury letter, he rests them on his shared beliefs with his letter's recipients ("Believing with you . . ."). To understand Jefferson's philosophical argument in support of the Danbury letter's "natural rights," accordingly, requires that we examine the Virginia Statute.

But what about the "wall of separation"? What did Jefferson mean to communicate by using that metaphor, which does not appear in the Virginia Statute? At first glance, it would seem that the "wall" refers to the three "useful truths and principles" articulated. Jefferson appears to instruct the American people that the First Amendment recognizes that religion lies between the individual and God, that individuals owe nobody an account of their religious faith, and that the First Amendment prohibits the government from legislating on matters of religious opinion. In other public

---

[18] For background information about the Danbury Baptist Association and their understanding of religious freedom, see Philip Hamburger, *Separation of Church and State* (Cambridge, MA: Harvard University Press, 2002), 163–80.

TABLE 2. *Danbury Baptists' Letter and The Virginia Statute*

Danbury Baptists' Letter	Jefferson's Virginia Statute
1. That religion is at all times and places a matter between God and individuals	1. No man shall be compelled to frequent or support any religious worship, place, or ministry whatsoever
2. That no man ought to suffer in name, person, or effects on account of his religious opinions	2. [No man] shall be enforced, restrained, molested, or burthened [sic] in his body or goods, nor shall otherwise suffer, on account of his religious opinions or belief
3. That the legitimate power of civil government extends no further than to punish the man who works ill to his neighbor	3. That it is time enough for the rightful purposes of civil government for its officers to interfere when principles break out into overt acts against peace and good order

statements, however, Jefferson interpreted the First Amendment in a strictly jurisdictional manner. In his second Inaugural Address, he offered what is perhaps his most succinct interpretation:

In matters of religion, I have considered that its free exercise is placed by the constitution independent of the powers of the general government. I have therefore undertaken, on no occasion, to prescribe the religious exercises suited to it; but have left them, as the constitution found them, under the direction and discipline of State or Church authorities acknowledged by the several religious societies.[19]

Jefferson paraphrased the Tenth Amendment to explain that he had not issued presidential religious proclamations because the national government – and, therefore, himself as president – lacked the constitutional power to do so.

Jefferson offered a more detailed defense of the same jurisdictional interpretation in a private letter to Reverend Samuel Miller, dated January 23, 1808. Miller wrote to Jefferson requesting him to designate a national fast day. Jefferson's response emphasized his lack of constitutional power to do so.

[19] Thomas Jefferson, second Inaugural Address, March 4, 1805, in *The Works of Thomas Jefferson*, federal edition, ed. Paul Leicester Ford (New York: G. P. Putnam's Sons, 1904–05), 10:131. I disagree, accordingly, with David N. Mayer, who interprets this passage from Jefferson's second Inaugural to reflect Jefferson's principled commitment to the separation of church and state. See David N. Mayer, *The Constitutional Thought of Thomas Jefferson* (Charlottesville: University Press of Virginia, 1994), 165.

The national government, Jefferson wrote, is "interdicted by the Constitution from intermeddling with religious institutions, their doctrines, discipline, or exercises." "This results," he continued, "not only from the provisions that no law shall be made respecting the establishment or free exercise of religion, but from that also which reserves to the States the powers not delegated to the United States." Since no power is delegated to the national government "to prescribe any religious exercise, or to assume authority in religious discipline," Jefferson explained, "it must then rest with the States, as far as it can be in any human authority." The authority of state governors to issue religious proclamations, Jefferson suggested later in the letter, has "led to the assumption of that authority by the General Government, without due examination, which would have discovered that what might be a right in a State government, was a violation of that right when assumed by another." "No authority to direct the religious exercises of his constituents," Jefferson concluded, has been given to the president of the United States.[20]

In his second Inaugural Address and in his letter to Reverend Miller, Jefferson interpreted the First Amendment as a particular example of the general constitutional doctrine affirmed by the Tenth Amendment: that the national government possesses only limited, delegated powers. The "intermeddling with religious institutions, their doctrines, discipline, or exercises," as he put it, is not one of those delegated powers. If Jefferson thought that the First Amendment directly prohibited him from issuing religious proclamations because of its substantive protection of the right to religious liberty, it seems that he would have advanced that interpretation in his second Inaugural Address and letter to Miller. But Jefferson did not take that approach; instead, he interpreted the First Amendment jurisdictionally.

His jurisdictional interpretation of the First Amendment may explain why Jefferson used the metaphor of a "wall of separation" in the Danbury Baptist letter. Contrary to first appearances, the "wall" may refer, as Daniel Dreisbach contends, only to the jurisdictional boundary between the federal government and religion.[21] Read this way, the First Amendment is an "expression . . . in behalf of the rights of conscience" because it reaffirms that the federal government lacks authority over religion and, therefore, that it cannot prescribe religious opinions or punish an

[20] Thomas Jefferson to Rev. Samuel Miller, January 23, 1808, in *Jefferson: Writings*, 1186–87.

[21] Daniel L. Dreisbach, *Thomas Jefferson and the Wall of Separation Between Church and State*, Chapter 4. For a different interpretation that emphasizes the political context of the Danbury letter, see James Hutson, "Thomas Jefferson's Letter to the Danbury Baptists," 776.

individual on account of his religious beliefs. A wall of federalism, in other words, effectively prohibits the national government from trespassing illegitimately into the realm of religious belief. To see the "wall" only as a reference to federalism, however, requires a careful parsing of the letter's text and reading it in the light of Jefferson's other interpretations of the First Amendment. Reading the Danbury letter alone could easily lead one to interpret the "wall of separation" to refer to the substantive principles that are also asserted.

In this context, it should also be noted that Jefferson's intention in writing the Danbury Baptist letter was not to offer a precise interpretation of the First Amendment's Establishment Clause. In a letter to his Attorney General Levi Lincoln, Jefferson explained that the purpose of his response to the Danbury Baptist Association was to sow "useful truths & principles among the people, which might germinate and become rooted among their political tenets."[22] He concluded the Danbury letter by referring to his "sincere satisfaction [with] the progress of those sentiments which tend to restore to man all his natural rights. . . ." Jefferson sought to teach that religion is a matter for the individual alone, that individuals are not accountable to others for their religious beliefs, and that the legitimate jurisdiction of any government extends to acts alone and not to beliefs. If the American people interpreted the "wall" to stand for these principles, he would have furthered his intention.[23] Even if the most accurate and precise interpretation of the "wall" is that it refers to federalism, it is not necessarily mistaken to regard it as a metaphor for a part of Jefferson's approach to church-state relations.

The Danbury Baptist letter, however, is not the document in which Jefferson most philosophically articulated that approach. While it may offer an irresistible image for judges in search of a legal doctrine, the Danbury letter does not merit status as the primary source of meaning for Jefferson's

---

[22] Thomas Jefferson to Attorney General Levi Lincoln, January 1, 1802, *The Writings of Thomas Jefferson*, library edition, ed. Andrew A. Lipscomb (Washington, DC: The Thomas Jefferson Memorial Association, 1903–05), 9:346.

[23] Regarding the intentions that animate Jefferson's writings, Philip Hamburger claims, Jefferson seems to have come to believe that he could liberate a people through his writings. He recognized his ability to write in prose that resonated with Americans, and he hoped that his words, together with those of his allies, could overturn prejudices and open the minds of the people to new ways of seeing their world – leading eventually to radical changes. . . . One of the ways Jefferson had long been revolutionizing or at least liberating the minds of Americans was by using familiar words in unfamiliar contexts, in which their meaning was altered and expanded so as to give the readers new ways of seeing themselves and their liberty. Hamburger, *Separation of Church and State*, 145–46.

thought on church and state. It reiterates doctrines that Jefferson set forth in the Virginia Statute for Religious Freedom. To understand how Jefferson attempted to build the "wall" philosophically, we must move beyond the Danbury Baptist letter to the Virginia Statute.

JEFFERSON'S PHILOSOPHY OF RELIGIOUS LIBERTY: THE VIRGINIA STATUTE FOR RELIGIOUS FREEDOM

Despite the relative lack of attention the Supreme Court has given the Virginia Statute, scholars have long noted its significance. Harvard historian Bernard Bailyn called it "the most important document in American history, bar none."[24] Jefferson biographer Dumas Malone offered similar praise: "[Jefferson's] bill for the establishing of religious freedom is, in my opinion, one of his most superb papers, and it is as fresh now as it was the day he wrote it."[25] The bill remains "fresh" because of the nature of its argument. In the Virginia Statute, Jefferson strives to articulate philosophically the grounds for the natural right of religious liberty, and, in doing so, to legislate for our times as well as his own.

The bill's concluding sentence discloses Jefferson's own ambitious judgment that he had drafted legislation for future generations:

[W]e are free to declare, and do declare, that the rights hereby asserted are of the natural rights of mankind, and that if any act shall be hereafter passed to repeal the present or to narrow its operation, such act will be an infringement of natural right.[26]

The bill explicitly recognizes that the legislature adopting it has "no power to restrain the acts of succeeding Assemblies"; nonetheless, it preemptively declares that any subsequent act that repeals or even only narrows the bill's operation would be "an infringement of natural right." The Virginia Statute thus invokes for its authority the unchanging principles of natural right and natural rights, invocations that invite us to focus on its philosophical

---

[24] See Daniel L. Dreisbach, "Religion and Legal Reform in Revolutionary Virginia," in *Religion and Political Culture in Jefferson's Virginia,* eds. Garrett Ward Sheldon and Daniel L. Dreisbach (Lanham, MD: Rowman & Littlefield, 2000), 211n.39 (quoting Bailyn).

[25] Dumas Malone, "Mr. Jefferson and the Traditions of Virginia," *Virginia Magazine of History & Biography* 75 (April 1967): 137.

[26] The text of the Virginia Statute can be found in Appendix C. Jefferson's original of the Virginia Statute was modified by the Virginia assembly. Since our purpose is to uncover Jefferson's thought, this chapter examines Jefferson's original text.

teaching. If the Virginia Statute persuasively articulates the philosophical grounds of the natural right to religious liberty and deduces from that philosophy the proper boundaries between church and state, then its enduring significance is unquestionable.

Identifying the Virginia Statute's philosophical teaching, however, is more complicated than it first appears.[27] The preamble's declaration of the freedom of the human mind precedes a one-sentence enacting paragraph, which contains the legal rules of the bill. The enacting paragraph is then followed by the aforementioned one-sentence concluding paragraph. The bill appears to contain the transparent structure of a legal argument: statement of principle, deductions from principle, and concluding statement of significance. The legal maxims in the second paragraph, however, are not straightforwardly deduced from the preamble's declaration of human freedom. Moreover, the preamble interweaves epistemological, theological, and prudential arguments. By carefully examining the preamble, we shall attempt to disentangle Jefferson's philosophical, theological, and prudential arguments and thereby determine to what extent he philosophically deduces the natural rights maxims he asserts.

The Preamble

Jefferson's manner of composition obscures the preamble's embedded structure. The one long sentence can be divided into three parts: the declaration of the freedom of the human mind, arguments against the imposition of religion, and arguments that religion should not define or determine the rights and privileges of political citizenship. The preamble of Jefferson's

---

[27] Thomas Buckley, S.J., speaking more generally about Jefferson's contribution to the achievement of religious freedom, nicely captures some of the complexities of understanding Jefferson's thought:

> The complexity of his [Jefferson's] achievement has not been fully appreciated, perhaps because of the paradoxical way in which he made his contribution. Jefferson repeatedly insisted that his religion was private, but drafted public documents with strong religious overtones. He thought theology of little or no academic value, yet issued profound theological statements. Some contemporaries considered his view the height of irreligion, but others found them deeply religious as well as political. He argued for separation of church and state based on the nature of religion itself, and founded a public policy for the United States on a theology. Those who opposed his views did so in the name of preserving religion, but it was his consistent approach to keep civil government away from religion in order to preserve religion truly.

> Thomas Buckley, S.J., "The Political Theology of Thomas Jefferson," in *The Virginia Statute for Religious Freedom: Its Evolution and Consequences in American History*, eds. Merrill D. Peterson and Robert C. Vaughan (Cambridge: Cambridge University Press, 1988), 77.

original draft can be outlined as follows. Because we are primarily concerned with Jefferson's thought, we shall focus on his unamended draft, the full text of which can be found in Appendix C.

I. Declaration of the freedom of the human mind
   A. Epistemological foundations
      1. Opinions and beliefs of men depend not on their own will, but form involuntarily from the evidence proposed to their minds
      2. The mind is altogether insusceptible to restraint
   B. Theological foundations
      1. Almighty God hath created the mind free
      2. All attempts to influence it by temporal punishments, or "burthens," or by civil incapacitations are a departure from the plan of the holy author of our religion

II. Arguments against the imposition of religion
   A. Imposition of religious belief and practice
      1. Irrational – tends to beget habits of hypocrisy and meanness
      2. Impious
         a. Almighty God chose not to propagate the mind by coercions, as was in his Almighty power to do, but to extend it by its influence on reason alone
         b. Legislators and rulers, civil as well as ecclesiastical, are fallible and uninspired
   B. Compelled financial support
      1. Sinful and tyrannical if one disbelieves and abhors the supported opinions
      2. Imprudent
         a. Deprivation of liberty of the individual to support the pastor he favors
         b. Withdraws inducement to virtue from clergy

III. Arguments against religion determining rights and privileges of citizenship
   A. Violation of "natural right"
      1. Our civil rights do not depend on our religious opinions
      2. Opinions are not the object of civil government, nor are they under its jurisdiction – rightful purposes of civil government and for its officers are to interfere when principles break out into overt acts against peace and good order

B. Imprudent
1. Corrupts religious faith of individuals
2. Inevitably threatens religious liberty
3. Unnecessary because truth is great and will prevail if left to herself

Jefferson's preamble begins with a resounding statement declaring the freedom of the human mind:

Well aware that the opinions and belief of men depend not on their own will, but follow involuntarily the evidence proposed to their minds; that Almighty God hath created the mind free, and manifested his supreme will that free it shall remain by making it altogether insusceptible of restraint. . . .

The Virginia Assembly eliminated the opening clause, starting the bill instead with the theological statement, "Almighty God hath created the mind free." Jefferson's unamended argument, as we shall explain, includes theological assertions, but his evidence for the freedom of the human mind rests primarily on epistemological grounds. His draft focuses on two related aspects of the mind's operations: that it involuntarily adheres to the evidence it finds persuasive, and that it cannot be restrained. Both observations follow the teachings of John Locke, who Jefferson carefully studied.[28] In *A Letter Concerning Toleration*, Locke claims, "It is only Light and Evidence that can work a change in Men[']s Opinions; which light can in no manner proceed from corporal Sufferings, or any other outward Penalties."[29] Accepting Locke's idea that evidence alone can persuade the mind, Jefferson recognizes that the mind cannot be compelled to belief: "All attempts to influence it [the mind] by temporal punishments, or burthens, or by civil incapacitations tend only to beget habits of hypocrisy and meanness." Coercive force can lead a man disingenuously to profess a belief or an opinion, but it cannot create

---

[28] See "Notes on Locke and Shaftesbury," in *The Papers of Thomas Jefferson*, ed. Julian P. Boyd (Princeton, NJ: Princeton University Press, 1953), 1:544–51. S. Gerald Sandler sets forth a side-by-side comparison of Locke's *Letter Concerning Toleration*, Jefferson's notes on the *Letter*, and Jefferson's "Bill for Establishing Religious Freedom" that demonstrates Jefferson's indebtedness to Locke. S. Gerald Sandler, "Lockean Ideas in Thomas Jefferson's Bill for Establishing Religious Freedom," *Journal of the History of Ideas* 21 (1960): 110–16. A more theoretical explanation of Jefferson's debt to Locke is set forth by Sanford Kessler, "Locke's Influence on Jefferson's 'Bill for Establishing Religious Freedom,'" *Journal of Church and State* 25 (1983): 231–52.

[29] John Locke, *A Letter Concerning Toleration*, ed. James H. Tully (Indianapolis: Hackett, 1983), 27.

inner conviction. The mind's insusceptibility to restraint and compulsion maintains its freedom even under duress.

Not only is the human mind impervious to force, it cannot reject evidence it finds persuasive. Jefferson states, "the opinions and belief of men depend not on their own will, but follow involuntarily the evidence proposed to their minds." Here he adopts a teaching articulated by Locke in *An Essay Concerning Human Understanding*. "[O]*ur will hath no power to determine the knowledge of the mind one way or another*," Locke writes, "that is done only by the objects themselves, as far as they are clearly discovered."[30] This aspect of the mind's freedom implies that, in one sense, the mind is radically determined. Individuals do not willfully choose or select their own opinions but, rather, opinions are the involuntary outcomes of an individual's perception of evidence.[31]

These two epistemological observations establishing the mind's freedom – its insusceptibility to coercion and its involuntary subjection to persuasive evidence – lie at the heart of Jefferson's philosophical argument for religious freedom. They also serve as the basis for Jefferson's subsequent theological assertions that "Almighty God hath created the mind free," and "all attempts to influence it by temporal punishments, or burthens [sic], or by civil incapacitations . . . are a departure from the plan of the holy author of our religion. . . ." Jefferson does not cite the Bible or a church authority to support his theology. He says that God created the mind free because he sees that it is free. He deduces the "plan of the holy author of our religion" in the same way. An omnipotent god, Jefferson says, could have coerced belief by infusing the mind directly with knowledge of divine things, but the "Almighty" left the mind to be influenced by reason alone. From these observable facts, he concludes that attempts to influence it by temporal punishments "are a departure from the plan of the holy author of our religion." This does not imply that the "Almighty God" that creates the mind cannot be the God of the Bible, but Jefferson's argument about the

---

[30] Emphasis in the original. *An Essay Concerning Human Understanding* (New York: Dover Publications, Inc., 1959), Book IV, Chapter 13, §2, 358. See also John Locke, *An Essay Concerning Human Understanding*, Book IV, Chapter 20, §16, 455: "As knowledge is no more arbitrary than perception; so, I think, assent is not more in our power than knowledge. When the agreement of any two ideas appears to our minds, whether immediately or by the assistance of reason, I can no more refuse to perceive, no more avoid knowing it, than I can avoid seeing those objects which I turn my eyes to, and look on in daylight; and what upon full examination I find the most probable, I cannot deny my assent to."

[31] The Virginia assembly also eliminated Jefferson's phrase, "and manifested his supreme will that free it shall remain by making it altogether insusceptible of restraint," thus eliminating Jefferson's statement about the mind's determinism from the bill's adopted text.

mind's freedom does not depend on that identification.[32] His theological assertions about the freedom of the mind are not taken from revelation. Observation of and rational reflection about natural phenomena are Jefferson's tools for theological inquiry.[33]

Having asserted the mind's freedom, the preamble moves to arguments against the imposition of religious beliefs and the compulsion of financial support for religion. Attempts to influence the mind by temporal punishments or penalties, Jefferson states, "tend only to beget habits of hypocrisy and meanness." A direct implication of the mind's freedom is that attempts to influence it by force necessarily must fail. Jefferson does not explicitly draw out the full implication of his argument, which is that lawmakers who legislate beliefs attempt to do what cannot be done and thus act irrationally.

The Virginia Statute instead turns to theological considerations. Jefferson denounces the "impious presumption" of rulers who assume "dominion over the faith of others." The presumption is made by civil and ecclesiastical rulers who are "themselves but fallible and uninspired men." Jefferson implies that God inspires no man, or at least no man that exercises civil or religious authority. Being uninspired, civil and ecclesiastical rulers – in this context, Jefferson does not distinguish between the two – lack legitimate authority to establish and impose their opinions as true and infallible. When they exercise "dominion over the faith of others," they do something that God Himself refuses to do because, according to Jefferson, "Almighty God" influences the human mind by reason alone. Civil and ecclesiastical

---

[32] One might question, of course, whether the Judeo-Christian God is as noncoercive as Jefferson suggests. The God of both the Hebrew scriptures and New Testament frequently uses miracles to draw in followers. Moreover, if the Bible is interpreted to support belief in a life after death where the individual is rewarded or punished for his beliefs, one might conclude that the God of the Bible, in some sense, does use punishments and incapacitations as a way to influence belief.

[33] For Jefferson's belief in the sovereignty of reason in matters of revelation, see Thomas Jefferson to Miles King, September 26, 1814, in *Jefferson's Extracts from the Gospels*, ed. Dickenson W. Adams (Princeton, NJ: Princeton University Press, 1983), 360–61; Thomas Jefferson to Peter Carr, August 10, 1787, in *Portable Thomas Jefferson*, 423–28; Jean M. Yarbrough, *American Virtues: Thomas Jefferson on the Character of a Free People* (Lawrence: University Press of Kansas, 1998), 182–86; Aristide Tessitore, "Legitimate Government, Religion, and Education: The Political Philosophy of Thomas Jefferson," in *History of American Political Thought*, eds. Bryan-Paul Frost and Jeffrey Sikkenga (Lanham, MD: Lexington Books, 2003), 139; Michael Zuckert, "Thomas Jefferson on Nature and Natural Rights," in *The Framers and Fundamental Rights*, ed. Robert A. Licht (Washington, DC: AEI Press, 1991), 141. For a discussion of how Jefferson used the word "rational," see Paul Conkin, "The Religious Pilgrimage of Thomas Jefferson," in *Jefferson Legacies*, ed. Peter S. Onuf (Charlottesville: University of Virginia Press, 1993), 25.

leaders who impose their own opinions as true and infallible, therefore, act impiously when they fail to recognize the limits of their own knowledge and fail to follow God's example of persuasion through reason alone.[34]

Not only is the imposition of religious opinions impious, Jefferson declares that compulsory financial support for the propagation of opinions that one "disbelieves and abhors" is "sinful and tyrannical." It is sinful, presumably, for the same reasons that the imposition of religious belief is an "impious presumption." Jefferson does not draw out clearly why such action is "tyrannical," but it seems to be related to man's lack of freedom over his own beliefs and opinions. Because an individual is not free to reject opinions he finds persuasive, financial compulsion to support opinions that one "disbelieves and abhors" forces that individual to sustain beliefs that he lacks the ability to favor. Just as it is irrational to attempt to compel beliefs, Jefferson declares that it is "tyrannical" to force a man to support beliefs about which he has no choice to accept or reject.

This reading of the "tyrannical" nature of compulsory support is bolstered by Jefferson's subsequent distinction between financial support for beliefs that one "disbelieves and abhors" and financial support for a teacher of one's own religious persuasion. Jefferson does not call the latter "tyrannical." Instead, he offers a separate, prudential rationale against compulsory support of one's own religion: that it deprives the individual of the "comfortable liberty" of favoring the pastor "whose morals he would make his pattern, and whose powers he feels most persuasive to righteousness," and that it withdraws from ministers the incentive of those "temporary rewards" that "are an additional incitement to earnest and unremitting labours for the instruction of mankind." From the distinction between the two types of compulsory financial support, it seems that Jefferson associates tyranny with forcing an individual to act financially in a manner that contradicts deeply held opinions. Compulsion to support a religion consistent with one's own opinions is portrayed differently: It may be unwise, but it does not force a man to act in a manner that imposes a contradiction between actions and opinions. We note in passing that Jefferson here employs a problematical definition of tyranny – one that he does not maintain in his educational thought, a point we shall return to in the latter part of this chapter.

---

[34] Jefferson seems to equate divine intention with the operations of nature, which would imply that piety requires that men respect how the mind has been created and that men approach it in light of its natural operations. Impiety and irrationality appear to be synonymous terms for Jefferson. For a discussion of how the laws of nature are identical to the laws of "nature's God" in Jefferson's thought, see Zuckert, "Thomas Jefferson on Nature and Natural Rights," 139–47.

Having argued that religion should be free from political control, Jefferson next attempts to liberate political rights from religious affiliation. His language becomes less theological and more philosophical, and his arguments reach back to the foundations of liberal political theory. "Our civil rights have no dependance [sic] on our religious opinions," Jefferson declares, "any more than our opinions in physics or geometry." Religious tests for public offices and emoluments, accordingly, deprive an individual "injuriously of those privileges and advantages to which, in common with his fellow citizens, he has a natural right." Here the Virginia Statute assumes the social contract philosophy of government implicit in the Declaration of Independence, among other places. Because government is created by free and equal individuals, it can legitimately exercise only those powers granted to it. Jefferson explains in *Notes on the State of Virginia* that the opinions of men cannot be the object of civil government or under its jurisdiction because "[O]ur rulers can have authority over such natural rights only as we have submitted to them. The rights of conscience we never submitted, we could not submit."[35] The rights of conscience cannot be submitted, Jefferson writes in *Notes*, because "We are answerable for them to our God." They also cannot be submitted, to return to the argument of the Virginia Statute, because man lacks sovereignty over his beliefs and opinions. Men cannot relinquish what they do not possess or control. Because opinions, unlike acts of the body, are not subject to the will, individuals cannot grant jurisdiction over them to the state.[36] The epistemological fact that limits governmental authority over opinions is that individuals do not govern their minds like they govern their bodies. Since individuals cannot grant the state authority over their opinions, "the rightful purposes of civil government [are] for its officers to interfere when principles break out into overt acts against peace and good order." The will's lack of sovereignty over beliefs leads Jefferson to draw a categorical distinction between the beliefs and opinions, on the one hand, and actions

---

[35] Jefferson, *Notes of the State of Virginia*, Query XVII, "Religion," in *Portable Thomas Jefferson*, 210. For background information relating to the composition of Query XVII see Bernhard Fabian, "Jefferson's *Notes on Virginia*: The Genesis of Query xvii, The Different Religions Received into That State?" *William and Mary Quarterly*, 3rd Series, 12, no. 1 (1955): 124–38.

[36] Cf. Locke in *A Letter Concerning Toleration*: "Nor can such power [care of souls] be vested in the Magistrate by the *consent of the People*; because no man can so far abandon the care of his own Salvation, as blindly to leave it to the choice of any other. . . . For no Man can, if he would, conform his Faith or Worship to the Dictates of another." Locke, *A Letter Concerning Toleration*, 26.

on the other. Beliefs and opinions lie outside the legitimate jurisdiction of government; actions can lie within it.[37]

Jefferson's categorical denial of governmental jurisdiction over the entire realm of opinions is the Virginia Statute's boldest claim and its fundamental philosophical teaching. It also is Jefferson's most unique contribution to the idea of religious liberty. As discussed previously, the Virginia Statute follows the epistemological and political thought of John Locke. Jefferson breaks from Locke, however, regarding the state's lack of jurisdiction over opinions. In *A Letter Concerning Toleration*, Locke grants toleration only to religious worship not "prejudicial to the commonweal of a people in the ordinary use," and to speculative religious opinions "which have no manner of relation to the civil rights of the subjects."[38] Moreover, Locke explicitly teaches that "no opinions contrary to human society, or to those moral rules which are necessary to the preservation of civil society, are to be tolerated by the [civil] magistrate."[39] The Lockean commonwealth retains jurisdiction over opinions because opinions affect moral action and moral action affects the peace of society, the primary concern of the state.[40] While not disagreeing with Locke about civil peace being a primary end of government, Jefferson goes further than Locke does in curtailing the legitimate means government may employ to secure that end. The Virginia Statute contends that not only are speculative religious opinions tolerated, but the freedom of the human mind demands that all opinions lie outside the jurisdiction of civil government.

Jefferson was conscious of his departure from Locke on this point. He took detailed notes on *A Letter Concerning Toleration*, much of which consisted of paraphrases of Locke's text. His notes on Locke's limitations regarding politically dangerous opinions are as follows. The brackets and the sentence within them are Jefferson's:

[Lo]cke denies toleration to those who entertain opns. contrary to those moral rules necessary for the preservation of society; as for instance, that faith is not to be kept

---

[37] The belief-action distinction does not imply that Jefferson believes that government can legitimately prohibit any action, but, rather, as he states in *Notes on the State of Virginia*, "The legitimate powers of government extend to such acts only as are injurious to others." Thomas Jefferson, *Notes on the State of Virginia*, Query XVII, in *Portable Thomas Jefferson*, 210.

[38] Locke, *A Letter Concerning Toleration*, 42, 46.

[39] Ibid., 49.

[40] Sanford Kessler remarks,

While Locke explicitly advocated the complete separation of church and state on one level in the *Letter*, he modified this principle at another level by teaching that government must have certain powers with regard to religion. . . . Perhaps the most important of these is the power to deny toleration to religious practices violating civil law and to religious doctrines leading to actions inimical to the public good.

See Kessler, "Locke's Influence of Jefferson's 'Bill for Establishing Religious Freedom,'" 235.

with those of another persuasion, that kings excommunicated forfeit their crowns, that dominion is founded in grace, or that obedience is due to some foreign prince, or who will not own & teach the duty of tolerating all men in matters of religion, or who deny the existence of a god. [It was a great thing to go so far (as he himself sais [sic] of the parl. who framed the act of tolern.) but where he stopped short, we may go on.]⁴¹

Locke "stopped short" because he only tolerated religious opinions that were consistent with liberal political principles. Jefferson says "we may go on" and grant liberty to all religious opinions because, as he states in the Virginia Statute, "the opinions of men are not the object of civil government, nor under its jurisdiction." The freedom of the mind that lies at the heart of Jefferson's philosophical argument for religious liberty requires that all opinions lie outside of government's jurisdiction.

The preamble concludes with three prudential arguments against civil rights being dependent on religious affiliation. Extending rights only to citizens of religious faith tends to "corrupt the principles of that very religion it is meant to encourage" by bribing external professions of faith with "worldly honours and emoluments." It inevitably threatens religious liberty, as civil magistrates will tend to make their own religious faith the "rule of judgment" for such rights. The true religion, moreover, does not need the support of government to flourish. "Truth is great and will prevail if left to herself," Jefferson declares, ". . . she is the proper and sufficient antagonist to error, and has nothing to fear from the conflict unless by human interposition disarmed of her natural weapons, free argument and debate. . . ."

The Enacting Paragraph

Despite the preamble's sweeping philosophical defense of complete freedom of opinions, the enacting paragraph, surprisingly, does not strictly follow the opinion-action distinction. Three of the five rights it lists pertain specifically to actions: the right not to frequent any religious worship, the right not to support financially any religious worship, and the right to profess and by argument maintain one's religious opinions.

In full, the enacting paragraph states the following:

---

⁴¹ "Notes on Locke and Shaftesbury," in *Papers of Thomas Jefferson*, 1:548, 551. A footnote by Jefferson follows, stating:

will not his own excellent rule be sufficient here too; to punish these as civil offences. e. gr. {sic} to assert that a foreign prince has power within this commonwealth is a misdemeanor. The other opns. may be despised. Perhaps the single thing which may be required to others before toleration to them would be an oath that they will allow toleration to others.

WE the General Assembly of Virginia do enact that no man shall be compelled to frequent or support any religious worship, place, or ministry whatsoever, nor shall be enforced, restrained, molested, or burthened in his body or goods, nor shall otherwise suffer, on account of his religious opinions or belief; but that all men shall be free to profess, and by argument to maintain, their opinions in matters of religion, and that the same shall in no wise diminish, enlarge, or affect their civil capacities.

Jefferson does not categorize or enumerate the bill's legal maxims, but a total of five overlapping limitations on state power can be identified:

1. No individual shall be compelled to frequent any religious worship, place, or ministry.
2. No individual shall be compelled to support any religious worship, place, or ministry.
3. No individual shall suffer or be punished on account of his religious opinions or beliefs.
4. All individuals shall be free to profess and by argument maintain their opinions in matters of religion.
5. An individual's civil capacities shall not be diminished, enlarged, or affected by his religious opinions.

The enacting paragraph does not directly connect the rights articulated to the preamble's arguments, but the claim that "the rights hereby asserted are of the natural rights of mankind" seems to imply that all the legal maxims are derived from the preamble's philosophical premises.

Not all of the bill's legal maxims, however, can be straightforwardly derived from the preamble's principled arguments. Only two provisions can be said to follow completely from the stated philosophy of the freedom of the human mind; another one can be derived with qualifications. The remaining two only follow from the preamble's prudential arguments. By not directly connecting the bill's legal provisions to specific arguments made in the preamble and by then asserting that the rights set forth are "of the natural rights of mankind," Jefferson obfuscates the difference between his principled and prudential arguments, which allows him to claim more than he actually demonstrates.

This confounding element of Jefferson's arguments becomes clear when we try to connect the bill's five legal maxims to the preamble's arguments. A direct connection can be made only between the preamble's declaration of the freedom of the mind and the enacting paragraph's third and fifth provisions. That an individual should not be punished (3) or have his civil capacities affected (5) on account of his religious opinions follows directly from the argument that "the opinions of men are not the object of civil government, nor under its jurisdiction" and from the corresponding finding that "our civil rights have no dependance [sic] on our religious opinions." As discussed, because the mind necessarily follows evidence it finds persuasive, individuals do not determine their own opinions and, therefore, they cannot grant authority over them to the state. Lacking such jurisdiction, the state, in turn, cannot legitimately punish individuals for their opinions as such or affect civil capacities on account of opinions.

The illegitimacy of punishment of religious opinions (3) and deprivations of civil capacities on account of religious opinions (5) supports the idea that individuals should be free to profess and, by argument, maintain their religious opinions (4), but with an important qualification. Punishing opinions and depriving civil rights on account of opinions is unjust because it holds individuals accountable for something over which they lack control. Speech is different. While a man may not control what he believes, he can control what he says. That an individual should be allowed to speak his mind and that viewpoints he asserts should not be punishable are consistent with the idea of the freedom of the human mind – if government lacks jurisdiction over opinions, then it would seem to lack authority to punish the viewpoint of speech as such – but because speech is subject to the will in a way that opinions are not, governmental regulation of speech does not irrationally hold an individual accountable for something he cannot control. Non-content-based restrictions on religious speech – such as time, place, and manner restrictions – are not unjust in the same way that punishments or deprivations on account of religious opinions are.

In contrast, a categorical prohibition against compulsory religious worship does not follow from the freedom of the human mind alone. The mind's freedom demonstrates the irrationality of compulsory worship only from a particular religious perspective and for religious reasons. Compulsory worship is irrational only if salutary religious devotion requires the sincere conviction of the worshiper. If the essence of religion is sincere faith, then the coercive force of law cannot command saving worship; but if saving religion is primarily a matter of works, then law, which can command actions, can direct individuals toward salvation. Jefferson's argument here assumes the Christian theological tenet that salvation is primarily a matter of sincere belief.

His argument also assumes that only religious purposes animate those who seek to coerce worship. Jefferson purports to demonstrate that the force of law cannot compel authentic worship and, therefore, that law cannot lead men to salvation. This may be true, but other, nonreligious reasons also might exist to coerce worship. The inability to lead men to salvation because of the freedom of the mind does not reveal the error of compelling worship for nonreligious reasons.

Perhaps because he was aware of the weakness of his philosophical argument on this point, Jefferson offers an alternative prudential consideration to support it. If a civil magistrate is allowed to evaluate religion on the supposition of its "ill tendency," he "will make his opinions the rule of judgment, and approve or condemn the sentiments of others only as they shall square with or differ from his own." The problem with political evaluations of religion, Jefferson says, is that they are always made in favor of the magistrate's own religion. Jefferson needs to introduce this prudential consideration to make a more complete argument against all compelled religious worship. The epistemological argument from the freedom of the mind requires the Christian theological premise that authentic religious practices require inner conviction, and it is only persuasive against compelling religious worship for religious reasons.

The illegitimacy of all coerced financial support for religion also cannot be derived from the freedom of the human mind alone. As discussed previously, the preamble declares only that compelled financial support for a religion that one "disbelieves and abhors" is "sinful and tyrannical." The enacting paragraph, however, categorically forbids all compulsory financial support of religion. The preamble's distinction between compulsory financial support that is wrong in principle (for a religion that one "disbelieves and abhors") and compulsory financial support that is imprudent (for one's own religion) disappears. Being forced to support one's own religion does not force an individual to act contrary to his professed beliefs and, thus, would not seem to violate the freedom of the mind. Again, Jefferson may have recognized this because he supports the point with the prudential argument that compulsory contributions deprive individuals from influencing ministers' behavior by granting or withholding financial support. He also claims that "truth is great and will prevail if left to herself," suggesting that truthful religions do not need the support of government.

Even the conclusion that it is tyrannical to force an individual to support a religion that he disbelieves and abhors is difficult to sustain. As explained previously, Jefferson's argument rests on the premise that it is tyrannical to force an individual to support financially a belief that he does not hold and that he is not free to accept or reject. Yet Jefferson writes that all opinions follow from the evidence that the mind finds persuasive, which means that an individual is not free to accept or reject *any* of the opinions he holds. If it is tyrannical for the state to compel an individual to support financially opinions with which he disagrees, government funding of any opinion that lacks unanimous assent would be tyrannical to some. Pushed to its logical conclusion, this maxim would make nontyrannical governmental action nearly impossible. It would forbid the state from using taxpayer dollars to fund any opinion with which the taxpayer disagreed. Only a radically libertarian state completely unconcerned with the cultivation of any opinions could attempt to meet such a criterion.

The Virginia Statute leans toward such libertarianism in stating that "the rightful purposes of civil government" are limited to restraining individuals when "principles break out into overt acts against peace and good order." In areas other than religion, however, Jefferson did not maintain this libertarian ideal. As we shall discuss later in this chapter, Jefferson was one of the fathers of public education in America, and his educational philosophy admits the legitimacy of governmental jurisdiction over and funding of particular opinions. This does not mean that Jefferson fails to offer any arguments against government funding of religion. As mentioned, he introduces prudential considerations against taxpayer support of religion. However, the Virginia Statute fails to offer a satisfactory philosophical argument against *all* taxpayer-funded support of religion, and Jefferson's argument against compulsory support of religion that one "disbelieves and abhors" rests on a limitation on state actions that he does not consistently maintain.

If this analysis of the Virginia Statute's philosophical argument is correct, we can conclude that it fails to demonstrate that the prohibitions against compulsory religious worship and compulsory financial support of religion are natural rights, at least if those natural rights are to be derived from the freedom of the human mind alone. These shortcomings result from the fact that the enacting paragraph's legal maxims protect actions in addition to opinions, whereas the preamble philosophically defends the freedom of opinion. The two legal maxims that involve beliefs alone – the nonpunishment of opinions and the nondeprivation of rights because of opinions – most clearly follow from the preamble's philosophy of the freedom of the human mind. Religious speech, which involves beliefs and actions, is partially protected. The two legal maxims that are more purely actions – the attendance of worship and the payment of religious taxes – are analytically less connected to the preamble's philosophical argument and, hence, less supported by it. Jefferson may offer solid prudential reasons for these prohibitions, but they do not follow from his epistemological starting point of the freedom of the human mind.

Different explanations might account for the discrepancy between what the Virginia Statute philosophically claims and what it philosophically demonstrates. Jefferson may have made an unintentional intellectual mistake in thinking that he could use epistemology alone to demonstrate the existence of all the natural rights to religious freedom. He may have been carried away by rhetorical excess. Both these possibilities, however, are doubtful. That Jefferson offered prudential considerations to substantiate the weakest points of his philosophical arguments suggests that he was aware that the freedom of the mind did not establish all the legal maxims that he asserted.

A deeper and more fundamental difficulty also exists with the Virginia Statute. The statute's epistemological argument has radically libertarian implications. From the starting point of the freedom of the human mind, Jefferson concludes that "the opinions of men are not the object of civil government, nor under its jurisdiction." If taken literally, that doctrine would seem to prohibit the state from undertaking any effort to influence (let alone punish) any type of opinion.[42] The Virginia Statute itself, however, belies that doctrine. The statute is an official state document that attempts to influence the opinions of those who read it. Jefferson, moreover, championed public education, and as we shall discuss next, he aimed to influence citizens' religious and political opinions through his system of public education. Unless we charge Jefferson with grossly contradicting himself – which, of course, he was capable of doing – it would seem that his final position cannot be that government lacks jurisdiction over all opinions, at least in the sense of the state being prohibited from trying to influence opinions. The freedom of the mind does not explain Jefferson's actual political efforts to separate church from state and to establish religious freedom.

We have attempted to take the Virginia Statute's philosophical argument seriously because Jefferson identified the statute as one of his three greatest accomplishments and because it purports to deduce the natural rights of religious freedom. Without questioning whether the mind actually is "free" in the way that Jefferson depicts it to be, I have attempted to show how only some of the statute's conclusions follow from its epistemological premises. Moreover, as I shall attempt to demonstrate in the next section, the Virginia Statute's doctrines do not explain Jefferson's own political activities. Throughout his political career, Jefferson sought to use state power to

---

[42] Cf. Lorraine Smith Pangle and Thomas L. Pangle, *The Learning of Liberty: The Educational Ideals of the American Founders* (Lawrence: University Press of Kansas, 1993), 193.

discourage some type of religious opinions and to encourage others. He may have declared that the opinions of men lie beyond the jurisdiction of government, but as we will attempt to document next, Jefferson did not act in a corresponding manner.

JEFFERSON'S ANTICLERICAL POLITICS OF RELIGIOUS LIBERTY

The Virginia legislature adopted an edited version of the Virginia Statute on January 16, 1786.[43] In a letter to James Madison written later that year, a proud Jefferson relayed the "infinite approbation" the bill had received in Europe. "[A]fter so many ages during which the human mind has been held in vassalage by kings, priests and nobles," he wrote, ". . . it is honorable for us [America] to have produced the first legislature who has had the courage to declare that the reason of man may be trusted with the formation of his own opinions."[44] Despite what he said in his draft of the Virginia Statute, Jefferson's idea of trusting men to form their own opinions did not mean that the state could not try to influence them. Throughout his political career, Jefferson drafted laws, executed acts, and proposed policies that aimed to shape individuals' opinions, including their religious opinions.

Public Education and Jefferson's Efforts to Shape the American Mind

Nowhere is this more apparent than in Jefferson's efforts to establish a system of public education. In 1778, one year after he composed "A Bill Establishing Religious Freedom," Jefferson drafted legislation proposing a general plan of public education for Virginia.[45] Like the Virginia Statute, "A Bill for the More General Diffusion of Knowledge" begins with an explanatory preamble. Jefferson declares that "the most effectual means of preventing" the political corruption that threatens individuals' natural rights is "to illuminate, as far as practical, the minds of the people at large." He proposes "to give them [the people] knowledge of those facts, which history exhibiteth that . . . they may know ambition under all its shapes, and prompt to exert their natural powers to defeat its purposes."[46] On a different

---

[43] For an excellent history of the politics surrounding the passage of Jefferson's bill, see Thomas E. Buckley, S.J., *Church and State in Revolutionary Virginia, 1776–1787* (Charlottesville: University Press of Virginia, 1977), especially Chapters 4 and 5.

[44] Thomas Jefferson to James Madison, December 16, 1786, in *Papers of Thomas Jefferson*, 10:604.

[45] "A Bill for the More General Diffusion of Knowledge," in *Jefferson: Writings*, 365–73. The Virginia legislature periodically took up Jefferson's proposal but never enacted its substance in full. In 1796, the legislature enacted some of the bill's provisions related to elementary schools.

[46] Ibid., 365.

occasion, he described the purpose of primary schools as "to instruct the mass of our citizens in these, their rights, interests and duties, as men and citizens . . . ."[47] In explaining the purposes of public education, Jefferson articulated a deliberate intention to shape the minds of American citizens.[48] He did not propose an educational scheme neutral in its political values or even one that led citizens to form their own, independent conclusions about the nature and purposes of government. He aimed, instead, to create citizens with the beliefs and habits of mind conducive to the maintenance of a liberal political order dedicated to the natural rights of mankind.

Jefferson's attention to the content of public education and the opinions it nurtures is most evident in his attempt to impose a political orthodoxy on the political philosophy curriculum at the University of Virginia.[49] "In the selection of our Law Professor," Jefferson wrote to James Madison, "we must be rigorously attentive to his political principles."[50] In an 1825 letter, Jefferson explained that for most subjects, the choice of textbooks should belong to the professor. He made one exception:

> But there is one branch [of science] in which we are the best judges, in which heresies may be taught, of so interesting a character to our own State and to the United States, as to make it a duty in us to lay down the principles which are to be taught. It is that of government. . . . It is our duty to guard against such principles being disseminated among our youth, and the diffusion of that poison, by a previous prescription of the texts to be followed in their discourses.[51]

The minutes of the University of Virginia's Board of Visitors meeting held later that year include Jefferson's syllabus of books and authors to be read. He prescribed John Locke's *Second Treatise on Government* and Algernon Sidney's *Discourses Concerning Government* to understand the general principles of liberty and the rights of man. Jefferson also specified for study: the Declaration of Independence, *The Federalist Papers*, the 1799 resolutions of

---

[47] Report of the Commissioners for the University of Virginia, August 4, 1818, in *Jefferson: Writings*, 459.

[48] For discussions of the specifics of Jefferson's plan for public education, see *Notes on the State of Virginia*, Query XIV, in *Portable Thomas Jefferson*, 193–99; Joseph F. Kett, "Education," in *Thomas Jefferson: A Reference Biography*, ed. Merrill D. Peterson (New York: Charles Scribner's Sons, 1986), 233–51; Pangle and Pangle, *The Learning of Liberty*, 106–24.

[49] Aristide Tessitore, "Legitimate Government, Religion, and Education," 145.

[50] Thomas Jefferson to James Madison, February 17, 1826, in *Jefferson: Writings*, 1513.

[51] Thomas Jefferson to an unknown recipient, February 3, 1825, in *Writings of Thomas Jefferson*, 3:397. Roy J. Honeywell identifies the recipient of the letter as Joseph C. Cabell. See Roy J. Honeywell, *The Educational Work of Thomas Jefferson* (New York: Russell & Russell, 1964), 97.

the Virginia Assembly on the Alien and Sedition Acts, and President Washington's "Farewell Address."[52] What students would read at the university was of highest importance because Jefferson envisioned it as the nursery for future office holders. "If we are true and vigilant in our trust," he wrote to Madison in 1826, "within a dozen or twenty years a majority of our own [Virginia] legislature will be from one school, and many disciples will have carried its doctrines home with them to their several States, and will have leavened thus the whole mass." As the training grounds for the future leaders of the republic, "it is in our seminary that the vestal flame [of republicanism] is to be kept alive. . . ."[53] Jefferson did not prohibit the assignment of any specific books, but by prescribing what students would study he clearly aimed to form the opinions of the university's students and, through their future political leadership, the nation as a whole.[54]

Jefferson's educational philosophy reveals that he was not devoted to the principle that government completely lacks jurisdiction over opinions. In the realm of education, he did not start from the Virginia Statute's premise of the freedom of the mind. Moreover, his efforts on behalf of public education reflect his attempt to form Americans' political opinions and to encourage the development of certain religious opinions while

[52] Minutes of the Board of Visitors, March 4, 1825, in *Jefferson: Writings*, 479. The Minutes of the Board of Visitors dated March 4, 1825 began as follows:

> A resolution was moved and agreed to in the following words: Whereas, it is the duty of this Board to the government under which it lives, and especially to that of which this University is the immediate creation, to pay especial attention to the principles of government which shall be inculcated therein, and to provide that none shall be inculcated which are incompatible with those on which the Constitutions of this State, and of the United States were genuinely based, in the common opinion; and for this purpose it may be necessary to point out specially where these principles are to be found legitimately developed. . . .

[53] Thomas Jefferson to James Madison, February 17, 1826, in *Jefferson: Writings*, 1514. See also Jefferson to William B. Giles, December 26, 1825, in *Jefferson: Writings*, 1512. According to Leonard Levy, "Where, therefore, Jefferson spoke of the law school of the University of Virginia as a seedbed of future political leaders of Whig persuasion, he meant the school to be an arm of his own party. He was seeking to proscribe the teaching of ideas antithetical to his own views of the federal system. The school was not to teach both Federalist and Republican views objectively or to avoid altogether a study of the American party system; it was to indoctrinate loyalty to Republicanism." Leonard W. Levy, *Jefferson and Civil Liberties*, 152–53.

[54] Elsewhere in his correspondence about political education, Jefferson denounces the "poison" of Hume's principles of government (Thomas Jefferson to William Duane, August 12, 1810, in *Jefferson: Writings*, 1228–29), speaks ill of Montesquieu's *Spirit of the Laws* (Jefferson to William Duane, August 12, 1810, in *Jefferson: Writings*, 1229–30), and deplores the "slide into torism" by lawyers influenced by "the honied Mansfieldism of Blackstone" (Thomas Jefferson to James Madison, February 17, 1826, in *Jefferson: Writings*, 1513).

hindering others. More specifically, Jefferson sought to discourage belief in what he considered to be nonrational religious opinions and to encourage belief in those simple religious precepts that he believed were confirmed by reason. By doing so, Jefferson aimed to marginalize the influence of sectarian religious clergy and to nurture the religious beliefs that he believed supported republican political principles. In practice, Jefferson's position on church and state was not that government lacked jurisdiction over opinions, but that government should cultivate those religious opinions that are conducive to human freedom and hinder the religious opinions, institutions, and individuals that threaten religious and political liberty.

Jefferson's Anticlericalism and the Religion of Reason

The religious opinions that Jefferson thought most threatened religious and political freedom were those advanced by ecclesiastical religions and their clergy. The first tenet of Jefferson's approach to church and state was that the establishment of religious freedom required the subjugation of ecclesiastical influence in American society. "History, I believe," Jefferson wrote in 1813, "furnishes no example of a priest-ridden people maintaining a free civil government."[55]

Jefferson never systematically developed his sweeping and generalized critique of religious clergy, which seems to apply to all clergymen. Its basic outline is that religious clergy use specious theological dogmas to keep their subjects in mental servitude and to enrich and empower themselves. It appears almost exclusively but with frequency in Jefferson's private correspondence. A few examples:

[B]ut a short time elapsed after the death of the great reformer of the Jewish religion before his principles were departed from by those who professed to be his special servants, and perverted into an engine for enslaving mankind, and aggrandizing their oppressors in church and state: that the purest system of morals ever before preached to man has been adulterated and sophisticated, by artificial constructions, into a mere contrivance to filch wealth and power to themselves, that rational men not being able to swallow their impious heresies, in order to force them down their throats, they raise the hue and cry of infidelity, while themselves are the greatest obstacles to the advancement of the real doctrines of Jesus, and do in fact constitute the real Anti-Christ.[56]

---

[55] Thomas Jefferson to Alexander von Humboldt, December 6, 1813, in *Jefferson: Writings*, 1311.

[56] Thomas Jefferson to William Baldwin, January 19, 1810, in *Jefferson's Extracts from the Gospels*, 345.

In extracting the pure principles which he [Jesus] taught we should have to strip off the artificial vestments in which they have been muffled by priests, who have travestied them into various forms, as instruments of riches and power to them.[57]

I abuse priests indeed, who have so much abused the pure and holy doctrines of their master [Jesus], and who have laid me under no obligations of reticence as to the tricks of their trade. The genuine system of Jesus, and the artificial structures they have erected to make him the instrument of wealth, power, and preeminence to themselves are as distinct things in my view as light and darkness.[58]

[The doctrines of Jesus] have been still more disfigured by the corruptions of schismatising [sic] followers, who have found an interest in sophisticating & perverting the simple doctrines he taught by engrafting on to them the mysticisms of a Grecian sophist, frittering them into subtleties, & obscuring them with jargon, until they have caused good men to reject the whole in disgust, & to view Jesus himself as an impostor.[59]

Jefferson believed that clergy acquired and maintained their power though legal privileges and, more fundamentally, by exerting mental tyranny over their subjects.[60] They used doctrines like the Trinity to lead men to abandon their reason. Having surrendered his reason, "[man] has no remaining guard against absurdities the most monstrous, and like a ship without a rudder is the sport of every wind. With such persons gullability [sic] which they call faith takes the helm from the hand of reason and the mind becomes a wreck."[61] With influence over the law through the unification of church and state, clergy also suppressed the intellectual freedom that might lead individuals to challenge them. In perhaps his most revealing public statement on the subject, Jefferson compared the "genuine fruit" of the alliance of church and state to the "barbarism and wretchedness" caused by Native Americans' veneration of their fathers. What "chains" those peoples like "our indigenous neighbors" Jefferson asked rhetorically, "but a bigoted veneration for the supposed superlative wisdom of their fathers, and the preposterous idea that they are to look backward for better things, and not forward . . . ?" What must be overcome is the idea that "we must tread with awful reverence in the footsteps of our fathers." This backward-looking, noxious doctrine, Jefferson continued, "is the genuine fruit of the alliance between Church and State; the tenants of which, finding themselves

---

57 Thomas Jefferson to John Adams, October 12, 1813, in *Jefferson's Extracts from the Gospels*, 352.
58 Thomas Jefferson to Charles Clay, January 29, 1815, in *Jefferson's Extracts from the Gospels*, 353.
59 "Syllabus of an Estimate of the Merits of the Doctrines of Jesus, Compared with Those of Others," April 1803, sent to Benjamin Rush, April 21, 1803, in *Jefferson: Writings*, 1125.
60 Philip Hamburger, *Separation of Church and State*, 148.
61 Thomas Jefferson to James Smith, December 8, 1822, in *Jefferson's Extracts from the Gospels*, 409.

but too well in their present condition, oppose all advances which might unmask their usurpations, and monopolies of honors, wealth, and power and fear every change, as endangering the comforts they now hold."[62]

Jefferson's anticlericalism follows the basic elements of the Enlightenment's critique of religion: Religious clergy invent theological doctrines to disarm human reason and then use those dogmas and the power of the state to suppress the ideas and individuals that might threaten clerical power and influence. Jefferson's efforts to suppress clerical authority, accordingly, involved the emancipation of human reason from clerical influence and the imposition of limitations on clerical access to political power. He had faith that, once liberated from "monkish ignorance," individuals would embrace what he considered to be the authentic teachings of Jesus. The "free exercise of reason," he wrote, "is all I ask for the vindication of the character of Jesus."[63] Jefferson placed enormous confidence in free inquiry because he believed "hocus-pocus phantasm[s]" like the doctrine of the Trinity could only be established and maintained by religious fanatics who possessed the sword of civil government.[64] Once clergy were stripped of political power and influence, such doctrines would evaporate: "A strong proof of the solidity of the primitive faith [of Christianity] is it's [sic] restoration as soon as a nation arises which vindicates to itself the freedom of religious opinion, and it's [sic] divorce from civil authority."[65] "If the freedom of religion, guaranteed to us by law *in theory*, can ever rise *in practice*," Jefferson claimed on a different occasion, ". . . truth will prevail over fanaticism, and the genuine doctrines of Jesus, so long perverted by his pseudo-priests, will again be restored to their original purity."[66]

Jefferson's anticipation of the restoration "of the genuine doctrines of Jesus" may sound orthodox, but it must be understood in light of his beliefs of who Jesus was and what Jesus taught. Jefferson did not believe in Jesus' divinity.[67] Among the "artificial systems, invented by ultra-Christians,"

---

[62] Ibid., 461–62. In a letter to William Short, Jefferson writes, "The serious enemies [of the University of Virginia] are the priests of the different religious sects, to whose spells on the human mind it's [sic] improvement is ominous." Thomas Jefferson to William Short, April 13, 1820, in *Jefferson's Extracts from the Gospels*, 392.

[63] Thomas Jefferson to William Short, August 4, 1820, in *Jefferson's Extracts from the Gospels*, 395–96.

[64] Thomas Jefferson to James Smith, December 8, 1822, in *Jefferson's Extracts from the Gospels*, 409.

[65] Ibid.

[66] Jefferson's emphasis. Thomas Jefferson to Jared Sparks, December 4, 1820, in *Jefferson's Extracts from the Gospels*, 402.

[67] For a discussion of this point and Jefferson's religious beliefs more generally, see Conkin, "The Religious Pilgrimage of Thomas Jefferson," especially p. 34.

Jefferson identified: "the immaculate conception of Jesus, His deification, the creation of the world by Him, His miraculous powers, His resurrection and visible ascension, His corporal presence in the Eucharist, the Trinity, original sin, atonement, regeneration, election, orders of Hierarchy, etc."[68] At most, Jefferson thought that Jesus may have deluded himself into believing that he was divine. In 1787, Jefferson counseled his nephew Peter Carr to keep his mind open to the possibility that Jesus was only "a man, of illegitimate birth, of a benevolent heart, enthusiastic mind, who set out without pretensions to divinity, ended in believing them, and was punished capitally for sedition by being gibbeted according to the Roman Law."[69] Toward the end of his life, in a revealing private letter, Jefferson wrote,

That Jesus did not mean to impose himself on mankind as the son of god physically speaking I have been convinced by the writings of men more learned than myself in that lore. But that he might conscientiously believe himself inspired from above, is very possible. The whole religion of the Jews, inculcated on him from his infancy, was founded in the belief of divine inspiration. . . . Elevated by the enthusiasm of a warm and pure heart, conscious of the high strains of an eloquence which had not been taught him, he might readily mistake the coruscations of his own fine genius for inspiration of an higher order. This belief carried, therefore, no more personal imputation, than the belief of Socrates, that himself was under the care and admonitions of a guardian Dæmon.[70]

Jefferson set forth what he considered to be the "primitive faith" and "genuine doctrines" of Jesus in an 1822 letter to Benjamin Waterhouse, a former professor of physics at Harvard and a pioneer in the use of vaccinations. "The doctrines of Jesus are simple," Jefferson wrote, listing the following three tenets: 1) that there is one God and he is all perfect; 2) that there is a future state of rewards and punishments; 3) that to love God with all thy heart, and thy neighbor as thyself is the sum of all religion.[71] In a letter written the previous year, he suggested that Jesus' "pure and simple" doctrines were supported by reason:

---

[68] Thomas Jefferson to William Short, October 31, 1819, in *Jefferson: Writings*, 1431.

[69] Thomas Jefferson to Peter Carr, August 10, 1787, in *Portable Thomas Jefferson*, 426.

[70] Thomas Jefferson to William Short, August 4, 1820, in *Jefferson's Extracts from the Gospels*, 397. See also Eugene Sheridan's discussion of Benjamin Rush's account of Jefferson's religious opinions of Jesus' divinity in his "Introduction" to *Jefferson's Extracts from the Gospels*, 17n.48. For a recent discussion of Jefferson's religious beliefs, see J. Judd Owen, "The Struggle between 'Religion and Nonreligion': Jefferson, Backus, and the Dissonance of America's Founding Principles," *American Political Science Review* 101, no. 3 (2007): 496–99.

[71] Thomas Jefferson to Benjamin Waterhouse, June 26, 1822, in *Jefferson's Extracts from the Gospels*, 405.

No one sees with greater pleasure than myself the progress of reason in it's [sic] advances toward rational Christianity. When we shall have done away with the incomprehensible jargon of the Trinitarian arithmetic, that three are one, and one is three; when we shall have knocked down the artificial scaffolding, reared to mask from view the simple structure of Jesus, when, in short, we shall have unlearned every thing which has been taught since his day, and got back to the pure and simple doctrines he inculcated, we shall then be truly and worthily his disciples: and my opinion is that if nothing had even been added to what flowed purely from his lips, the whole world at this day would have been Christian.[72]

Jefferson's faith that the free exercise of reason would lead most individuals to embrace a simple version of demystified Christianity reflects his confidence in the ease of distinguishing Jesus' authentic teachings from the "artificial scaffolding" erected by priests. Toward the end of his life, Jefferson repeatedly wrote that within a generation he expected the nation to accept Unitarianism. In December 1822, he claimed, "The pure and simple unity of the creator of the universe is not all but ascendant in the Eastern states; it is dawning in the West, and advancing towards the South; and I confidently expect that the present generation will see Unitarianism become the general religion of the United states [sic]."[73] Earlier that year, he had written, "I rejoice that in this blessed country of free inquiry and belief, which has surrendered it's [sic] creed and conscience to neither kings nor priests, the genuine doctrine of only one God is reviving, and I trust that there is not a *young man* now living in the US. who will not die a Unitarian."[74] For Jefferson, Unitarianism was not just one sect among many; it signified the rejection of the Trinity and the ascendance of reason over ecclesiastical religion. "[T]he Athanasian paradox that one is three, and three but one," Jefferson wrote of the Trinity, "is so incomprehensible to the human mind that no candid man can say he has any idea of it, and how can he believe what presents no idea? He who thinks he does only deceives himself."[75] Jefferson's prediction of a general acceptance of Unitarianism was grounded in his faith that educated individuals would follow his example and recognize the

---

[72] Thomas Jefferson to Timothy Pickering, February 27, 1821, in *Jefferson's Extracts from the Gospels*, 402–03.

[73] Thomas Jefferson to James Smith, December 8, 1822, in *Jefferson's Extracts from the Gospels*, 409.

[74] Jefferson's emphasis. Thomas Jefferson to Benjamin Waterhouse, June 26, 1822, in *Jefferson's Extracts from the Gospels*, 405–06. For Jefferson's view of the advantages of free inquiry in matters of religion see also *Notes on the State of Virginia*, Query XVII, in *Portable Thomas Jefferson*, 210–13.

[75] Thomas Jefferson to James Smith, December 8, 1822, in *Jefferson's Extracts from the Gospels*, 409.

reasonable – and, hence, the authentic – teachings of Christianity, thereby disregarding the false doctrine perpetuated by priests.

The ease with which Jefferson expected reason to reform Christianity can be seen in his description of how he constructed the "Jefferson Bible." While president, Jefferson pieced together his own version of the New Testament. Calling it "The Philosophy of Jesus," he extracted passages from the Gospels "whose style and spirit proved them [to be] genuine." Despite saying his work "of one or two evenings only" was "too hastily done," he described the process as uncomplicated, "as they [Jesus' genuine sayings] are as distinguishable from the matter in which they are imbedded as diamonds in the dunghills."[76] Jefferson repeated a similar view of the New Testament on a different occasion:

We find in the writings of his [Jesus'] biographers matter of two distinct descriptions. First a ground work of vulgar ignorance, of things impossible, of superstitions, fanaticisms, and fabrications. Intermixed with these again are sublime ideas of the supreme being, aphorisms and precepts of the purest morality and benevolence, sanctioned by a life of humility, innocence, and simplicity of manners, neglect of riches, absence of worldly ambition and honors, with an eloquence and persuasiveness which have not been surpassed. These could not be inventions of the groveling authors who relate them. They are far beyond the powers of their feeble minds. They shew [sic] that there was a character, the subject of their history, whose splendid conceptions were above all suspicion of being interpolations from their hands. Can we be at a loss in separating such materials, and ascribing each to it's [sic] genuine author? The difference is obvious to the eye and to the understanding, and we may read, as we run, to each his part; and I will venture to affirm that he who, as I have done, will undertake to winnow this grain from it's [sic] chaff, will find it not to require a moment's [sic] consideration. The parts fall asunder of themselves as would those of an image of metal and clay.[77]

Even accounting for hyperbole, Jefferson's comments attest to his untroubled confidence in the ability of reasonable individuals, such as himself, to distinguish the true teachings of Jesus from the "artificial scaffolding" added by priests.[78]

---

[76] Thomas Jefferson to Francis Adrian Van der Kemp, April 25, 1816, in *Jefferson's Extracts from the Gospels*, 369. Jefferson also describes his compilation of "The Philosophy of Jesus," in a letter to John Adams, October 12, 1813, and a letter to William Short, October 31, 1819. Both letters are available in *Jefferson's Extracts from the Gospels*. For a scholarly account of Jefferson's construction of "The Philosophy of Jesus," see Eugene R. Sheridan, "Introduction," in *Jefferson's Extracts from the Gospels*, 26–29.

[77] Thomas Jefferson to William Short, August 4, 1820, in *Jefferson's Extracts from the Gospels*, 396.

[78] Thomas Jefferson to John Adams, October 12, 1813, in *Jefferson's Extracts from the Gospels*, 369.

Jefferson's Educational and Legal Efforts
to Subjugate Clerical Influence

Jefferson had great faith in human reason, but he believed that education had to be emancipated from irrational religious influences for reason to be set free. He devised his system of public education to subvert clerical authority. On more than one occasion, he attempted to impose direct legal disabilities on clergymen, actions that stand in direct contradiction to the natural rights doctrines articulated in the Virginia Statute for Religious Freedom.

Jefferson's effort to weaken clerical influence can be seen in how he designed the curriculum at the University of Virginia. In his original proposal for the school, he excluded a divinity professor, instead proposing a professor of ethics whose subjects would include "the proofs of the being of a God, the creator, preserver, and supreme ruler of the universe, the author of all the relations of morality, and of the laws of obligations these infer. . . ."[79] Jefferson designed the curriculum to teach the existence of a god and of moral obligations – about which, he said, "all sects agree" – but not the dogmas of any particular faith. This would allow the university to teach morality without sectarianism and, most importantly, without religious clergy.

Among evangelical Christians, the exclusion of a divinity professor raised doubts about the character of the university, suspicions they saw confirmed by Jefferson's recruitment of Dr. Thomas Cooper to become the university's professor of chemistry and law. An English Unitarian whom Jefferson described as "the greatest man in America in the powers of mind and acquired information," Cooper was known for his heterodox religious opinions, in part because of his inflammatory writings.[80] In an appendix to a volume of the writings of Dr. Joseph Priestly, Cooper had written, "The times seems to have arrived, when the separate existence of the human soul, the freedom of the will, and the eternal duration of future punishments, like the doctrines of the Trinity and transubstantiation, may no longer be entitled to public discussion."[81] That

---

[79] In the Rockfish Gap report, Jefferson proposed ten professorships, each of which would encompass a different "branch of learning": 1. Languages, ancient; 2. Languages, modern; 3. Mathematics, pure; 4. Physico-mathematics; 5. Physics or Natural Philosophy; 6. Botany, Zoology; 7. Anatomy, Medicine; 8. Government, Political Economy, Law of Nature and Nations, History; 9. Law, municipal; 10. Ideology, General Grammar, Ethics, Rhetoric, Belles Lettres, and the fine arts. *Jefferson: Writings*, 462–64.

[80] Thomas Jefferson to Joseph C. Cabell, March 1, 1819, in *Early History of the University of Virginia, as Contained in the Letters of Thomas Jefferson and Joseph C. Cabell*, 169. Also see Peterson, *Thomas Jefferson and the New Nation*, 977.

[81] Quoted in Malone, *Jefferson and His Times*, 6:376.

comment and others like it were publicized by Presbyterian minister John H. Rice, who, in two articles criticizing Cooper's appointment, argued that it would be improper for the university to employ a professor who would teach heretical ideas and be intolerant of those who disagreed with him.[82] Rice's criticism and the stir it created contributed to Cooper's resignation before the university opened its doors, much to Jefferson's disappointment.[83] Cooper was not Jefferson's only controversial faculty choice. His pursuits of George Ticknor, who was Harvard's first professor of modern languages, and Nathaniel Bowditch, a mathematician who some credit with being the founder of modern maritime navigation, were also derailed, in part, because of the candidates' objectionable religious opinions.[84] By 1821, evangelical Christians' distrust of Jefferson's plans for the university ran so deep that Joseph Cabell, Jefferson's legislative ally in establishing the university, warned Jefferson that the Presbyterian clergy believed "that the Socinians [Unitarians] are to be installed at the University for the purpose of overthrowing the prevailing religious opinions of the country."[85]

It was in this context of distrust that Jefferson proposed in 1822 to invite sectarian divinity schools to locate "on the confines" of the university.

[82] John H. Rice, "Review; Memoirs of Dr. Joseph Priestly. . . and Observations of His Writings, by Thomas Cooper," *The Virginia Evangelical and Literary Magazine* (February 1820): 63–74. For a discussion of Cooper's appointment and Rice's criticism of it, see Dumas Malone, *The Public Life of Thomas Cooper* (New Haven, CT: Yale University Press, 1926), 239–46; Malone, *Jefferson and His Times*, 6:376–80; West, *The Politics of Reason and Revelation*, 61–64. For a more general discussion of Rice's views on the University of Virginia, see Addis, *Jefferson's Vision for Education*, 74–82.

[83] In May 1820, lamenting the loss of Cooper, Jefferson wrote to General Robert B. Taylor, "I have looked to him as the corner-stone of our edifice" (quoted in Philip Alexander Bruce, *History of the University of Virginia: 1818–1919*, centennial edition [New York: The Macmillan Company, 1920], 1:205). Cooper became president of South Carolina College in 1821. According to Daniel Walker Howe, Cooper was forced to resign in 1834, in part because of opposition from Presbyterian clergy who opposed him on account of his "tactless denunciations of Christianity." See Daniel Walker Howe, "Church, State, and Education in the Young American Republic," *Journal of the Early Republic* 22 (Spring 2002): 12. Robert P. Forbes writes that Cooper "displayed a hostility toward the clergy and religion perhaps more extreme than any other man in American public life." Robert P. Forbes, "Slavery and the Evangelical Enlightenment," in *Religion and the Antebellum Debate Over Slavery*, eds. John R. McKivigan and Mitchell Snay (Athens: The University of Georgia Press, 1998), 87.

[84] Bell, *Church, State, and Education in Virginia*, 374. Also see Joseph Cabell's letter to Thomas Jefferson, January 14, 1822, in *Early History of the University of Virginia, as Contained in the Letters of Thomas Jefferson and Joseph C. Cabell*, 231–37.

[85] Cabell to Jefferson, August 5, 1821, in West, *Politics of Reason and Revelation*, 63n.265. According to Cameron Addis, Cabell was a "dyed-in-the-wool Republican who 'bordered on the gloomy verge of atheism' as an undergraduate at William and Mary in the late 1790s." Addis, *Jefferson's Vision for Education*, 41 (quoting Joseph Cabell to David Watson, March 4, 1798, David Watson Papers, Library of Congress).

Jefferson set forth the idea in an 1822 Board of Visitors report, in which he also defended his previous exclusion of a divinity professor. The report stated that by the exclusion of a divinity professor "it was not . . . to be understood that instruction in religious opinion and duties was meant to be precluded by the public authorities, as indifferent to the interests of society." Jefferson claimed that the exclusion was made to be "in conformity with the principles of our constitution, which places all sects of religion on an equal footing," and because it was thought that "the entrustment to each [religious] society of its own doctrine, were evils of less danger than a permission to the public authorities to dictate modes or principles of religious instruction."[86] He proposed that the establishment of private, sectarian divinity schools near the university "would offer the . . . advantage of enabling the students of the University to attend religious exercises with the professors of their particular sect" and would "complete the circle of the useful sciences embraced by this institution."[87]

Jefferson's divinity school proposal might seem to indicate that he did not believe in a strict separation between church and state. But evaluated in light of its context, the proposal reveals a calculated plan to defuse evangelical criticism without allowing a sectarian divinity professor to join the university's faculty. In a private letter to Cooper, Jefferson described the plan as a way to "silence this calumny," suggesting that he proposed it for reasons of expediency. In the same letter he offered another reason for the invitation to the divinity schools, moreover, a reason that did not appear in any public document but the one that may have been decisive to Jefferson. "And by bringing the sects together, and mixing them with the mass of other students," Jefferson

---

[86] Minutes of the Board of Visitors, October 7, 1822, in *Jefferson: Writings*, 477. In the October 1822 Board of Visitors Report, Jefferson quotes the constitutional reasons for the exclusion of a divinity professor that he originally set forth in the 1818 Rockfish Gap report, the report he drafted to propose the university to the Virginia legislature. At the time, Article XVI of the Virginia Declaration of Rights declared: "That religion, or the duty which we owe to our Creator and the manner of discharging it, can be directed by reason and conviction, not by force or violence; and therefore, all men are equally entitled to the free exercise of religion, according to the dictates of conscience; and that it is the mutual duty of all to practice Christian forbearance, love, and charity towards each other." In both the Rockfish Gap report and the 1822 Board of Visitors report, Jefferson said that the exclusion of a divinity professorship was also in conformity "with the sentiments of the legislature in freedom of religion, manifested on former occasions," which would seem to be an allusion to the Virginia Statute for Religious Freedom. Jefferson's constitutional reasoning suggests that the selection of one divinity professor would impermissibly favor one sect over all others. He does not offer an explanation as to why exactly a divinity professor would have violated the principles of the Virginia Statute. For background on the legislative authorization of the University of Virginia and drafting of the Rockfish Gap report, see Honeywell, *Educational Work of Thomas Jefferson*, 67–87.

[87] Minutes of the Board of Visitors, October 7, 1822, in *Jefferson: Writings*, 478.

wrote, "we shall soften their asperities, liberalize and neutralize their prejudices, and make the general religion a religion of peace, reason, and morality."[88] To his fellow Unitarian, Jefferson praised the divinity school plan because it offered the possibility of reforming the divinity students' religious beliefs. His letter to Cooper suggests that he invited the divinity schools to locate next to campus not to accommodate the university students' religious practices but rather to bring divinity students to the University of Virginia's campus so the divinity students' religious beliefs could be "liberalize[d] and neutralize[d]." His apparent concession to evangelical criticism became part of his strategy to transform the religious beliefs of the nation.[89]

Further evidence of Jefferson's design to minimize sectarian clerical influence at the University of Virginia is evinced by his efforts to keep religious worship off campus. In 1820, chapel was required at all public and private American colleges.[90] Consistent with this practice, in 1824 the Board of Visitors had approved a room in the yet-to-be-completed rotunda building for religious services.[91] After the university had begun instruction but before the completion of the rotunda, Jefferson, who was rector at the time, received a proposal from the university's bursar to permit the use of a lecture room in one of the university's pavilions for prayer and preaching on Sundays. Jefferson denied the request. In his letter of denial, he explained that the 1818 Rockfish Gap report, the report submitted to the Virginia legislature to charter the university, proposed a building to be used for religious worship *"under such impartial regulations as the Visitors should prescribe."* The legislature, Jefferson claimed, neither sanctioned nor rejected that proposal. He then interpreted the divinity school plan to supersede the original proposal that allowed religious worship in a campus building. Citing the "caution" with which the "board of Visitors thinks it a duty to observe this delicate and jealous subject," Jefferson concluded, "[the] proposition therefore leading to an application of the University buildings to other than University purposes, and to a partial regulation in favor of two particular sects, would be a deviation from the course which they think it their duty to observe."[92]

---

[88] Thomas Jefferson to Dr. Thomas Cooper, November 2, 1822, in *Jefferson: Writings*, 1465.

[89] Although the invitation was issued, divinity schools were never established near the university.

[90] Addis, *Jefferson's Vision for Education*, 55.

[91] Regulations Adopted by the Board of Visitors of the University of Virginia, October 4, 1824, reprinted in Honeywell, *Educational Work of Thomas Jefferson*, 275.

[92] Jefferson's emphasis. Thomas Jefferson to Arthur S. Brokenbrough, April 21, 1825, in Anson Phelps Stokes, *Church and State in the United States* (New York: Harper and Brothers, 1950), 2:633.

Jefferson's implication that religious services were not part of the university's "purposes" is extraordinary given that in 1824 – in the same report that authorized a room in the yet-to-be-completed rotunda to be used for religious services – the Board of Visitors declared that the university's regular students "will be free, and expected to attend religious worship at the establishment of their respective sects. . . ."[93] Not only did Jefferson make it more difficult for students to meet those religious expectations, he went out of his way to prevent them from doing so on campus.

Jefferson's actions concerning religion at the University of Virginia reflect his intention to move the religious views of the new nation away from ecclesiastical sectarianism toward a more generic nondenominationalism. Perhaps his boldest attack on traditional religion involved elementary education. Jefferson sought to prevent Bible reading in the first stages of public education, where he hoped "the great masses of the people will receive their instruction."[94] Young children's judgments, he said, "are not sufficiently matured for religious inquiries." He recommended instead that children's memories be filled with "the most useful facts from Grecian, Roman, European and American history."[95] If historical examples were used to teach morality instead of the Bible, children's minds and imaginations more likely would be kept free of miraculous truths and revealed dogmas, beliefs that might inhibit the critical and rational analysis of clerical religion Jefferson intended more advanced students to undertake later in life.[96]

Jefferson revealed his idea of how older students should be taught religion in the aforementioned letter to his nephew Peter Carr. "Your reason is now mature enough," Jefferson wrote to the seventeen-year-old, "to receive this object [religion]." Jefferson counseled against piety or reverence.

---

[93] Regulations adopted by the Board of Visitors of the University of Virginia, October 4, 1824, in Honeywell, *Educational Work of Thomas Jefferson*, 274–75.

[94] Notes on the State of Virginia, Query XIV, in *Portable Thomas Jefferson*, 197.

[95] Ibid.

[96] Jefferson's concern was not primarily that he thought much of the Bible was fiction. Rather, he feared that children's minds would be prepared for clerical tyranny by reading the Bible at too early an age. In one of his earliest preserved letters on education, Jefferson praises the ability of books of fiction to awaken the moral imagination. When we read good literature, including fiction, he says, "the spacious field of imagination is thus laid open to our use, and lessons may be formed to illustrate and carry home to the mind every rule of moral life." Thomas Jefferson to Robert Skipwith, August 3, 1771, in *Portable Thomas Jefferson*, 350–51. For an excellent discussion of Jefferson's understanding of the imagination in relation to the development of moral character, see Yarbrough, *American Virtues*, 40–43.

Instead, he exhorted to his nephew: "Question with boldness even the existence of a god"; "read the bible then as you would read Livy or Tacitus";
your own reason, "the only oracle given you by heaven," is "to call to her
tribunal every fact, every opinion." The purpose of the study of religion,
Jefferson instructed, should not be to accept or reject religious belief, but
rather to "lay aside all prejudice on both sides, and neither believe nor reject
any thing because any other person, or description of persons have rejected
or believed it."[97] Jefferson anticipated that such an inquiry would lead
individuals to reject clerical religion and adopt a rational religion such as
Unitarianism.

Jefferson's Advocacy of Legal Disabilities on Clergymen

Jefferson expected clerical influence to be overcome primarily through
proper education, but he did not rely on education alone. Jefferson went
so far as to sponsor the imposition of direct legal disabilities on clergymen.
In his 1783 draft constitution for Virginia, he proposed to exclude "ministers of the Gospel" from eligibility for election to the general assembly.[98] As
we discussed in Chapter 1, James Madison criticized the provision
for violating "a fundamental principle of liberty by punishing a religious
profession with the privation of a civil right." Madison also said that the
exclusion violated a different provision in the same constitution, which
declared that the general assembly should not have power "to abridge the
civil rights of any person on account of his religious belief."[99] Minister
exclusions from public office were not uncommon in state constitutions in
the founding era, but Jefferson's provision was not just a by-product of
colonial tradition. In 1776, he had drafted a different proposed constitution
for Virginia.[100] That draft did not include a minister exclusion provision,
which means that Jefferson decided to add the minister exclusion between
1776 and 1783. At the same time that he declared in the Virginia Statute
that an individual's religious opinions "shall in no wise diminish, enlarge, or
affect their civil capacities" and specifically denounced religious tests for
office, he sought to impose a religious test to exclude clergy from the right
to be eligible for elective office. When asked about the exclusion by the

---

[97] Thomas Jefferson to Peter Carr, August 10, 1787, in *Portable Thomas Jefferson*, 425–27.
[98] *Papers of Thomas Jefferson*, 6:297. Jefferson published his draft constitution as an appendix to *Notes on the State of Virginia*.
[99] James Madison, *The Writings of James Madison*, ed. Gaillard Hunt (New York: G. P.
Putnam's Sons, 1900–10), 5:288.
[100] "Draft Constitution for Virginia," 1776, in *Portable Thomas Jefferson*, 242–50.

Frenchman Jean de Chastellux, Jefferson responded in a revealingly straightforward manner:

The clergy are excluded, because, if admitted into the legislature at all, the probability is that they would form it's [sic] majority. For they are dispersed through every county in the state, they have influence with the people, and great opportunities of persuading them to elect them in the legislature. This body, tho shattered, is still formidable, still forms a *corps*, and is still actuated by the *esprit de corps*. The nature of that spirit has been severely felt by mankind, and has filled the history of ten or twelve centuries with too many atrocities not to merit a proscription from meddling with government.[101]

In a private letter written in 1800, Jefferson recanted his proposed clergy exclusion, but he did not explain the change as reflecting his renewed appreciation for the principles of the Virginia Statute. He explained:

[In] the same scheme of a constitution [for Virginia which I prepared in 1783, I observe] an abridgment of the right of being elected, which after 17 years more of experience & reflection, I do not approve. It is the incapacitation of a clergyman from being elected. The clergy, by getting themselves established by law, & ingrafted into the machine of government, have been a very formidable engine against the civil and religious rights of man. They are still so in many countries & even in some of these United States. Even in 1783 we doubted the stability of our recent measures for reducing them to the footing of other useful callings. It now appears that our means were effectual. The clergy here seem to have relinquished all pretensions to privilege, and to stand on a footing with lawyers, physicians, &c. They ought therefore to possess the same rights.[102]

Jefferson does *not* express misgivings about having transgressed the principles he stated in the Virginia Statute. Quite the opposite; he concludes that clergy "ought . . . to possess the same rights" only because "our measures for reducing them" have been "effectual." His statement suggests that if the clergy had not been "reduced," then their rights should still be curtailed. Jefferson, in fact, would later reverse his position again. His 1817 "Act for Establishing Elementary Schools" explicitly prohibited clergy from serving as overseeing "visitors" of Virginia's public schools.[103]

---

[101] Thomas Jefferson to Chastellux, September 2, 1785, in *Papers of Thomas Jefferson*, 8:470.

[102] Thomas Jefferson to Jeremiah Moor, August 14, 1800, in *Works of Thomas Jefferson*, 9:143.

[103] "An Act for Establishing Elementary Schools," 1817, in *Writings of Thomas Jefferson*, 9:490.

Jefferson's Philosophy of Religious Freedom in Light of His Politics of Church and State

Jefferson's attempts to impose legal disabilities on religious clergy cannot be reconciled with the Virginia Statute's natural rights teachings that an individual's civil capacities should not be diminished on account of his religious beliefs and that individuals ought to be free to profess and argue to defend their religious opinions. His approach to public education, moreover, belies the understanding of the human mind articulated in the Virginia Statute. In practice, Jefferson did not start from the premises that individuals' opinions are insusceptible to coercion or that they are an involuntary product of persuasive evidence. He did not act as if opinions were beyond the legitimate jurisdiction of government. Rather, Jefferson took cognizance of how early childhood education can exert extraordinary influence on intellectual development, and he recognized how authoritative opinions and individuals can shape beliefs. Jefferson sought to use the power of the state to liberate individuals from what he believed to be the irrationalities of clerical education and theological superstition. Through public education and targeted legal disabilities on clergy, he sought to develop minds that could be free and that would be guided by reason alone.

It must be mentioned that Jefferson's desire to minimize the influence of religious clergy does not mean that he was simply hostile toward all religion. He sought only to overcome what he considered to be the antirational elements of religion and the attendant oppressive designs of religious clergy. He believed that a simple and reasonable Christianity would emerge when individuals were liberated from irrational theological dogmas and from clerical influence. This version of demystified Christianity would, in Jefferson's view, be sufficient to sustain the moral knowledge necessary for a free society because nature and nature's god imparted to man a moral sense. "The practice of morality being necessary for the well-being of society," Jefferson claimed, "he [our creator] has taken care to impress it's [sic] precepts so indelibly on our hearts that they shall not be effaced by the subtleties of our brain."[104] A full discussion of Jefferson's conception of the moral sense lies beyond the scope of this chapter, but his belief in it helps

---

[104] Thomas Jefferson to James Fishback, September 27, 1809, in *Papers of Thomas Jefferson*, Retirement Series, ed. J. Jefferson Looney (Princeton, NJ: Princeton University Press, 2004), 1:266. For excellent discussions of Jefferson's understanding of the moral sense see Yarbrough, *American Virtues*, 27–54; Michael P. Zuckert, *The Natural Rights Republic* (Notre Dame, IN: University of Notre Dame Press, 1996), 68–72.

to explain why he thought that a moral society did not require the precepts of nonrational religious beliefs or religious authorities.

Jefferson also thought his version of rational Christianity would support democratic citizenship. "And can the liberties of a nation be thought secure when we have removed their only firm basis, a conviction in the minds of the people that these liberties are of the gift of God? That they are not to be violated but with his wrath?" Jefferson famously asks in *Notes on the State of Virginia*.[105] He does not actually answer his own questions, but they indicate that he thought the state could endorse religious precepts that he believed to be supported by reason, such as the existence of a creator god that endows individuals with rights. Jefferson sought to suppress ecclesiastical influence in American society, not "reasonable" religious beliefs compatible with the rights of man.

CONCLUSION

When we consult the philosophical epistemology of the Virginia Statute for Religious Freedom, Jefferson's doctrine for church-state relations is that government jurisdiction extends to actions alone and not to opinions. Jefferson's approach to church-state relations in practice, however, was different. First and foremost, he believed that clerical influence on American society had to be reduced, an intention that can be seen in the Virginia Statute itself. The document makes a philosophical argument against state jurisdiction over opinions, but then it proceeds to limit state activity over opinions *and actions*. And the actions it limits, laws compelling attendance and financial support of religion, are exactly the ones by which clergy maintained their power and prestige. The statute's two political maxims that cannot be derived from the starting point of the freedom of the mind make sense in light of Jefferson's anticlerical objectives.

Jefferson primarily aimed to subvert clerical influence, however, through his system of public education, which he designed to nurture belief in a simple, demystified, rational version of Christianity and to lead students to eschew belief in traditional Christian dogmas. Jefferson believed that a properly designed system of public education could free America from the mental tyranny imposed by religious clergy and ecclesiastical religion, allowing its citizens to "burst the chains under which monkish ignorance and superstition had persuaded them to bind themselves."[106] Toward this end,

---

[105] Notes on the State of Virginia, Query XVIII, in *Portable Thomas Jefferson*, 215.
[106] Thomas Jefferson to Roger C. Weightman, June 24, 1826, in *Portable Thomas Jefferson*, 585.

he also attempted to impose prohibitions against clergymen holding public office, a disability that violated the principles of the Virginia Statute. When clergy were sufficiently "reduced" and no longer politically dangerous, Jefferson suggested they then might enjoy equal political rights. However, he seems not to have believed that America had reached that point in his own lifetime, as he proposed legal disabilities on clergy as late as 1817 and one of his last actions as rector at the University of Virginia was to prohibit Sunday services on campus.

Despite his desire to be remembered for his authorship of the Virginia Statute for Religious Liberty, Jefferson's own commitment to religious freedom was not grounded on the statute's philosophical epistemology. He did not attempt to build a politics on the premise that "Almighty God hath created the mind to be free." His own actions to establish religious freedom belied his declaration that "the opinions of men are not the object of civil government, nor under its jurisdiction." Jefferson aimed to construct a political community that would emancipate the human mind from what he considered to be nonrational influences. The fundamental basis of the "natural rights" to religious freedom for Jefferson was his commitment to the idea that individuals and political communities should be guided by reason alone. Unfortunately, he never provided a systematic defense of how to distinguish reasonable from irrational religious opinions. He seems to have thought that all men of good sense would be able to differentiate the one from the other, just as he easily had distinguished the "diamonds" from the "dunghill" when editing the New Testament. His faith "that truth is great and will prevail if left to herself" may explain why he never provided the argument necessary to substantiate the premise on which his politics of church-state separation was based. Whatever the reason, this lacuna in his political thought means his argument for the rights of religious liberty lies on an unsecured foundation. Ironically, the American Founder who was perhaps the most dedicated to a politics based on reason alone appears to have left his position dependent on others' faith in its reasonableness.

In Chapter 4, we shall attempt to convert Jefferson's approach to church-state relations into a workable judicial doctrine. For now, we can point out that his politics do not easily translate into an unchanging legal rule. Jefferson approached religious freedom as a project to be pursued in different stages. He sought to establish religious liberty, first, by transforming Americans' religious opinions and by suppressing clerical power and privilege. Once that was achieved, he suggested that the state might equally protect the natural rights of religious liberty. The protection of these rights, however, was conditional. As society became less influenced by religious clergy and more rational,

Jefferson expected that disabilities on clergy and the irrational elements of religion could be lessened and the availability of rights expanded. But as long as ecclesiastical clergy and their religious institutions remained dangerous, Jefferson thought it necessary to target them for specific disabilities.

As we shall discuss in the next three chapters, a contemporary application of Jefferson's thought would not necessarily extol the idea of state neutrality toward all religions or among different religions. It could maintain a posture of state antagonism toward nonrational theological dogmas and toward religions with ecclesiastical hierarchies, especially in educational matters. The approach also could allow the state to endorse "rational" religious sentiments that support liberal political ideas – such as the idea that "Almighty God hath created the mind free." Sectarianism might be used as a rough approximation to distinguish the types of religious beliefs that Jefferson thought were dangerous from those he thought were reasonable and politically useful. The state, in this view, could encourage nonsectarian sentiments like belief in "nature and nature's God" but discourage sectarian religious beliefs that privilege a class of believers over unbelievers or that favor the establishment of ecclesiastical hierarchies.

Jefferson believed America to be embroiled in a battle between religious superstition and intolerance on the one hand and reason and freedom on the other.[107] He sought to achieve a decisive victory by using state power to nurture the rational religious beliefs that he believed supported reason and freedom and to suppress the irrational dogmas and institutions that he believed to be hostile to liberty. To help determine whether this understanding and approach to religious freedom is worthy of adoption today, we can turn to constitutional law and attempt to apply Jefferson, Madison, and Washington to legal issues faced by the modern Supreme Court.

---

[107] Owen, "The Struggle between 'Religion and Nonreligion': Jefferson, Backus, and the Dissonance of America's Founding Principles," 498.

PART II

THE FOUNDERS AND THE FIRST AMENDMENT
RELIGION CLAUSES

4

Madison's, Washington's, and Jefferson's Church-State Doctrines

The preceding three chapters attempted to articulate the different church-state political philosophies of James Madison, George Washington, and Thomas Jefferson. The next three chapters translate these philosophies into judicial doctrines and then apply those doctrines to leading church-state constitutional questions. Applying the Founders' approaches to legal cases helps to clarify their positions by showing how they might resolve specific constitutional questions. It also reveals how and when these leading Founders agree and disagree, which, in turn, can help us determine the degree to which their ideas remain relevant and persuasive today. This chapter attempts to deduce legal doctrines from each Founder. Chapters 5 and 6 apply those doctrines to Establishment Clause and Free Exercise Clause constitutional controversies, respectively.

THE FOUNDERS' CHURCH-STATE DOCTRINES

To apply the Founders' ideas to church-state constitutional controversies requires that their political theories be translated into legal doctrines. As constitutional scholar Keith E. Whittington states, "In order for the [Constitution's] text to serve as law, it must be rulelike."[1] The most useful judicial rules are sufficiently abstract to cover a multitude of similar

---

[1] Keith E. Whittington, *Constitutional Interpretation: Textual Meaning, Original Intent, and Judicial Review* (Lawrence: University Press of Kansas, 1999), 6. In full, the passage from which the quotation is taken is as follows:

In order for the [Constitution's] text to serve as law, it must be rulelike. In order to be a governing rule, it must possess a certain specificity in order to connect it to a given situation.

situations yet specific enough to indicate a decision in a given case. Without requisite specificity and sufficient abstraction, those who interpret the Constitution are left without a standard or too vague of a standard to apply to a given set of circumstances. This necessarily increases the interpreter's discretion – which, for the judiciary, may or may not be attractive, depending on one's conception of the judicial role – but a corollary of increased discretion is decreased guidance by the rule that purportedly governs the case.

An overly simplified example might help to illustrate this point. The rule, "the state must safeguard religious liberty," accurately captures the intentions of Madison, Washington, and Jefferson. Its vagueness, however, makes the rule almost meaningless when applied to any specific case. Does a nonsectarian prayer in a public school violate religious liberty? Without further clarification of what Madison, Washington, or Jefferson meant by "safeguard religious liberty," it is impossible to determine. To resolve the case, a judge would have to introduce a secondary rule to specify what "safeguarding religious liberty" means, and this secondary rule – and not necessarily the position of any of the Founders – effectively would determine whether prayer in public school violated religious liberty. For any of the Founders' approaches to determine actual judicial decision-making, their political philosophies must be translated into judicial doctrines that can cover a multitude of different situations yet be specific enough to indicate an actual decision for a given set of circumstances.

This requirement demands the following caveat be mentioned. The application of general principles to a specific set of facts requires interpretive judgments. In what follows, I have attempted to be as transparent as possible when I have made such judgments either to translate the Founders' political philosophies into judicial doctrines or to apply those doctrines to the facts of a specific case. I attempt to render as accurately as possible how the Madisonian, Washingtonian, and Jeffersonian approaches would adjudicate the cases discussed in Chapters 5 and 6. With regard to Washington and Jefferson in particular, both the translation of their political philosophies to

Further, it must indicate a decision with a fair degree of certainty. Such certainty and specificity need not be absolute, but the law does need to provide determinate and dichotomous answers to questions of legal authority. In order for the Constitution to be legally binding, judges must be able to determine that a given action either is or is not allowed by its terms. Similarly, the Constitution is binding only to the extent that judges do not have discretion in its application. Although the application of the law may require controversial judgments, the law nonetheless imposes obligations on the judge that are reflected in the vindication of the legal entitlements of one party or another. For the Constitution to serve this purpose, it must be elaborated as a series of doctrines, formulas, or tests.

requisitely specific judicial doctrines and the application of those doctrines to the facts of specific cases is more of an art than a science.

The Madisonian Approach

Madison offers a straightforward approach to church-state constitutional questions. Madison argued that the nature of religious beliefs and duties makes their exercise an "unalienable" natural right and, therefore, that religion must remain beyond the state's cognizance. A Madisonian approach to the First Amendment, accordingly, would require the state to remain noncognizant of religion. The government could not use religion as a basis for classifying citizens. Religion as such could not be the cause of state action, be the subject of criminal sanctions or government regulations, or be used to determine eligibility for governmental benefits. To borrow from contemporary civil rights discourse, the Madisonian position would require the state to remain "religion blind." Madison's doctrine can be stated as follows:

The Madisonian Doctrine:

Government must remain noncognizant of religion as such and of the religious beliefs and affiliation of individual citizens.

The Washingtonian Approach

A Washingtonian approach to church and state constitutional questions would focus on the purposes or ends of state action. Washington held that the state could support or burden religion as long as it did so in light of a legitimate civic interest. He thought good citizenship to be a fundamental civic interest, and he believed religion to be an essential aid in developing the moral character on which good citizenship depended. The Washingtonian approach, therefore, would allow the state to endorse and to financially support religion as a means to encourage good citizenship or to advance legitimate civic interests.

Because Washington premised government support on a religion's support of legitimate civic interest, Washingtonianism would not require the state to support all religions equally. Those religions that failed to support good citizenship or other legitimate civic interests would not need to be treated equally to those that did. The Washingtonian approach also would allow the state to impose civic obligations on religious individuals even if those obligations conflicted with perceived religious tenets. Religious individuals could be relieved of such burden by legislative or executive accommodations – in his letter to the Quakers, Washington expresses that this was his "wish and desire" – but Washingtonianism would not recognize such accommodations as part of the right to religious freedom. As long as the state remained within the sphere of legitimate civic action, it would not have a constitutional duty to recognize or tolerate religiously based claims for exemptions from burdensome laws. The Washingtonian approach would hold that, within the realm of legitimate civic interests, state authority trumps perceived religious obligations.

As a judicial doctrine, Washingtonianism usually would defer to legislative determinations of civic interests, but it would not hold that any civic interest asserted by the legislature actually is legitimate. Washington declared that every man is "accountable to God alone for his religious opinions" and that men "remain responsible only to their Maker for the Religion, or modes of faith, which they may prefer or profess."[2] As discussed in Chapter 2, Washington understood the right of religious freedom to protect individuals from compulsion to practice a mode of faith in which they do not believe. His position also would prohibit the state from judging, evaluating, or being concerned with the truth or falsity of religious opinions and religious practices as such. State actors could not attempt to lead citizens to adopt religious beliefs or practices because the state thought them to be religiously true. Washington's position, similarly, denies the legitimacy of state discouragement of religion as such. Governmental aid or hindrance of religion would only be permissible in light of a legitimate civic interest, which means aid to religion or burdens on religion could never be the sole purpose of state action.

The civic interest that animates a given policy might also determine the degree of permissible sectarianism under the Washingtonian approach. Washington aimed to minimize the tension between governmental policies that supported religion and individuals' own religious professions. If the state used religion to further civic purposes, he wanted the state to support all the religions that furthered that civic purpose. His official public actions in support of religion reveal how he thought state endorsement of religion ought, as much as possible, to be of a general character. We might label this part of Washington's position "ecumenicalism" – government policies

---

[2] George Washington to the United Baptist Churches of Virginia, May 1789, *Papers of George Washington*, Presidential Series, ed. Dorothy Twohig (Charlottesville: University Press of Virginia, 1987–), 2:424. George Washington to the Society of Quakers, October 1789, *Papers of George Washington*, Presidential Series, 4:266.

should be as ecumenical as possible in light of the legitimate civic end being advanced. Washingtonian ecumenicalism would not require the state to treat all religions equally or prohibit state support of specific religions, but it would require that state support be extended as widely as possible in light of the end of the policy in question.

We can set forth Washington's doctrine as follows:

The Washingtonian Doctrine:

1. State action must have a civic purpose.
2. State action may support or burden religion as a means to further that interest, but the state may not compel an individual to practice a religion in which he does not believe. The state may neither seek to discourage religion as such nor judge, evaluate, or be concerned with the truth or falsity of religious opinions and practices as such.
3. State endorsement of religion ought to be as ecumenical as possible in light of the civic purpose being advanced.

The Jeffersonian Approach

Converting Jefferson's approach into a legal doctrine is more complicated than translating Madison's or Washington's approach. If we limited our view to Jefferson's professed philosophical teaching in the Virginia Statute for Religious Freedom, a Jeffersonian approach to church-state constitutional questions would focus on the distinction between acts and opinions and prohibit the state from exercising jurisdiction over the opinions. But for the reasons discussed in Chapter 3, the act-opinion distinction fails to fully capture how Jefferson actually addressed church-state matters. Jefferson aspired to create a society in which clergy and sectarian theological dogmas did not guide human thinking. He wanted individuals to embrace what he considered to be rational religious beliefs – like the existence of a creator god that grants men rights – and to eschew irrational beliefs – such as Jesus' resurrection and the Trinity. Only when society developed to the point where it was free from the influence of sectarian religious dogmas and the mental tyranny that clergy imposed did he believe that the "natural rights" principles articulated in the Virginia Statute could be implemented equally for everyone. The Jeffersonian project to establish religious freedom, accordingly, is an evolving process that requires, first, freedom *from* certain types of religious beliefs and, then, the separation of civil rights and privileges from all religious beliefs.

The developmental nature of Jefferson's project means that it cannot be translated into a judicial doctrine that applies to all individuals equally. It also means that it might yield different results for similar sets of circumstances at different points in time. Context mattered for Jefferson, and the primary contextual consideration was the danger that religious sectarianism posed to society. His changing position on minister exclusions from public office reflects the evolutionary aspect of his thought. As discussed in Chapter 3, Jefferson's 1777 draft of the Virginia Statute asserted that individuals' civil capacities should not be affected by their religious opinions. In his 1783 draft constitution for Virginia, Jefferson sought to exclude religious ministers from eligibility for some political offices. In 1800, Jefferson wrote in a private letter that he had changed his position on minister exclusions because ministers' "measures for reducing them to the footing of other callings . . . were effectual."[3] Seventeen years later, however, he once again changed course and proposed to exclude clergymen from serving as overseeing visitors from public schools. These apparently contradictory policies can be reconciled if they are seen in light of Jefferson's intention to establish a society free of overbearing clerical influence. To the extent that clerical influence in society was "reduced," he thought clergy could be treated the same as other citizens. But to the extent that their influence posed a danger to society, he thought clergy ought to be subject to specific legal disabilities. While the end of reducing clerical influence remained consistent, the means Jefferson employed to achieve that end varied according to circumstances.

A necessary focus on context would seem to make it impossible to identify a single Jeffersonian rule that would be specific enough to determine constitutional decision-making in a variety of different circumstances. "Minimize clerical influence when it is dangerous to society" might be a consistent doctrine, but it is not one that can determine the outcome of specific cases with any regularity or predictability. Its vagueness would make the secondary judgments of those applying the doctrine determinative of the outcome of any given case. However, toward the end of his life, Jefferson described a level of societal and religious development that we can use to mark "sufficient progress" toward overcoming clerical influence from the Jeffersonian point of view. Jefferson predicted a general acceptance of Unitarianism. For him, Unitarianism represented the overcoming of traditional Christian dogmas like the Trinity – that is, irrational religious dogmas.

---

[3] Thomas Jefferson to Jeremiah Moor, August 14, 1800, in *Papers of Thomas Jefferson,* ed. Barbara Oberg (Princeton, NJ: Princeton University Press, 2005), 32:103.

Jefferson thought a "mature" society was one in which religion was limited to beliefs and practices confirmed by reason alone.

It is not easy to measure with precision the general societal or religious development of a nation. The religious revivals of the nineteenth century and the significant political influence of traditional religious clergy and orthodox religious beliefs throughout the twentieth century, however, suggest that the United States has never reached the point of religious development that Jefferson anticipated to be within a generation of his death.[4] Given the continued political influence of religious clergy and sectarian theological dogmas, a contemporary application of Jefferson's position might view religious freedom as still in the process of being established. Let me acknowledge explicitly that this is an inference from Jefferson's thought, not a necessary conclusion from it. If one concluded that religious clergy and nonrational religious beliefs no longer posed a danger to American society, then a Jeffersonian approach would focus on the impropriety of government affecting an individual's civil rights on account of religion. But it seems that Americans, by and large, have not accepted Jefferson's religion of reason alone. A contemporary application of his approach to church-state relations, accordingly, might remain particularly cognizant of the potential danger that clerical influence poses to society.

Religious sectarianism might be used to approximate the type of religious belief that Jefferson considered irrational and, thus, prone to clericalism and clerical misuse. Especially in matters of education, but not only in such matters, Jeffersonianism would seek to discourage clerical and sectarian influences on American society. It would not allow the state to advance or to finance through tax dollars sectarian religious opinions or sectarian institutions. Jeffersonian nonsectarianism contrasts with Washingtonian ecumenicalism. Washington thought it permissible for the state to support sectarian religious beliefs, but, at the same time, he wanted to minimize the potential tensions between governmental support of religion and individuals' own religious professions. Jefferson's concern was different. He sought to end state support for nonrational religious creeds. The Jeffersonian approach, thus, would categorically prohibit the kinds of state support of religion that Washingtonianism would allow.

Jeffersonianism, however, would not require that the state take affirmative action against every type of religious expression or all religious

---

[4] For a discussion of this point, see J. Judd Owen, "The Struggle between 'Religion and Nonreligion': Jefferson, Backus, and the Dissonance of America's Founding Principles," *American Political Science Review* 101, no. 3 (August 2007): 499–501.

institutions. Jefferson sought to free American society only from clerical and irrational religious influences, not from rational religious beliefs that could be politically useful. Under Jeffersonianism, the state could advance and endorse nonsectarian religious ideas and opinions consistent with the Jeffersonian ideal of "rational" Christianity. The approach would not demand governmental neutrality toward all religious beliefs or between religion and irreligion. It would require, instead, that the state act affirmatively against clerical and sectarian religion but allow the state to endorse "rational" religious beliefs that support liberal democratic political principles. For constitutional controversies that do not involve religious clergy, sectarian religious ideas, or sectarian religious institutions, the Jeffersonian approach could recur to the primary principle Jefferson articulated in the Virginia Statute for Religious Freedom: The state may not punish or affect an individual's or an institution's civil rights on account of religious opinions, religious professions, or religious worship (or lack thereof).

This multifaceted approach, which requires different types of analysis for different types of religious beliefs and different classes of individuals and institutions, reflects Jefferson's anticlerical politics, his endorsement of "rational" religion, and his qualified commitment to the natural rights principles articulated in the Virginia Statute. We can summarize the approach with the following two prongs:

The Jeffersonian Doctrine:

1. The state should not advance and may curtail the influence of religious clergy, sectarian religious beliefs, and sectarian religious institutions. No individual shall be compelled to support financially any religious worship, place, or ministry. The state may advance nonsectarian religious ideas and institutions.
2. Excluding individuals and institutions covered by the rule above, the state should not affect an individual's or institution's civil rights on account of religious opinions, religious professions, or religious worship (or lack thereof).

With the Madisonian, Washingtonian, and Jeffersonian legal doctrines articulated, we can attempt to apply these Founders' approaches to the First Amendment's Religion Clauses. The next chapter discusses how Madisonianism, Washingtonianism, and Jeffersonianism would adjudicate the different types of Establishment Clause cases that have come before the Supreme Court. Chapter 6 extends the analysis to Free Exercise Clause cases. As we shall see, in many cases the Founders' church-state political philosophies would lead to different jurisprudential results.

5

Madison, Washington, Jefferson, and the Establishment Clause

The previous chapter extrapolated legal rules from Madison's, Washington's, and Jefferson's church-state philosophies. This chapter attempts to apply those rules to a sample of historical cases adjudicated under the First Amendment's Establishment Clause. Unfortunately, no commonly accepted typology of Establishment Clause cases exists. In fact, whether a given set of facts qualifies a case for consideration under the Establishment Clause, Free Exercise Clause, or Free Speech Clause can be contentious and highly determinative of a case's outcome.[1] Nonetheless, three general types of cases cover most disputes adjudicated under the Establishment Clause:

1. Religion in public schools
2. Governmental support of private religious schools
3. The presence of religion in the public square, including the participation of religious individuals and organizations in generally available state programs

While not exhaustive, this categorization will let us apply Madison, Washington, and Jefferson to the most fundamental Establishment Clause issues that have come before the Supreme Court. In what follows, I briefly describe examples of each type of case and then explain how each Founder's approach would adjudicate those cases. Tables comparing the Founders'

---

[1] Consider, for example, *Rosenberger v. Rectors of the University of Virginia*, 515 U.S. 819 (1995). The Court's five-member majority reached its decision using the Free Speech Clause. Dissenting opinions argued, among other things, that the case involved an Establishment Clause violation. Arguably, the case might have been most properly adjudicated under the Free Exercise Clause.

jurisprudential results and a discussion of the most notable differences among the Founders round out the chapter.

RELIGION IN PUBLIC SCHOOLS

Prayer in public school has perhaps been the most enduring source of controversy involving the Establishment Clause. As discussed in Chapter 3, Thomas Jefferson argued against Bible reading in his early nineteenth-century plan for elementary schools. Jefferson's view, however, did not take hold, and daily Bible reading and teacher-led prayers were common in American public schools until they were declared unconstitutional by the Supreme Court in the early 1960s.

In *Engle v. Vitale* (1962), the Supreme Court found unconstitutional teacher-led prayer. The case involved the New York public schools, which began the day with the following nondenominational prayer:

Almighty God, we acknowledge our dependence upon Thee, and we beg Thy blessings upon us, our parents, our teachers and our Country.

No student was compelled to say the prayer, which had been composed by the New York State Board of Regents. The Court declared that the state lacked authority "to prescribe by law any particular form of prayer which is to be used as an official prayer in carrying on any program of governmentally sponsored religious activity."[2]

The following year, in *Abington School District v. Schempp* (1963), the Court found unconstitutional daily Bible readings and recitations of the Lord's Prayer in public schools. Pennsylvania law at the time required at least ten verses from the Holy Bible to be read without comment at the opening of each school day. In Maryland, official policy led most of Baltimore's public schools to begin the day by reading, without comment, one chapter of the Bible and/or the recitation of the Lord's Prayer. In both localities, parents could request their children be excused from the religious exercise. The *Schempp* Court said Establishment Clause precedents, including *Vitale*, required state action to possess a secular purpose and to have the primary effect of neither advancing nor inhibiting religion. Bible reading and recitation of the Lord's Prayer, the Court found, failed both requirements.[3]

More than twenty years later, the Court found itself faced with a new type of prayer in public school case. Partially in response to *Vitale* and *Schempp*, in

[2] *Engle v. Vitale*, 370 U.S. 421, 430 (1962).
[3] *Abington School District v. Schempp*, 374 U.S. 203, 222–25 (1963).

1978 the Alabama state legislature authorized a one-minute period of silence "for meditation" during the public school day. The state legislature modified the law in 1981 to authorize a period of silence "for meditation and voluntary prayer." This modified law was challenged and came before the Supreme Court in *Wallace v. Jaffree* (1985). Following its earlier precedents, the Court found that the amended Alabama law lacked a secular purpose and unconstitutionally endorsed religion.[4] Then–Associate Justice William Rehnquist used the case to write a vehement critique of the Court's entire body of separationist jurisprudence, setting forth nonpreferentialism as the more historically accurate interpretation of the Establishment Clause.[5]

In *Lee v. Weisman* (1992), the Court extended its ban on prayer in public school to include recitations of nondenominational prayers at middle and high school graduation ceremonies. The case evaluated a Providence, Rhode Island, school district policy that permitted school principals to invite clergy members to offer invocation and benediction prayers at graduation. The principal named in the case, Robert E. Lee, invited a Jewish rabbi to offer opening and closing prayers for a middle school graduation. Before the ceremony, Principal Lee gave the rabbi a pamphlet, entitled "Guidelines for Civic Occasions," prepared by the National Council of Christians and Jews. Following the pamphlet's instructions, the rabbi offered a nondenominational invocation and benediction at the graduation ceremony.[6] The Court found Principal Lee's actions and the school district policy that permitted them to be

---

[4] *Wallace v. Jaffree*, 472 U.S. 38, 56–61 (1985).
[5] Ibid., 98–100.
[6] The prayers led by the rabbi were as follows:

Invocation: God of the Free, Hope of the Brave: For the legacy of America where diversity is celebrated and the rights of minorities are protected, we thank You. May these young men and women grow up to enrich it. For the liberty of America, we thank You. May these new graduates grow up to guard it. For the political process of America in which all its citizens may participate, for its court system where all may seek justice, we thank You. May those we honor this morning always turn to it in trust. For the destiny of America, we thank You. May the graduates of Nathan Bishop Middle School so live that they might help to share it. May our aspirations for our country and for these young people, who are our hope for the future, be richly fulfilled. Amen.

Benediction: O God, we are grateful to You for having endowed us with the capacity for learning which we have celebrated on this joyous commencement. Happy families give thanks for seeing their children achieve an important milestone. Send Your blessings upon the teachers and administrators who helped prepare them. The graduates now need strength and guidance for the future; help them to understand that we are not complete with academic knowledge alone. We must each strive to fulfill what You require of us all: to do justly, to love mercy, to walk humbly. We give thanks to You, Lord, for keeping us alive, sustaining us, and allowing us to reach this special, happy occasion. Amen.

Lee v. Weisman, 505 U.S. 577, 582 (1992).

unconstitutional on account of the psychological religious coercion the prayers might have imposed on impressionable students.[7]

Following *Lee*, the Court next found officially sanctioned student-led prayers unconstitutional. In *Santa Fe Independent School District v. Doe* (2000), the Court struck down a Texas school district policy that permitted students to deliver a prayer over the public address system before varsity football games. The prayer leaders were elected by the student body, which also voted on whether a nonsectarian and nonproselytizing prayer would be said at all. The Court found that, since the prayer was authorized by a government policy and took place on government property at a government-sponsored, school-related event, it was not protected private speech. According to the Court, the prayer had "the improper effect of coercing those present to participate in an act of religious worship" and thus violated the Establishment Clause.[8]

Citing *Lee v. Weisman's* psychological coercion test and the Court's previous use of the "Lemon" test and "endorsement" test, a three-judge panel of the Ninth Circuit Court of Appeals in 2002 ruled the recitation of the Pledge of Allegiance unconstitutional in public schools. That court found dispositive the fact that the United States Congress added the phrase "under God" to the Pledge in 1954. If a once-a-year nondenominational prayer at a nonmandatory graduation ceremony is unconstitutional, the circuit court reasoned, so, too, is a daily recital in the classroom that employs religious language.[9] In *Elk Grove School District v. Newdow* (2004), the Supreme Court set aside that decision on narrow technical grounds, avoiding the Establishment Clause issue brought up in the original case.[10]

While prayer in public schools has been one of the more enduring Establishment Clause issues, constitutional questions involving religion and public schools have not been limited to it. Two of the Court's first modern-day Establishment Clause cases involved the facilitation of religious education by public schools. In *McCollum v. Board of Education* (1948), the Court evaluated an Illinois school district policy that allowed religious instruction in public schools during the school day. The religion classes were taught by nonschool faculty employed by a private Jewish, Roman Catholic, and Protestant voluntary association. The teachers, who included a Jewish rabbi and Catholic priests, were provided at no expense to the school

[7] Ibid., 593–94.

[8] *Santa Fe Independent School District v. Doe*, 530 U.S. 290, 312 (2000).

[9] *Newdow v. U.S. Congress*, 328 F.3d. 466, 486–88 (2002).

[10] *Elk Grove Unified School District v. Newdow*, 542 U.S. 1, 16–18 (2004).

district, but the instructors were subject to the approval and supervision of the superintendent of schools. Only students whose parents requested they participate attended the weekly classes, which lasted for thirty to forty-five minutes. Students who did not take the religious instruction were required to leave their classrooms and go to another part of the school.[11] The Supreme Court struck down the school district policy eight to one. Justice Hugo Black's majority opinion found that the program was "beyond all question a utilization of the tax-established and tax-supported public school system to aid religious groups to spread their faith" and therefore clearly trespassed the "wall of separation" interpretation of the Establishment Clause that the Court had issued only one year earlier in *Everson v. Board of Education.*[12]

In response to the *McCollum* decision, school districts around the nation began operating "released time" programs. In *Zorach v. Clauson* (1952), the Court evaluated a New York City school district policy that allowed students to be dismissed from classroom activities to attend religious instruction off school grounds. Participation required written parental permission. Students who did not attend religious education classes were not excused from school. A six-member Court majority upheld the program, finding the case distinguishable from *McCollum*, in part, because religious instruction did not occur on school grounds and because the "released time" reflected more of an accommodation of religious instruction than a promotion of it.[13]

The legal questions presented in these cases and the Supreme Court's answers can be summarized as follows:

- Can state-composed, teacher-led prayers be recited in public schools? (*Vitale*) No.
- Can devotional Bible reading and religious exercises be directed by public schools? (*Schempp*) No.
- Can public schools encourage and facilitate private prayer? (*Jaffree*) No.
- Can public schools include prayers in graduation ceremonies or at extra-curricular activities? (*Lee, Santa Fe*) No.
- Can "under God" be included in public school recitations of the Pledge of Allegiance? (*Newdow*) Not decided.
- Can public schools facilitate on-campus devotional religious instruction? (*McCollum*) No.
- Can public schools facilitate off-campus devotional religious instruction? (*Zorach*) Yes.

[11] *McCollum v. Board of Education*, 333 U.S. 203, 207–09 (1948).
[12] Ibid., 210.
[13] *Zorach v. Clausen*, 343 U.S. 306, 316 (1952).

The Madisonian Approach to Religion in Public Schools

Madisonianism prevents the state from recognizing religion. It would address prayer in public school in the same way that Madison viewed government-funded military chaplains and religious proclamations made by the president: Religion, Madison said, comprises no part of the social compact and, therefore, the state lacks authority to recommend religious exercises as such. Direct efforts to include prayer as part of the public school day or public school events would be impermissible. State-composed and teacher-led prayer (*Vitale*), state-sponsored Bible readings (*Schempp*), state-directed graduation prayers (*Lee*), and state-arranged student-led prayers (*Santa Fe*) would all violate Madisonian noncognizance.

Even though students alone voted to have prayer and elected those who led the prayer in *Santa Fe*, the school became cognizant of religion when it established the scheme to hold a special vote on the question of holding prayer. Similarly, in *Wallace v. Jaffree*, the Alabama state legislature took cognizance of religion when it recognized a special time "for prayer" and explicitly facilitated religious devotion. The original 1978 policy, however, which required only an unexplained moment of silence, would not seem to trespass the Madisonian position.

The religious instruction policies at issue in *McCollum* and *Zorach* would not be permissible under the Madisonian approach. In both cases, public school districts crafted policies to facilitate religious instruction as such. In *McCollum*, instruction took place in public school facilities; in *Zorach*, religious instruction took place off campus, but only students attending religion classes were allowed to leave school early. Madisonianism would allow a public school to teach about religion as part of a history or literature curriculum and would also allow school districts to end the school day early to allow students to pursue after-school activities, whatever those activities might be. But Madisonian noncognizance would prevent public schools from adopting policies that have the purpose of facilitating religious instruction as such. It therefore would not allow in-school religious instruction, as in the case of *McCollum*, or release students for the sole purpose of religious instruction, as in *Zorach*.

Even though the legal doctrine of religious noncognizance would not allow public schools to sponsor prayers or to facilitate devotional religious instruction, it would not require school officials to eliminate all possible references to religion or exercises of religious faith on public school grounds. For example, if a student was selected to speak at graduation for reasons unrelated to religion – say on account of being the class valedictorian – school officials could not prevent that student from expressing religious convictions. Students who used unstructured free time to study the Bible, to take another example, could not be prevented from doing so. Similarly, if school rules allowed students to form activity clubs, students could not be prevented from forming religiously themed clubs. Just as noncognizance prevents public school officials from taking cognizance of religion to promote religion, the doctrine forbids state actors from recognizing religion to suppress it.

"Under God" in the Pledge of Allegiance presents a difficult case for the Madisonian approach. Unlike the prayers in the other cases discussed, reciting the Pledge is not clearly a religious exercise. "One nation under God" could indicate that America occupies a chosen place in God's providential order. Thus interpreted, the phrase would seem to have a religious meaning and, thereby, be impermissible from the Madisonian point of view. Alternatively, "under God" might be interpreted more politically. The phrase could be seen to acknowledge that American law recognizes a higher authority and that this authority limits the scope and authority of American law.[14] Interpreted politically, "under God" would be seen as similar to Madison's use of the word "Creator" in the "Memorial and Remonstrance." The "Memorial's" acknowledgment of the "duties which we owe to our Creator" does not take cognizance of religion in a religious way; rather, it uses the conception of Creator to defend the inalienability of the right to religious freedom and, thereby, to justify the reason why government cannot take cognizance of religion. If "under God" is understood to be a statement about the limits of legitimate political authority, it would not trespass Madisonian noncognizance.

The Madisonian approach itself does not dictate which way the phrase should be interpreted. Congress adopted "under God" in 1954, in part to distinguish America from the Soviet Union and its atheistic, communistic philosophy of history.[15] The legislative history itself does not clearly resolve the question of whether "under God" is most accurately interpreted as a religious or a political statement. Given the ambiguous nature of the meaning of "under God," it would seem that Madisonianism could either uphold or strike down the phrase. The approach can frame the legal questions to be asked and structures the type of legal inquiry that would be needed to resolve the issue, but without a further factual determination of whether

[14] For a discussion of the political reading of "under God," which interprets the phrase to refer to limited government and inalienable rights, see Thomas C. Berg, "The Pledge of Allegiance and the Limited State." *Texas Review of Law and Politics* 8 (2003): 52–58.

[15] See Richard J. Ellis, *To the Flag: The Unlikely History of the Pledge of Allegiance* (Lawrence: Kansas University Press, 2004), Chapter 5.

"under God" is best understood as a religious or a political statement, it does not resolve the issue. As we shall discuss in the Conclusion, the Pledge case exposes the limits of Madisonianism.

In summary, the Madisonian approach would answer questions about religion in public schools as follows:

- Can state-composed, teacher-led prayers be recited in public schools? (*Vitale*) No.
- Can devotional Bible reading and religious exercises be directed by public schools? (*Schempp*) No.
- Can public schools encourage and facilitate private prayer? (*Jaffree*) No.
- Can public schools include prayers in graduation ceremonies or at extra-curricular activities? (*Lee, Santa Fe*) No.
- Can "under God" be included in public school recitations of the Pledge of Allegiance? (*Newdow*) Unclear.
- Can public schools facilitate on-campus devotional religious instruction? (*McCollum*) No.
- Can public schools facilitate off-campus devotional religious instruction? (*Zorach*) No.

The Washingtonian Approach to Religion in Public Schools

Unlike Madisonian noncognizance, the Washingtonian approach to religious freedom would allow the state to become cognizant of religion to foster legitimate civic purposes such as the cultivation of good citizenship and moral behavior. Regarding religion in public schools, the approach would impose two limits: Students could not be compelled to participate in religious exercises in which they did not believe, and school policies ought to be as ecumenical as possible in light of the purposes those policies seek to further. None of the constitutional cases discussed would clearly violate a Washingtonian interpretation of the Establishment Clause, although some of the programs might have to be broadened to meet the demands of requisite ecumenicalism.

The school prayers struck down by the Court in *Vitale* and *Lee* were similar to the prayers that Washington himself composed for public occasions. In a patriotic and nonsectarian manner, they recognized dependence on God and expressed gratitude for His blessings. In its entirety, the prayer at issue in *Vitale* was

Almighty God, we acknowledge our dependence upon Thee, and we beg Thy blessings upon us, our parents, our teachers and our Country.

The invocation read by the rabbi in *Lee* thanked the "God of the Free, Hope of the Brave" for, among other things, "the legacy of America where diversity is celebrated," "the liberty of America," and the "court system where all may seek justice." The rabbi's benediction expressed gratefulness to "God" for "the capacity of learning," asked for His blessing on the teachers and administrators of the school, and gave thanks to the "Lord" "for keeping us alive, sustaining us, and allowing us to reach this special, happy occasion."[16] Similar sentiments are found in Washington's public prayers. The same also can be said for the inclusion of "under God" in the Pledge of Allegiance, which also would not be problematic from a Washingtonian point of view.

The Bible readings and recitations of the Lord's Prayer struck down by the Supreme Court in *Schempp* would likely pass Washingtonian scrutiny, although with some modification. Washington wanted government-supported religion to reflect the religious beliefs of those supported. When he commanded his troops to attend religious services, for example, he sought to provide them chaplains of their own denominations. Following this example, Washingtonianism would require that prayers and religious readings reflect, as much as possible, the beliefs of the community in which they are said. While the Lord's Prayer might properly reflect some community's beliefs, it might not be appropriate for others. Local community beliefs could guide the permissible character of state encouragement. The Alabama policy of a moment of silence for voluntary prayer or meditation struck down by the Court in *Wallace v. Jaffree* clearly would be in line with the spirit of the Washingtonian approach due to its ecumenical character.

One way to reflect local community beliefs is to institute policies of community or individual choice. The voting arrangement struck down by the Court in *Santa Fe* would be the type of policy that Washingtonian ecumenicalism recommends. As noted already, students voted whether to have a prayer before their football games and then, if they voted in favor of pre-game prayer, they voted again to elect student prayer leaders. These choice elements are consistent with the Washingtonian policy of encouraging moral behavior by fostering citizens' own religious sentiments. The religious education programs at issue in *McCollum* and *Zorach* also included choice provisions that ensured that the state supported the religions of the program's participants. Jewish, Catholic, and Protestant students received religious education in their own religious traditions. As long as such programs were expandable in ways to match local school populations (and remained consistent with the purposes of fostering good citizenship and

---

[16] For the complete text of the rabbi's invocation and benediction, see note 6.

character development), they would meet the Washingtonian requirement of ecumenicalism.

In summary, the Washingtonian approach would answer religion in public school constitutional questions as follows:

- Can state-composed, teacher-led prayers be recited in public schools? (*Vitale*) Yes.
- Can devotional Bible reading and religious exercises be directed by public schools? (*Schempp*) Yes, with ecumenical modification.
- Can public schools encourage and facilitate private prayer? (*Jaffree*) Yes.
- Can public schools include prayers in graduation ceremonies or at extra-curricular activities? (*Lee*, *Santa Fe*) Yes.
- Can "under God" be included in public school recitations of the Pledge of Allegiance? (*Newdow*) Yes.
- Can public schools facilitate on-campus devotional religious instruction? (*McCollum*) Yes.
- Can public schools facilitate off-campus devotional religious instruction? (*Zorach*) Yes.

The Jeffersonian Approach to Religion in Public Schools

A Jeffersonian approach would focus on the extent to which the presence of religion in public schools advances the influence of religious clergy and nonrational religious dogmas. Regarding prayers, the inquiry necessarily would require an examination of their content and their manner of delivery. Jefferson thought it easy to distinguish the reasonable teachings of "rational" religion from the irrational dogmas invented by religious clergy. Despite his confidence in the obviousness of the distinction, to determine constitutional decisions on it would seem to demand a type of theological and philosophical inquiry that would stretch the competence of many judges. In discussing moral education at the University of Virginia, however, Jefferson indicated the type of religious beliefs he thought confirmed by reason and, hence, appropriate for state support. He authorized a professor of ethics to teach "the proofs of the being of a God, the creator, preserver, and supreme ruler of the universe, the author of all the relations of morality, and of the laws and obligations these infer." With these obligations, he said, "all sects agree."[17] Following this example, the Jeffersonian approach

---

[17] Rockfish Gap Report, August 4, 1818, in *Thomas Jefferson: Writings*, ed. Merrill D. Peterson (New York: The Library of America, 1984), 467.

would allow public school prayers that affirm the existence of God, divine providence, and the existence of a God that grants rights and corresponding duties – the exact political theology that informs the Declaration of Independence. Jefferson associated these ideas with nonsectarianism, which might serve as an approximation of the type of prayer that meets Jeffersonian scrutiny.

A Jeffersonian approach would also require that prayers in public schools not augment the influence of religious clergy. Again consulting Jefferson's own actions is helpful. In designing the faculty at the University of Virginia, Jefferson sought to keep a professor of divinity off the faculty, in part because the position would be occupied by a member of the clergy. Since a primary purpose of Jeffersonian nonsectarianism is to minimize clerical influence in society, the approach suggests a prohibition against clergy-led prayers or instruction in public schools.

These prohibitions do not mean that Jeffersonianism necessarily would strike down all the prayers in the cases we have discussed. The nondenominational prayer authorized for classroom use in *Engle v. Vitale*, for example, contains the simple acknowledgment of divine authority that Jefferson thought useful. The moment of silence "for prayer or meditation" in *Jaffree* similarly could be understood to encourage the development of religious sentiments without augmenting clerical influence and without reference to sectarian dogmas. *Newdow* presents a complication because, as discussed previously, the meaning of "one nation, under God" in the Pledge of Allegiance is not without ambiguity. The phrase could indicate that America occupies a chosen place in God's providential order or, alternatively, it could mean that America as a nation recognizes that a higher law exists and that that law limits the scope and authority of American law. Regardless, both meanings reflect a belief in a providential God who authors a moral law, a belief that Jefferson thought was consistent with the development of religious freedom and, therefore, appropriate for state endorsement. "Under God" in the Pledge, along with the prayer in *Vitale* and the moment of silence for prayer in *Jaffree*, could pass Jeffersonian scrutiny.

The school prayers in *Vitale*, *Santa Fe*, and *Newdow* also meet the second prong of the Jeffersonian doctrine, which requires that an individual's civil rights remain unaffected by their religious professions or lack thereof. If students were deprived of an otherwise available privilege or subject to a particular punishment – for example, by suspension from school or by exclusion from graduation ceremonies for not praying – the policies would violate the Jeffersonian approach. But in all three cases, no penalties resulted from a failure to pray.

Some prayer in public school cases would not survive Jeffersonian scrutiny. The approach would likely strike down the Bible readings and recitations of the Lord's Prayer at issue in *Schempp*, although the case is not as straightforward as it might first appear. The text of the Lord's Prayer, which does not mention Jesus Christ, does not contain ideas contrary to Jefferson's own version of "rational" religion. Nonetheless, the prayer can be viewed as sectarian insofar as it is a traditional prayer of Christianity alone. Catholics and Protestants, moreover, recite different versions of the prayer, which makes a nonsectarian recitation of it more difficult. The different versions could be recited on alternate days – for example, the Protestant version on Monday, the Catholic version on Tuesday, and so on – but this would amount to the recitation of different sectarian prayers, not the recitation of a nonsectarian prayer. The same type of problem arises in Bible readings. The texts that belong to the sacred traditions of Judaism, Catholicism, and Protestantism are not all the same. Different translations of the Bible, moreover, are associated with different sects. And while some books of the Hebrew Bible lie within the traditions of Judaism, Catholicism, and Protestantism, they do not belong to other religions such as Buddhism and Hinduism. For these reasons, the Lord's Prayer and Bible readings might be considered to be inherently sectarian and, consequently, constitutionally impermissible. Jefferson himself, furthermore, specifically sought to prevent elementary age children from reading the Bible because he feared that belief in the Bible's miraculous stories would prepare children to accept irrational clerical dogmas. The idea of divinely inspired scripture is opposed to Jeffersonian rationalism. Even without comment, to read the Bible in a classroom might suggest to students the truth of miracles and suprarational dogmas, beliefs that Jefferson intended to keep out of public schools. These considerations suggest that Bible reading in public schools is incompatible with Jefferson's project to establish religious freedom.

The graduation prayer in *Lee v. Weisman* would be unconstitutional for a different reason. The prayers recited were nonsectarian, but students were led in prayer by a Jewish rabbi, who was chosen on account of his religious position. Clergy-led prayer would seem to pose an inherent risk of augmenting clerical influence and thus would be ripe for prohibition by the Jeffersonian approach. Nondenominational prayers led by students, however, would not pose the same risk. Student-led prayers such as those struck down by the Court in *Santa Fe* could be upheld, as long as the prayers remained nonsectarian.

The "released time" programs evaluated in *McCollum* and *Zorach* would fail Jeffersonian scrutiny. Both programs integrated sectarian religious education within the public school day. They opened public schools to exactly the type of religious education that Jefferson hoped his system of public schools would displace. Such programs, moreover, are prone to clerical participation, especially by Catholics. Furthermore, by separating religious instruction students from their classmates and by segregating the religious students by their particular faiths, such programs encourage students to develop a sense of sectarian identity, which in turn can augment clerical influence. Most fundamentally, religious classes would likely teach theological dogmas incompatible with the Jeffersonian pursuit of religious freedom. For these reasons, sectarian religious instruction facilitated by public schools would seem to be anathema to the Jeffersonian approach to church-state separation and not permitted by it.

In summary, the Jeffersonian approach would answer religion in public school constitutional questions as follows:

- Can state-composed, teacher-led prayers be recited in public schools? (*Vitale*) Yes, if they are of a rationalist character and nonclerical.
- Can devotional Bible reading and religious exercises be directed by public schools? (*Schempp*) No.
- Can public schools encourage and facilitate private prayer? (*Jaffree*) Yes, if they are of a rationalist character and nonclerical.
- Can public schools include prayers in graduation ceremonies or at extracurricular activities? (*Lee, Santa Fe*) Depends. No, if led by a member of the clergy; yes, if they are of a rationalist character and nonclerical.
- Can "under God" be included in public school recitations of the Pledge of Allegiance? (*Newdow*) Yes.
- Can public schools facilitate on-campus devotional religious instruction? (*McCollum*) No.
- Can public schools facilitate off-campus devotional religious instruction? (*Zorach*) No.

GOVERNMENT SUPPORT OF PRIVATE RELIGIOUS SCHOOLS

Parallel to the question of religion's presence in public schools is the issue of government support of private religious schools, the second type of Establishment Clause case we shall discuss. Catholic schools, in particular, have brought forth questions regarding whether taxpayer money can be used to support private religious education, and, if it can, with what limitations and restrictions. Since *Everson v. Board of Education* (1947), the Supreme Court repeatedly has faced the issue, without definitively resolving how such cases should be decided.

Everson involved a New Jersey statute that authorized local school districts to reimburse parents for costs incurred for transporting their children to public or nonprofit private schools. Pursuant to the law, the township of Ewing, New Jersey, authorized the reimbursement of transportation costs to parents who sent their children to either public or Catholic schools.[18] A five-member Court majority found the reimbursements constitutional, although all nine members of the Court agreed that the Establishment Clause erected a "wall of separation" between church and state.

Perhaps the most famous aid to religious schools case is *Lemon v. Kurtzman* (1971), a case that examined Rhode Island and Pennsylvania school aid policies. The Rhode Island statute in question provided a 15 percent salary supplement to nonpublic school teachers who taught courses that were equivalent to those offered in public schools. Teachers receiving the salary supplement could not teach religion courses and their schools had to have levels of per-pupil expenditures on secular education at or below the public school average. All 250 teachers who had received salary supplements by the time the case reached the Supreme Court taught at Roman Catholic schools. The Pennsylvania program in question authorized the state Superintendent of Public Instruction to "purchase" certain "secular educational services" from nonpublic schools. The state reimbursed private schools directly for teacher salaries, textbooks, and instructional materials for courses in mathematics, modern foreign languages, physical science, and physical education. "Purchased" textbooks and materials had to be approved by the school officials and no payment could be made for any course containing "any subject matter expressing religious teaching, or the morals or forms of

---

[18] The Court seems to have viewed the township's identification of public and Catholic schools as equivalent to identifying all the schools in the township. According to Justice Black's majority opinion, the case record did not indicate that there were any children in the township who attended or would have attended, but for want of transportation, any school but a public or Catholic school. *Everson v. Board of Education*, 330 U.S. 1, 5n.2 (1947). Comments Justice Black would later make in his dissenting opinion in *Board of Education v. Allen* (1968) support this finding. Commenting on his opinion in *Everson*, Justice Black said:

That law [in question in *Everson*] did not attempt to deny the benefit of its general terms to children of any faith going to any legally authorized school. Thus, it was treated in the same way as a general law paying the streetcar fare of all school children, or a law providing midday lunches for all children or all school children, or a law to provide police protection for children going to and from school, or general laws to provide police and fire protection for buildings, including, of course, churches and church school buildings as well as others. *Board of Education v. Allen*, 392 U.S. 236, 252 (1968).

worship of any sect."[19] Most of the educational services "purchased" were from Roman Catholic schools.

The Supreme Court struck down both the Rhode Island and the Pennsylvania programs, articulating the three-pronged "Lemon" test to do so. According to the test, for a state action to be constitutional: 1) it must have a secular legislative purpose, 2) its principal or primary effect must be one that neither advances nor inhibits religion, and 3) the state action must not foster an excessive government entanglement with religion. The Court found that both policies in question violated the test's "excessive entanglement" prong.

Lemon established the high water mark – perhaps we should say, the "high brick point" – in the strict separationist interpretation of the Establishment Clause. Under William Rehnquist, who became chief justice in 1986, the Court began chipping away at the "wall" in various ways. Toward the end of Chief Justice Rehnquist's tenure, the Court upheld different forms of state aid to religious schools. In *Mitchell v. Helms* (2000), a four-judge plurality modified *Lemon*, effectively eliminating independent "excessive entanglement" scrutiny, to uphold a federal program that allowed federal funds to flow to private religious schools.[20] Known as "Chapter 2," the federal government made funds available to state and local educational agencies for the acquisition and use of instructional educational materials, such as library services, maps, assessment tools, computer hardware and software, projection screens, and video cassette recorders. With "Chapter 2" funds, nonprofit private schools, including religiously affiliated schools, were eligible to acquire "services, materials and equipment" that were "secular, neutral, and nonideological."[21] In *Zelman v. Simmons-Harris* (2002), Chief Justice Rehnquist wrote a five-member majority opinion that upheld a Cleveland "school choice" program. The program provided parents a tuition voucher of up to $2,250 a year to be used at private schools, including religiously affiliated schools. Participating schools had to agree not to discriminate on the basis of race, religion, or ethnic background or to "advocate or foster unlawful behavior or teach hatred of any person or group on the basis of race, ethnicity, national origin, or religion."[22] Eligible schools also had to accept students using rules and procedures established by the state superintendent. In the program's five years of existence before reaching the Supreme Court, 96 percent of the

[19] *Lemon v. Kurtzman*, 403 U.S. 602, 610 (1971). The facts of the case are set forth in the Court's opinion on pages 602–03, 607–10.
[20] *Mitchell v. Helms*, 530 U.S. 793, 808–09 (2000).
[21] Ibid., 802.
[22] *Zelman v. Simmons-Harris*, 536 U.S. 639, 645 (2002).

3,700 students who received vouchers used them to attend religiously affiliated schools. In both *Mitchell* and *Zelman*, the Court majorities emphasized that the funds were directed to religious schools as a result of private choices and, therefore, that the programs reflected governmental neutrality toward religion.[23]

The legal questions presented in these cases and the Supreme Court's answers can be summarized as follows:

- Can the state pay the costs to transport children to private religious schools if it does the same for public school pupils? (*Everson*) Yes.
- Can the state supplement private religious schools' nonreligion teachers' salaries and "purchase" secular educational services from private religious schools? (*Lemon*) No.
- Can private religious schools participate in state programs that fund educational services, materials, and equipment that are secular, neutral, and nonideological? (*Mitchell*) Yes.
- Can private religious schools receive state-funded tuition vouchers provided to parents to send their children to private schools? (*Zelman*) Yes.

The Madisonian Approach to Government Support of Private Religious Schools

Madisonian noncognizance would prohibit the state from using religious affiliation as a criterion for either including or excluding an institution from state funding. Under Madison's rule, the state could not fund private schools because they are religious, but it also could not not fund schools on account of religious affiliation. The state would not be obliged to fund private schools, but if the state did fund private schools, it could not adopt eligibility standards that took cognizance of religion for inclusion or exclusion in the program.

Using Madison's rule, religious schools could have received the state aid offered in *Lemon*, *Mitchell*, and *Zelman*. In none of those cases did religious schools qualify for state funding on account of their religious affiliation. Even if a large percentage of state funding goes to Catholic schools, as was the case in *Lemon* and *Zelman*, the Constitution would not be breached as long as a school's religious identity remains incidental to eligibility for state support. The only constitutionally questionable aspect of

[23] *Mitchell v. Helms*, 530 U.S. 793, 830 (2000); *Zelman v. Simmons-Harris*, 536 U.S. 639, 662–63 (2002).

these programs from a Madisonian view would have been the regulations that explicitly prohibited state funds from supporting religious instruction. In *Lemon*, for example, Rhode Island teachers who received salary supplements for teaching public school equivalent classes could not teach religion classes. In the Pennsylvania program, state funds could not be used to purchase materials for use in courses containing "any subject matter expressing religious teaching, or the morals or forms of worship of any sect."[24] Such regulations would be unconstitutional under the Madisonian approach. Consistent with noncognizance, a state could constitutionally limit aid to support specific subjects – such as math, foreign language, or physical science – but it could not use religion as such as a category for exclusion. In *Lemon*, the state of Rhode Island trespassed noncognizance when it prohibited teachers who received state salary supplements from teaching religion classes, and Pennsylvania trespassed noncognizance when it prohibited the "purchase" of materials "expressing religious teachings."

Everson presents a minor but clear violation of the Madisonian approach in this regard. New Jersey law allowed local school districts to make rules and contracts for the transportation of children to and from public and nonprofit private schools. That provision would have been unproblematic under Madisonian noncognizance. The township of Ewing, however, authorized transportation reimbursement to parents of children who sent their children to public or Catholic schools. The identification of "Catholic" in the township's policy would have been a facial violation of Madisonian noncognizance. It appears that the transportation policy easily could have been made compatible with the rule with a slight adjustment. According to Justice Black's majority opinion, there was nothing in the record to suggest that there were any children in the township who attended any schools except public and Catholic schools.[25] The identification of "Catholic" schools in the township's policy, accordingly, does not seem to have indicated that the schools were eligible for transportation reimbursements because they were Catholic; rather, "Catholic" seems to have been used to designate all the township's nonpublic private schools. A change in the township's language, substituting "private" for "Catholic," would have made the policy compatible with the Madisonian approach and allowed the township's Catholic school students to still receive the transportation subsidy.

[24] *Lemon v. Kurtzman*, 403 U.S. 602, 610 (1971).
[25] *Everson v. Board of Education*, 330 U.S. 1, 5 (1947).

In summary, the Madisonian approach would answer government support of private religious school constitutional questions as follows:

- Can the state pay the costs to transport children to private religious schools if it does the same for public school pupils? (*Everson*) Yes, so long as religious schools are not funded on account of their religious affiliation.
- Can the state supplement private religious schools' nonreligion teachers' salaries and "purchase" secular educational services from private religious schools? (*Lemon*) Yes, and the state cannot explicitly prohibit the use of such funds for religious purposes as such.
- Can private religious schools participate in state programs that fund educational services, materials, and equipment that are secular, neutral, and nonideological? (*Mitchell*) Yes.
- Can private religious schools receive state-funded tuition vouchers provided to parents to send their children to private schools? (*Zelman*) Yes.

The Washingtonian Approach to Government Support of Private Religious Schools

The Washingtonian approach would evaluate state aid to private religious schools in light of Washington's belief that the cultivation of republican morality grounded on religious faith is a legitimate civic end of government. As Washington declared in his Farewell Address, "Of all the dispositions and habits which lead to political prosperity, Religion and morality are indispensable supports."[26] As long as religious education could be connected to the cultivation of moral characteristics consistent with republican political principles, state aid to religious schools could be considered to have a legitimate civic interest. The state-funded programs at issue in *Everson*, *Lemon*, *Mitchell*, and *Zelman* all could pass constitutional muster under these terms.

Each of these programs also might be defended in light of their advancement of a nonreligious secular purpose, but the Washingtonian approach would not require that. The Pennsylvania program struck down in *Lemon*, for example, was defended in the Pennsylvania legislature as a way to combat

---

[26] George Washington, Farewell Address, September 19, 1796, in *The Writings of George Washington*, ed. John C. Fitzpatrick (Washington, DC: United States Government Printing Office, 1940), 35:229.

the rising costs of private education.[27] The Washingtonian approach would not require the elaboration of "secular" purposes unrelated to religion. It would consider the nurturing of religious belief itself a legitimate civic purpose on the premise that most religious belief supports good citizenship. The transportation subsidy in *Everson*, to take another example, could be defended as a way to protect student safety – students arguably would be safer riding a bus rather than walking to school – but the Washingtonian approach could also justify the transportation subsidy in terms of the state's legitimate interest to nurture good citizenship supported by religious education. The programs at issue in *Mitchell* and *Zelman* could be defended in a similar manner.

While the Washingtonian approach would require programs of state funding of religious schools to be as ecumenical as possible, it would not necessarily require the state to support all religious education equally if it supported any religious education at all. Washington thought the state ought to encourage religion because he believed religious morality supported republican citizenship. If a religious school did not support good citizenship, the state would not be obligated to include it in a program funding religious schools. Under the Washingtonian approach, the state could discriminate among religions in light of their perceived contribution to the civic good. As we shall discuss in the Conclusion, Washingtonianism's tolerance of some religious discrimination distinguishes it from the nonpreferentialism championed by Justice Rehnquist.

In summary, the Washingtonian approach would answer government support of private religious school constitutional questions as follows:

- Can the state pay the costs to transport children to private religious schools if it does the same for public school pupils? (*Everson*) Yes.
- Can the state supplement private religious schools' nonreligion teachers' salaries and "purchase" secular educational services from private religious schools? (*Lemon*) Yes.
- Can private religious schools participate in state programs that fund educational services, materials, and equipment that are secular, neutral, and nonideological? (*Mitchell*) Yes.
- Can private religious schools receive state-funded tuition vouchers provided to parents to send their children to private schools? (*Zelman*) Yes.

---

[27] *Lemon v. Kurtzman*, 403 U.S. 602, 609 (1971).

The Jeffersonian Approach to Government Support of Private Religious Schools

Jefferson intended public education to replace the type of religious education that he believed suppressed intellectual and political freedom. Jeffersonianism, accordingly, would mandate that public education be civic and exclude all sectarianism. The approach would forbid tax dollars from funding any religious education that advanced clerical religious dogmas or clerical influence, including funding of Bible-based schools and devotional study of the Bible. Jeffersonianism, however, would not necessarily prohibit all state funding of religious education. As discussed regarding prayer in public schools, the key question for the Jeffersonian approach is whether state action advances the influence of religious clergy and nonrational religious dogmas. Taxpayer dollars could be used to support private religious schools that taught "rational" religion in the way that Jefferson designed it to be taught by a professor of ethics at the University of Virginia. As in the case with prayer in public schools, the Jeffersonian concern with distinguishing nonclerical from clerical religion might be approximated by distinguishing nonsectarian from sectarian religious education. Thus applied, the state could not aid sectarian private schools, including Bible-based schools.

Jefferson's intention to minimize clerical influence in education also suggests that the state should not fund nonreligious instruction that takes place in sectarian schools. Money, personnel, and equipment are fungible. While a math textbook might reasonably be expected to be used to support mathematical education, every math textbook the state buys for a sectarian school allows that school to save resources, resources that, in turn, can be directed toward sectarian education. If one takes a broad view of the dangers of sectarian education – which Jefferson himself certainly did – any and all government support of sectarian schools can be considered to advance the mission of religious schools and, therefore, to trespass Jefferson's doctrine.

The facts of *Everson, Lemon, Mitchell,* and *Zelman* help to further illustrate how Jeffersonian nonsectarianism might be applied in practice. In *Everson,* government funds were used to reimburse the transportation costs of parents who sent their children to public and Catholic schools. This made it less expensive for parents to send their children to Catholic schools, which would be an impermissible subsidization of sectarian education under the Jeffersonian view. The salary supplements and state "purchased" educational materials challenged in *Lemon* would be unconstitutional for the same reason. In the Rhode Island program, teachers receiving the salary supplement could not teach religion courses, but the teachers themselves could be religious. In a Catholic school, they might be a nun or a priest. A Jeffersonian approach would not allow state money to be used to fund instruction by members of the clergy.

It also would not allow state money to "purchase" nonreligious educational materials for sectarian schools, as was done in the Pennsylvania program. Even though the policy allowed only the "purchase" of materials for specific nonreligious subjects, the state aid freed school resources for sectarian uses. For the same reason, the "secular, neutral, and nonideological" materials that the Court allowed sectarian schools to obtain using state money in *Mitchell* also would not be allowed.

The school voucher program upheld in *Zelman* would be a clear violation of Jeffersonianism. The program used state funds to send children to sectarian schools with no limitations on the religious education children would receive. An overwhelming majority of the vouchers were used to fund a type of religious education that Jefferson thought was incompatible with religious freedom and, ultimately, with free political institutions.

In summary, the Jeffersonian approach would answer government support of private religious school constitutional questions as follows:

- Can the state pay the costs to transport children to private religious schools if it does the same for public school pupils? (*Everson*) No.
- Can the state supplement private religious schools' nonreligion teachers' salaries and "purchase" secular educational services from private religious schools? (*Lemon*) No.
- Can private religious schools participate in state programs that fund educational services, materials, and equipment that are secular, neutral, and nonideological? (*Mitchell*) No.
- Can private religious schools receive state-funded tuition vouchers provided to parents to send their children to private schools? (*Zelman*) No.

RELIGION IN THE PUBLIC SQUARE

A third type of Establishment Clause case involves the permissibility of various types of government support or recognition of religion in what is frequently called "the public square." A variety of cases fall into this category, including instances when taxpayer dollars are received by religiously based institutions or organizations and when a governmental entity sponsors or facilitates the creation of religiously themed public displays.

On one end of the public funding spectrum lies direct and exclusive state funding of religion. Nebraska's taxpayer-funded legislative chaplaincy, which was upheld by the Supreme Court in *Marsh v. Chambers* (1983), is an example of this type of program. The chaplain, whose functions included beginning each legislative session with a prayer, was selected biennially by an executive board of the Nebraska legislature. At the time of litigation, a Presbyterian minister, Robert E. Palmer, had served as chaplain for more than sixteen years at a salary of $319.75 per month for each month the legislature was in session.[28] A six-member Court majority found the chaplaincy constitutional, citing the history and tradition of legislative chaplaincies dating back to the American founding.[29]

Direct funding of religion as such is not common in modern constitutional litigation. More typically cases lie closer to the other end of the funding spectrum, where religious individuals or organizations receive (or seek to receive) governmental aid on the basis of nonreligious criteria. In *Rosenberger v. Rectors of the University of Virginia* (1995), students who published a Christian newspaper sued the public university to gain access to student activity funds. University policy authorized funds to pay outside contractors for the printing costs of student publications. Publications associated with "religious activities," however, were excluded from eligibility.[30] Following this rule, the university denied a Christian student group's funding request to publish its newspaper. According to the Court's record, the publication, *Wide Awake: A Christian Perspective*, sought "to challenge Christians to live, in word and deed, according to the faith they proclaim and to encourage students to consider what a personal relationship with Jesus Christ means."[31] A five-member Court majority ruled in favor of the Christian students under the Free Speech Clause, citing the government's obligation to be "viewpoint neutral" when regulating speech.[32] The four dissenting judges – Justices Stevens, Souter, Breyer, and Ginsburg – found the university's exclusion of religious groups from student activity funds to be required by the Establishment Clause.[33]

A similar issue also has come before the Court in cases that do not involve the distribution of taxpayer funds. In *Good News Club v. Milford Public School District* (2001), a Christian organization challenged a public school board community use policy. The policy allowed local residents

---

[28] *Marsh v. Chambers*, 463 U.S. 783, 784–85 (1983).
[29] Ibid., 786–92.
[30] The university defined "religious activity" as any activity that "primarily promotes or manifests a particular belie[f] in or about a deity or an ultimate reality." *Rosenberger v. University of Virginia*, 515 U.S. 819, 825 (1995).
[31] Ibid., 826.
[32] Ibid., 829.
[33] Ibid., 863–64.

to use school facilities for a variety of purposes – including "instruction in any branch of education, learning or the arts" and "social, civic and recreational meetings" – but prohibited uses for "religious purposes."[34] Following the policy, school district officials denied a use permit to a local Good News Club, a Christian organization that taught Bible verses to children ages six to twelve. The Supreme Court, citing its decision in *Rosenberger*, sided with the Christian group on free speech grounds.[35]

Another type of religion in the public square case involves religious displays on government property. These cases usually do not involve significant public expenditures and the displays themselves are often unremarkable. The cases, however, tend to receive significant attention because of their symbolic meaning and because many believe they represent how the Constitution should (or should not) allow state endorsement of religion. *Lynch v. Donnelly* (1984), one of the first significant display cases to reach the Supreme Court, involved a challenge to an annual Christmas display erected by the city of Pawtucket, Rhode Island. The display consisted of figures and decorations traditionally associated with Christmas, including a Santa Claus house, reindeer pulling Santa's sleigh, and a crèche depicting the birth of Jesus Christ. A five-member Court majority found the display constitutional because it met the requirements of the Lemon test.[36] In *County of Allegheny v. Greater Pittsburgh ACLU* (1989), the Court evaluated two recurring holiday displays located on public property in downtown Pittsburgh, a crèche placed on the Grand Staircase of the Allegheny County Courthouse, and an eighteen-foot Chanukah menorah placed just outside the City-County Building next to a forty-five–foot decorated Christmas tree. A divided Court ruled the crèche display unconstitutional but the menorah display constitutional. The context of the former was found to endorse Christianity. The menorah display, however, did not endorse religion, according to the Court, because it did not contain exclusively religious content.[37] The Court also reached a split decision in 2005 when it evaluated the constitutionality of public postings of the Ten Commandments. Different five-member majorities ruled displays of the Ten Commandments posted in two Kentucky county courthouses unconstitutional (*McCreary County v. American Civil Liberties Union of Kentucky*) but found constitutional a Ten Commandments monument on the grounds

---

[34] *Good News Club v. Milford Central School District*, 533 U.S. 98, 102–03 (2001).
[35] Ibid., 111–12.
[36] *Lynch v. Donnelly*, 465 U.S. 668 (1984).
[37] *County of Allegheny v. Greater Pittsburgh ACLU*, 492 U.S. 573, 621 (1989).

of the Texas State Capitol (*Van Orden v. Perry*). Justice Stephen Breyer, who was the fifth vote in both cases, found that the Kentucky courthouse displays caused political divisiveness along religious lines, whereas the Texas Ten Commandments monument did not.[38]

The legal questions presented in these cases and the Supreme Court's answers can be summarized as follows:

- Can the state fund legislative chaplains? (*Marsh*) Yes.
- Can the state exclude religious college students/groups from receiving state funds if the students are eligible for those funds on the basis of nonreligious criteria? (*Rosenberger*) No.
- Can the state exclude religious groups from using public facilities open to nonreligious groups? (*Good News Club*) No.
- Can the state erect religious holiday displays? (*Lynch*, *Allegheny*) Depends on if they endorse religion.
- Can the state post the Ten Commandments? (*McCreary*, *Van Orden*) Depends on divisiveness.

The Madisonian Approach to Government Support of Religion in the Public Square

The principle of noncognizance prohibits the state from singling out religious institutions or individuals for legal benefits or legal disabilities. The Nebraska taxpayer-funded legislative chaplaincy upheld by the Supreme Court in *Marsh* v. *Chambers* exemplifies an impermissible privilege. Nebraska became cognizant of religion in two ways: It hired an employee on the basis of religious affiliation – a prerequisite for the chaplain position, no doubt, was that one was a religious minister – and it employed an individual specifically to conduct a religious exercise, opening each legislative session with prayer.

Rosenberger and *Good News Club* are examples of impermissible religious discrimination under Madison noncognizance. In *Rosenberger*, the

---

[38] In *McCreary County v. American, Civil Liberties Union*, 545 U.S. 844 (2005), Justice Breyer signed on to Justice Souter's majority opinion, which emphasized divisiveness in explaining the Establishment Clause violation committed. In *Van Orden v. Perry*, 545 U.S. 677 (2005), Justice Breyer wrote his opinion explaining how divisiveness did not lead to a constitutional violation in that case. For further discussion of these cases, see Vincent Phillip Muñoz, "Thou Shall Not Post the Ten Commandments? *McCreary*, *Van Orden*, and the Future of Religious Display Jurisprudence," *Texas Review of Law and Politics* 10 (2003): 357–400.

Christian student group was excluded from receiving an otherwise available subsidy on account of the religious content of its publication. In *Good News Club*, religious groups were explicitly excluded from using public school facilities after school hours solely because they sought to use them for religious purposes. Public universities and school districts need not subsidize student periodicals or open facilities to community groups, but if they do, under Madisonianism they cannot exclude religious groups on account of their religious character.

State-sponsored religious displays also would be impermissible under Madisonian noncognizance, although whether any given display is religious is not always a straightforward question. The Madison approach would allow religious material to be a part of a nonreligious display if it was included for a nonreligious purpose. George Washington's Bible, for example, could be included in a historical display depicting the life of Washington because it would serve historical and educational purposes. The determinative question for any public display under the Madisonian doctrine would be, Does the display take cognizance of religion as such? The answer in any given case would seem to depend on a display's context.

Displays that celebrate a religious holy day with corresponding religious symbols would seem to be religious by definition and, therefore, be impermissible. The crèche at issue in *Allegheny County*, which was placed in the county courthouse during the Christmas season, would be an example. "Holiday" displays set up during Christmas that feature a mixture of religious and nonreligious symbolism would seem to be less religious. However, the fact that they are set up in conjunction with a religious holy day would seem to indicate their religious character and, thus, their unconstitutionality. The Christmas display upheld by the Court in *Lynch v. Donnelly* – which contained a Santa Claus, reindeer, and a crèche – and the Chanukah menorah in *Allegheny County* placed next to a Christmas tree would be examples of this type of unconstitutional display.

The displays of the Ten Commandments at issue in *McCreary County* and *Van Orden* are similar to the phrase "under God" in the Pledge of Allegiance. The displays could be considered to be religious and, thus, fail Madisonian noncognizance. Alternatively, the displays might be considered historical or educational. Such an interpretation would not deny that the Ten Commandments are religious but would find that the reason for their posting was not religious but rather related to history or education. Madisonian noncognizance does not provide one uniform answer to the question of whether any particular display of the Ten Commandments is most properly viewed to be religious or historical/educational. To suggest that it does would be to ask more of the approach than it can deliver. As discussed with regard to "under God" in the Pledge of Allegiance, at most Madisonianism can dictate the line of legal inquiry by which to assess the facts of Ten Commandments and other similar displays. If an evaluation of the context of the displays reveals them to take cognizance of religion as such, then they would be unconstitutional.

With that reservation noted, a Madisonian analysis of the generating history and the stated purpose of the displays of the Ten Commandments evaluated in *McCreary County* reveal initial state cognizance of religion but then a movement away from such cognizance. The Kentucky counties initially posted a large, gold-framed copy of the Ten Commandments alone, and they seemed to do so for religious reasons.[39] That display was dismantled and, after an intervening display was set up and taken down, a third display was erected in which the Ten Commandments was one of nine documents posted. The third display, titled "The Foundation of Law and Government Display," included both religious and nonreligious documents and had a purportedly educational purpose. If the Kentucky counties' litigation position was found to be true – that the third display was not intended to be religious in nature – it would pass Madisonian scrutiny. The unique generating history of the display, however, makes the true nature of the display difficult to determine.

The Ten Commandments monument at issue in *Van Orden v. Perry* had a much more straightforward history. The monument was donated by a civic group and was one of seventeen monuments and twenty-one historical markers on the capital grounds that commemorated the "people, ideals, and events that compose Texan identity."[40] Given this context, Texas arguably did not take cognizance of religion when it accepted and displayed the monument.

But even if the third display of the Ten Commandments in *McCreary* or the Ten Commandments monument in *Van Orden* were found to be constitutional, not all displays of the Ten Commandments would be allowed under the rule of noncognizance. Context matters for the Madisonian approach. Governmental displays that aim to recognize religion as such would be impermissible.

In summary, the Madisonian approach would answer religion in the public square cases as follows:

---

[39] For further discussion of the particular facts in *McCreary County* and *Van Orden*, see Muñoz, "Thou Shall Not Post the Ten Commandments?," 360–63.
[40] H.R. 38, 77th Leg. (Texas 2001), cited in *Van Orden v. Perry*, 545 U.S. 677, 681 (2005).

- Can the state fund legislative chaplains? (*Marsh*) No.
- Can the state exclude religious college students/groups from receiving state funds if the students are eligible for those funds on the basis of nonreligious criteria? (*Rosenberger*) No.
- Can the state exclude religious groups from using public facilities open to nonreligious groups? (*Good News Club*) No.
- Can the state erect religious holiday displays? (*Lynch*, *Allegheny*) Depends on context, but not in the cases discussed.
- Can the state post the Ten Commandments? (*McCreary*, *Van Orden*) Depends on context.

The Washingtonian Approach to Government Support of Religion in the Public Square

As was the case with religion in public schools, a Washingtonian approach would allow the state to support religion in the public square on the grounds that the cultivation of moral character is a legitimate end of government. The approach would impose only two limitations: that government support of religion be as ecumenical as possible given the purposes of the state action, and that government support of religion not compel an individual to practice a religion in which he or she does not believe.

The state-funded chaplaincy for the Nebraska legislature could be defended on the same grounds that Washington defended military chaplains – religious belief and practice might encourage public officials to fulfill their civic duties better. The Washingtonian approach would scrutinize the specifics of any particular chaplaincy to ensure that it was as ecumenical as necessary. Following Washington's handling of military chaplains, chaplains ought to be available to minister to all members of the legislature, whatever their faith. As long as this ecumenical consideration was met, state-funded chaplaincies would be constitutional.

A legitimate concern to nurture moral character and good citizenship would also justify the state support for student religious periodicals in *Rosenberger* and the religious uses of public facilities at issue in *Good News Club*. To be sufficiently ecumenical, the state programs would need to be available to all religious groups, with the caveat that the Washington approach also would tolerate the noninclusion of those whose beliefs or actions were viewed to be incompatible with the civic ends being pursued by the policy. These cases do not involve coercion because the religious groups in question chose to participate in the programs of public funding.

The cultivation of moral character also could sustain the religious displays at issue in *Lynch*, *Allegheny*, *McCreary*, and *Van Orden*. The passive nature of the displays would eliminate all possible concerns about religious coercion. The displays might be scrutinized, however, to ensure that they comply with the Washingtonian demand of requisite ecumenicalism. Unlike the Jeffersonian approach, the Washingtonian approach would not impose a rule of strict nonsectarianism. It would counsel that displays reflect, as much as possible, the beliefs of the local community or, given the purposes of the display, the civic end being advanced. Christmas or Chanukah displays like the ones challenged in *Lynch* and *Allegheny* could contain exclusively Christian and Jewish symbolism given that their purposes are to celebrate specific religious holidays. Displays of the Ten Commandments, if they are judged by local officials to reflect local religious sentiment, also could be upheld.

In summary, the Washingtonian approach would answer religion in the public square cases as follows:

- Can the state fund legislative chaplains? (*Marsh*) Yes.
- Can the state exclude religious college students/groups from receiving state funds if the students are eligible for those funds on the basis of nonreligious criteria? (*Rosenberger*) No.
- Can the state exclude religious groups from using public facilities open to nonreligious groups? (*Good News Club*) No.
- Can the state erect religious holiday displays? (*Lynch*, *Allegheny*) Yes.
- Can the state post the Ten Commandments? (*McCreary*, *Van Orden*) Yes.

The Jeffersonian Approach to Government Support of Religion in the Public Square

A Jeffersonian approach to religion in the public square would focus on the content of the religious material in question. Similar to prayer in public school cases and public aid to private school cases, vigorous nonsectarianism might be used to implement the Jeffersonian rule. Religion in the public square would not be unconstitutional per se, but state-sponsored sectarianism would be impermissible.

A Jeffersonian approach would clearly prohibit the legislative chaplaincy upheld by the Court in *Marsh v. Chambers*. Jefferson thought the establishment of religious freedom required overcoming clerical influence in American society and politics. A state-funded legislative chaplain stands directly opposed to the Jeffersonian project. Unlike prayer, moreover, a chaplain cannot easily be made nonsectarian. By definition, a minister is a minister of a particular religion and, therefore, a chaplaincy with a single minister would necessarily give the impression of favoring the chaplain's own denomination. Periodic rotation among chaplains of different denominations or the employment of multiple chaplains would not resolve the problem for the same reason discussed regarding minister-led prayers in public schools. A multiplicity of sectarian appointments is not nonsectarian but, rather, multiple instances of sectarianism.

For similar reasons, a Jeffersonian approach would not allow state funding of sectarian student publications or the use of state facilities by sectarian organizations even if the state-funded nonsectarian publications or state facilities were used by nonsectarian groups. Jeffersonianism does not require the state to treat sectarian groups equally to nonsectarian organizations. The approach aims not at equality but rather to suppress the ideas, institutions, and clerical authority associated with sectarianism. In *Rosenberger* and *Good News Club*, accordingly, the Jeffersonian approach would have reached different conclusions than the Court and ruled against the religious litigants.

Religious display cases also would be adjudicated with a view toward prohibiting state-sponsored sectarianism. In practice, this would mean that most, though not necessarily all, religious displays would fail Jeffersonian scrutiny. Religious displays are more similar to chaplains and less similar to prayers insofar as it is easier to compose a nonsectarian prayer than to construct a nonsectarian religious display or nonsectarian chaplaincy. No commonly accepted symbols exist to represent "almighty God" or "the Creator," language that can be used to compose nonsectarian prayers that reflect Jeffersonian "rational" religion. Communities might attempt to erect inclusive displays by including multiple symbols from different religions, but this does not create a nonsectarian display as much as it does a multisectarian display – a sectarian symbol does not cease to be sectarian simply because it is placed next to another sectarian symbol. Even symbols that are not inherently religious, such as a tree for Christmas or a bunny for Easter, arguably can acquire sectarian meaning to the extent that they are exclusively associated with a sectarian religious celebration – a Christmas tree is a *Christmas* tree, an Easter bunny is an *Easter* bunny. A strict application of Jeffersonian nonsectarianism would prohibit any state-sponsored display from containing sectarian symbolism. Admittedly, the precise point at which any particular display becomes sectarian is not one that the Jeffersonian approach itself determines. A blanket prohibition against all sectarian symbols, however, might be the most effective rule to accomplish the Jeffersonian end of minimizing clerical influence in

American society. Thus interpreted, the crèche in the *Lynch v. Donnelly* Christmas display and the crèche and menorah in the *Allegheny* displays would be unconstitutional under the Jeffersonian approach as these symbols are clearly sectarian.

The displays of the Ten Commandments in *McCreary* and *Van Orden* would also be unconstitutional. The Ten Commandments do not belong to one religion alone, but their display necessarily becomes sectarian if the text is written out, as was the case in both displays. Catholics on the one hand and Jews and Protestants on the other count the commandments differently, which makes drafting a nonsectarian version impossible. A display that left out the text and included only two tablets with Roman numerals counting to ten, however, could be constitutional. A nontextual display could be considered a nonsectarian representation of divine law reflecting the idea of a providential god, a type of religious belief that the Jeffersonian approach allows the state to endorse.

In summary, the Jeffersonian approach would answer religion in the public square questions as follows:

- Can the state fund legislative chaplains? (*Marsh*) No.
- Can the state exclude religious college students/groups from receiving state funds if the students are eligible for those funds on the basis of nonreligious criteria? (*Rosenberger*) Yes.
- Can the state exclude religious groups from using public facilities open to nonreligious groups? (*Good News Club*) Yes.
- Can the state erect religious holiday displays? (*Lynch*, *Allegheny*) No.
- Can the state post the Ten Commandments? (*McCreary*, *Van Orden*) No, if the text is included.

The Founders and the Establishment Clause

The tables that follow summarize the jurisprudential results for the Establishment Clause cases discussed in this chapter.

For Tables EC 2, EC 3, and EC 4, an "X" in the left-hand side of the column under each case indicates a vote to uphold the state action in question. In *Vitale*, for example, Jefferson's and Washington's doctrines would have found the prayer in question constitutional, whereas the Madisonian doctrine would have agreed with the Supreme Court and struck down the prayer at issue.

TABLE EC 1. *Establishment Clause Results*

	Supreme Court	Madison	Washington	Jefferson
Religion in Public Schools				
Can state-composed, teacher-led prayers be recited in public schools?	No	No	Yes	Yes*
Can devotional Bible reading and religious exercises be directed by public schools? (*Schempp*)	No	No	Yes	No
Can public schools encourage and facilitate private prayer? (*Jaffree*)	No	No	Yes	Yes*
Can public schools include prayers in graduation ceremonies or at extracurricular activities? (*Lee, Santa Fe*)	No	No	Yes	Depends
Can "under God" be included in public school recitations of the Pledge of Allegiance? (*Newdow*)	Not decided	Unclear	Yes	Yes
Can public schools facilitate on-campus devotional religious instruction? (*McCollum*)	No	No	Yes	No
Can public schools facilitate off-campus devotional religious instruction? (*Zorach*)	Yes	No	Yes	No
Government Support of Private Religious Schools				
Can the state pay the costs to transport children to private religious schools if it does the same for public school pupils? (*Everson*)	Yes	Yes**	Yes	No
Can the state supplement private religious schools' nonreligion teachers' salaries and "purchase" secular educational services from private religious schools? (*Lemon*)	No	Yes	Yes	No

continued

TABLE EC 1 *(continued)*

	Supreme Court	Madison	Washington	Jefferson
Can private religious schools participate in state programs that fund educational services, materials, and equipment that are secular, neutral, and nonideological? (*Mitchell*)	Yes	Yes	Yes	No
Can private religious schools receive state-funded tuition vouchers provided to parents to send their children to private schools? (*Zelman*)	Yes	Yes	Yes	No
Religion in the Public Square				
Can the state fund legislative chaplains? (*Marsh*)	Yes	No	Yes	No
Can the state exclude religious college students/ groups from receiving state funds if the students are eligible for those funds on the basis of nonreligious criteria? (*Rosenberger*)	No	No	No	Yes
Can the state exclude religious groups from using public facilities open to nonreligious groups? (*Good News Club*)	No	No	No	Yes
Can the state erect religious holiday displays? (*Lynch, Allegheny*)	Depends	No	Yes	No
Can the state post the Ten Commandments? (*McCreary, Van Orden*)	Depends	Unclear	Yes	No

* For Jeffersonian approval of prayer in public schools, the prayers must accord with Jeffersonian rationalism, be nonsectarian, and not increase the influence of religious clergy.

** Madisonian approval of state funding of private religious education requires that the private institutions qualify for state aid based on nonreligious criteria.

Table EC 6 presents the ratio of cases decided in favor of the religious litigants for the nineteen cases discussed in this chapter. Because the Supreme Court decided *Newdow* on standing grounds, it rendered decisions on the

TABLE EC 2. *Religion in Public Schools*

	Vitale	Schempp	Jaffree	Lee	Santa Fe	Newdow*	McCollum	Zorach
Supreme Court	X	X	X	X	X	?	X	X
Madison	X	X	X	X	X	?	X	X
Washington	X	X	X		X	X	X	X
Jefferson	X	X	X	X	X	X	X	X

* Madisonianism does not render a clear decision in *Newdow*. The Supreme Court decided *Newdow* on standing grounds and did not render a decision on the merits of the Establishment Clause challenge at issue.

TABLE EC 3. *Government Aid to Private Religious Schools*

	Everson		Lemon		Mitchell		Zelman	
Supreme Court	X			X	X		X	
Madison*	X		X		X		X	
Washington	X		X		X		X	
Jefferson		X		X		X		X

* In *Everson*, the Madisonian approach would have required that the transportation policy refer to "private schools" instead of "Catholic" schools. In *Lemon*, the Madisonian approach would have upheld the funding of religious schools but not restrictions attached to that funding that took cognizance of religion.

merits in only eighteen of the Establishment Clause cases discussed, deciding in favor of the religious litigants in nine-and-a-half of those cases. The half decision refers to *Allegheny*, in which the Supreme Court upheld only one of the two religious displays it scrutinized. The Madisonian approach would have ruled in favor of the religious litigants in at least six of the cases discussed. For the reasons discussed previously, Madisonianism does not render a definitive decision in *Newdow*, *McCreary*, and *Van Orden*, which is why the Madisonian ratio has a denominator of sixteen cases. If "under God" and public postings of the Ten Commandments were judged not to take cognizance of religion, the Madisonian approach would uphold nine of the nineteen cases examined. In no case, with the possible exception of *Newdow*, would the approaches of all three Founders have reached a unanimous result.[41]

Washingtonianism Would Favor Religion the Most, Jeffersonianism the Least

Perhaps the most striking finding revealed in Tables EC 1 and EC 6 is that the Washingtonian approach would have favored the religious litigants in every case involving public support to religion, whereas Jeffersonianism would have favored religion in only four of those nineteen cases. These ratios point to our first notable finding about the Founders' differences, namely that the Washingtonian approach would allow the most governmental support of religion and the Jeffersonian approach would allow the least.

Washington viewed religion far more positively than did Jefferson. The Washingtonian approach presumes that most religions will further civic interests and it allows the state to utilize religion to further civic interests.

---

[41] If an application of the Madisonian approach were to find "under God" to remain non-cognizant of religion, all three approaches would uphold "under God" in public school recitations of the Pledge of Allegiance.

TABLE EC 4. *Religion in the Public Square*

	Marsh	Rosenberger	Good News Club	Lynch	Allegheny*	McCreary	VanOrden
Supreme Court	X		X	X	X X	X	X
Madison**	X	X	X		X	?	?
Washington	X	X	X	X	X	X	X
Jefferson	X	X	X	X	X	X	X

* In *Allegheny*, the Court upheld one holiday display but struck down another.
** Madisonianism does not render a clear decision in *McCreary* or *Van Orden*.

TABLE EC 5. *Ratio of Agreement between the Founders*

	Madison and Washington	Madison and Jefferson	Washington and Jefferson
Religion in public schools	0/7	4/7	4/8
Government aid to private religious schools	4/4	0/4	0/4
Religion in the public square	2/5	3/5	0/7
Ratio of agreement*	6/16	7/16	4/19

* Because Madisonianism does not render a clear decision in *Newdow, McCreary,* and *Van Orden,* only sixteen cases are available from cross comparison for Madison with Washington and Jefferson.

TABLE EC 6. *Ratio of Establishment Clause Cases Decided in Favor of Religious Litigants*

	Supreme Court	Madison	Washington	Jefferson
Religion in public schools	1/7	0/7	8/8	4/8
Government aid to private religious schools	3/4	4/4	4/4	0/4
Religion in the public square*	5.5/7	2/5	7/7	0/7
Decisions in favor of religious litigants	9.5/18	6/16	19/19	4/19

* In *Rosenberger* and *Good News Club,* a vote against the state action is counted as a vote for the religious litigants.

It does not forbid governmental entanglement with religion, and it permits church and state to become interdependent if such a relationship furthers civic interests. Because it presumes that most state endorsements of religion will further civic interests, Washingtonianism is jurisprudentially deferential to legislatures and their findings of how and when religion might support civic ends. As discussed in Chapter 2, the only limitations Washingtonianism places on governmental support of religion is that the support be as ecumenical as possible given the civic purposes of the state action in question and that the state not judge the truth or falsity of a religion as such.

Jeffersonianism, by contrast, aims to suppress clerical religious influence and, therefore, takes an antagonistic view toward state advancement of most (though not all) religion. It does not allow the state to use religion to further civic purposes if by doing so the state would augment the influence of religious clergy or clerical theological dogmas. The approach, accordingly, does not allow the state to fund religious instruction in public schools by members of the clergy (e.g., *McCollum*) or the state to fund sectarian private schools (e.g., *Zelman*). Jeffersonianism only allows the state to endorse religious beliefs compatible with Jefferson's own version of rationalized and demystified Christianity, such as the nondenominational Regents prayer in *Engle v. Vitale* and "under God" in the Pledge of Allegiance (*Newdow*). Whereas the Washingtonian approach emphasizes how religion can contribute to the civic good, the Jeffersonian approach is attentive to how religion can threaten individual and political freedom. While not completely hostile toward all religious sentiments, Jeffersonianism sees a basic incompatibility between liberal democratic political principles and the structures and beliefs of ecclesiastical religions.

Madison Would Prevent the State from Engaging Religion Directly

The Madisonian approach is different from both the Washingtonian and Jeffersonian approaches insofar as it is not primarily concerned with the purposes or effects of state support of religion. Whereas Washingtonianism encourages a cooperative relationship between church and state by allowing the state to employ religion for civic purposes and Jeffersonianism develops an antagonistic relationship between church and state by placing the state in a hostile position toward certain religious beliefs and institutions, Madisonianism attempts to prohibit an unfiltered relationship between church and state. Madisonian noncognizance prevents the state from making religion an object of direct state concern.

Establishment Clause cases that pass Madisonian scrutiny involve instances when religious schools or groups participate in state programs on the basis of a nonreligious criterion. In *Rosenberger*, for example, the Madisonian approach would have allowed tax dollars to fund a religious periodical because the University of Virginia had a policy of funding a wide variety of school publications and the religious periodical qualified for funding on the basis of nonreligious criteria. Unlike the Jeffersonian view, the Madisonian approach does not require – and in fact would prevent – the state from excluding religion from programs of taxpayer funding on account of the danger of increasing clerical influence.

Madison's difference from Washington can be seen in the ten cases that Madisonianism would have struck down, including all the religion in public school cases. Unlike Washingtonianism, Madisonianism does not allow the state to become cognizant of religion even if doing so serves otherwise legitimate civic interests. Political utility for Madison is not the primary measure of constitutional validity.

The Jeffersonian and Madisonian Approaches Would Often Lead to Different Results

Since *Everson v. Board of Education* (1947), Jefferson's and Madison's church-state positions often have been thought to be the same. As Table EC 5 indicates, however, in only seven of the sixteen cases discussed would the Jeffersonian and Madisonian positions clearly reach the same results. Jeffersonianism actually would be more lenient than Madisonianism regarding religion in public schools. The Jeffersonian approach allows the state to encourage religious tenets similar to Jefferson's own version of rational Christianity and therefore would allow prayers like the ones at issue in *Vitale, Jaffree,* and *Santa Fe*; Madisonianism, by contrast, does not allow the state to encourage any religious beliefs as such directly and therefore does not allow any form of state-directed prayer in public schools.

Madisonianism would be more lenient than Jeffersonianism, however, regarding state actions that provide support to private religious schools and toward the presence of religion in the public square. The Jeffersonian concern to prevent clerical influence leads that approach to prohibit sectarian schools from participating in programs of general funding or availability. It treats clerical institutions and individuals unequally. Madisonian noncognizance is different. It prohibits the state from excluding sectarian schools from generally available programs on account of their religious character. More than Jeffersonianism, Madisonianism prohibits the state from treating religion unfavorably. In cases such as *Zelman* and *Good News Club*, for example, the Jeffersonian approach would exclude religious institutions from participating in programs of general applicability on account of the potential for state advancement of clerical influence, while Madisonian noncognizance would forbid the state from excluding religion from such programs, regardless of the degree to which religious interests were advanced.

Madison's, Washington's, and Jefferson's Legal Doctrines would Lead to Different Results for Establishment Clause Cases

Even with their significant differences, Madisonianism and Jeffersonianism appear to stand in greater agreement with one another (seven out of the sixteen cases we discussed) than either approach does with Washingtonianism. Madisonianism and Washingtonianism would reach the same result in only six of the sixteen cases. Jeffersonianism and Washingtonianism, as discussed previously, would reach the same result in only four of the nineteen cases discussed.[42] As displayed in Tables EC 1, EC 2, and EC 5, Madisonian noncognizance would reach a different result from the Washingtonian doctrine in every prayer in public school case: Madisonianism would find all the prayers unconstitutional, whereas Washingtonianism would allow them all. Jeffersonianism would agree with Washingtonianism in four of the prayer in public school cases, but in every other Establishment Clause case discussed, these two Founders' doctrines would lead to divergent results.

In Chapter 7 we will compare the results of the Madisonian, Washingtonian, and Jeffersonian approaches with the results reached by the Supreme Court. We will also compare the Founders' projected votes with the actual votes of prominent twentieth-century Supreme Court justices. For now, we can summarize what the foregoing discussion should have made obvious. When we apply the Founders to actual constitutional cases, we see that their different understandings of the right to religious liberty produce different kinds of Establishment Clause jurisprudence. The Founders' competing doctrinal tests would require judges to engage in divergent kinds of legal inquiry to resolve cases. They also would produce different results for questions pertaining to religion in public schools, government support for private religious schools, and the presence of religion in the "public square." Washingtonianism would most favor religion and allow the state to create an interdependent relationship between church and state if doing so furthered civic interests. Jeffersonianism would favor religion the least and erect an antagonistic relationship between certain types of religion and state power. Madisonianism would attempt to sever any type of direct relationship between church and state. It would deny religion state funding in instances where Washingtonianism would allow it, but allow religious participation in general state programs that Jeffersonianism would prohibit.

[42] If the Madisonian approach was interpreted to find "under God" constitutional in *Newdow* and to find the Ten Commandments postings in *McCreary* and *Van Orden* constitutional, then it would be more in agreement with Washingtonianism (9/19) than Jeffersonianism (7/19).

6

Madison, Washington, Jefferson, and the Free Exercise Clause

The previous chapter applied the Founders' legal doctrines to a sample of cases arising under the Establishment Clause. This chapter does the same for the Free Exercise Clause.

Similarly to Establishment Clause jurisprudence, no generally recognized taxonomy exists for Free Exercise cases.[1] For the purposes of our analysis, free exercise cases can be grouped into three general categories:

1. Direct burdens on religious exercise.
2. Indirect burdens on religious exercise, including obligations of citizenship that conflict with religious precepts and state actions that disparately impact religious individuals or religious organizations.
3. Identification of religion for regulation or preferential exemptions.

Direct burden cases include the criminalization of religious practices as such and the imposition of civil disabilities on religious individuals on account of their religion or religious beliefs. They are distinguishable from indirect burden cases in that the former involve state actions that specify or target religion whereas the latter involve state actions that do not specify religion but incidentally affect it through generally applicable statutes or regulations. To make a Catholic mass illegal is an example of a direct burden; a generally applicable building code that limits the construction size

---

[1] Many scholars discuss the Court's free exercise jurisprudence historically, which has the advantage of highlighting the Court's development of doctrine. It has the disadvantage, however, of obscuring the different categories of legal questions posed. An excellent historical discussion is offered by Henry J. Abraham and Barbara A. Perry, *Freedom and the Court: Civil Rights and Liberties in the United States*, 7th edition (New York: Oxford University Press, 1998), 235–65.

of a new Catholic church is an indirect burden. Identification cases are similar to direct burden cases insofar as they involve state action that identifies religion; but, unlike direct burden cases, identification cases involve policies that use religion as a basis for regulatory classification or privilege. Building regulations that regulate houses of worship as such or regulations that exempt houses of worship from generally applicable rules are examples of identification cases.

These three categories may not cover every conceivable free exercise controversy, but dividing free exercise cases in this way facilitates the application of the Founders' doctrines to the vast majority of contemporary free exercise constitutional issues. Following the pattern of the previous chapter, the relevant facts of a handful of actual Supreme Court cases are presented for each type of Free Exercise Clause case, and then how the Founders' different doctrines would adjudicate those cases is discussed. The chapter includes tables presenting these outcomes and a discussion of the similarities and differences between the Founders' approaches to the Free Exercise Clause.

DIRECT BURDENS ON RELIGIOUS EXERCISE

Direct burden cases can be subdivided into two general categories: the criminalization of religion and the deprivation of otherwise available rights and privileges on account of religion.

The criminalization of religious practices and beliefs has been relatively rare in the United States, but it is not unheard of. In 1993, the Supreme Court evaluated the constitutionality of a Florida city's attempt to outlaw the animal sacrifice practices of Santeria, an Afro-Caribbean–based religion dating back to the nineteenth century. After Santeria practitioners leased land and announced plans to establish a house of worship, school, and museum in Hialeah, Florida, members of the Hialeah City Council passed three ordinances regulating and banishing religious animal sacrifice.[2] In *Church of the Lukumi Babalu Aye v. City of Hialeah* (1993), a unanimous Supreme Court struck down the ordinances for their lack of neutrality and lack of general applicability. The Court noted that city's resolutions and ordinances used the words "sacrifice" and "ritual" and that they were gerrymandered in such a way to proscribe religious killings of animals by

---

[2] The Hialeah City Council's three ordinances can be found in David M. O'Brien, *Animal Sacrifice and Religious Freedom: Church of the Lukumi Babalu Aye v. City of Hialeah* (Lawrence: University of Kansas Press, 2004), 163–68.

Santeria church members but to allow almost all other animal killings.[3] Assuming the accuracy of the Supreme Court's factual finding "that Santeria alone was the exclusive legislative concern" of the Hialeah City Council, the case presents an example of the criminalization of religious practice as such.[4]

A deprivation of rights case reached the Supreme Court in *McDaniel v. Paty* (1978). The case involved a Tennessee constitutional provision that excluded "Ministers of the Gospel or priests of any denomination whatever" from eligibility for state legislative office.[5] The Tennessee legislature applied the exclusion to candidates for delegates to the state's 1977 constitutional convention. The Tennessee Supreme Court subsequently found Paul McDaniel, an ordained Baptist minister, ineligible for the delegate position to which he had been elected. The Tennessee Supreme Court accepted the state's argument that no actual burden on religious freedom had been imposed because the state did not prohibit the minister from exercising his religion or from serving as a delegate. It only prohibited him from doing both at the same time. The Court also found that the minister exclusion provision was rationally related to the state's legitimate interest in maintaining the separation of church and state.[6] A unanimous United States Supreme Court decision overturned the Tennessee Supreme Court's ruling, although four separate opinions were written to explain why Tennessee violated the First Amendment.[7]

McDaniel brought forth the specific question of whether religion can be used legitimately as an eligibility requirement for public office. A more general version of the same question is whether the state can use a religiously

---

[3] *Church of the Lukumi Babalu Aye v. City of Hialeah*, 508 U.S. 520, 534–36 (1993).

[4] Ibid., 534–36. The district court interpreted the ordinances differently, upholding them, in part, because it found that the Hialeah City Council did not aim to exclude Santeria from the city but rather to end all animal sacrifice practices, regardless of the reasons that motivated them. The district court's ruling is summarized by the Supreme Court in *Church of the Lukumi Babalu Aye v. City of Hialeah*, 508 U.S. 520, 529–30. See also O'Brien, *Animal Sacrifice and Religious Freedom*, 74–93. For a critical evaluation of the Supreme Court's factual findings in the case, see Lino Graglia, "Church of the Lukumi Aye: Of Animal Sacrifice and Religious Persecution," *Georgetown Law Journal* 85 (November 1996): 1–69.

[5] The Tennessee Constitution stated:

Whereas Ministers of the Gospel are by their profession, dedicated to God and the care of Souls, and ought not to be diverted from the great duties of their functions; therefore, no Minister of the Gospel, or priest of any denomination whatever, shall be eligible to a seat in either House of the Legislature.

Tennessee Constitution, Article VIII, §1 (1796).

[6] *Paty v. McDaniel*, 547 S.W. 2d 897, 903, 905 (1977).

[7] *McDaniel v. Paty*, 435 U.S. 618 (1978).

based classification to disadvantage individuals. Can the state, for example, deprive religious individuals of a civil right or an otherwise available privilege on account of religious beliefs, practices, or pursuits? The Supreme Court addressed the question in *Locke v. Davey* (2004). As a high school senior, Joshua Davey won a "Promise" scholarship, a renewable $1,125 state-funded grant that could be used at any public or private accredited institution of higher education in the state of Washington. He enrolled at Northwest College, an accredited Bible college affiliated with the Assembly of God, and declared a double major in pastoral ministries and business management. Davey's declared major violated the terms of the "Promise" scholarship, which specified that no scholarship funds could be awarded to a student pursuing a degree in "theology." The state included the prohibition to comply with the Washington State Constitution's "Blaine" provisions, which declared: "No public money or property shall be appropriated for or applied to any religious worship, exercise, or instruction, or the support of any religious establishment,"[8] and "All schools maintained or supported wholly or in part by the public funds shall be forever free of sectarian control."[9] Seven members of the Supreme Court rejected Davey's argument that Washington violated the Free Exercise Clause by revoking his scholarship. Chief Justice Rehnquist's majority opinion found that the state possessed legitimate "antiestablishment interests" that allowed it to "disfavor" religion.[10] To support that conclusion, the chief justice cited the Founding Fathers and what he said were their efforts to end direct taxpayer support of religion, claiming that several state constitutions at the time of the founding "prohibited *any* tax dollars from supporting the clergy."[11]

The legal questions presented in direct burden free exercise cases and the Supreme Court's answers to those questions can be summarized as follows:

- Can the state criminalize religious practices as such? (*Lukumi Babalu Aye*) No.
- Can the state use religion as a qualification/nonqualification for public office? (*McDaniel*) No.

---

[8] Washington State Constitution, Article 1, §11.
[9] Washington State Constitution, Article 9, §4. For a brief description of the history surrounding the proposal of the "Blaine" amendment at the national level, see Philip Hamburger, *Separation of Church and State*, Chapter 11. For a survey of state "Blaine" amendments, including Washington State's "Blaine" amendments, see Mark Edward DeForrest, "An Overview and Evaluation of State Blaine Amendments: Origins, Scope, and First Amendment Concerns," *Harvard Journal of Law and Public Policy* 26 (2003): 551–626.
[10] *Locke v. Davey*, 540 U.S. 712, 722 (2004).
[11] Emphasis in the original. Ibid., 723.

- Can the state employ a religiously based classification to disadvantage individuals? (*Davey*)? Yes.

The Madisonian Approach to Direct Burdens

Madison's doctrine of state noncognizance of religion would adjudicate these cases in a relatively straightforward manner, prohibiting all direct burdens on religion. In *Church of the Lukumi Babalu Aye*, the Supreme Court's factual finding that Santeria was the "exclusive legislative concern" of the city of Hialeah's ordinances amounts to state cognizance of religion as such.[12] Consistent with the Madisonian approach, the city could have banned the killing of animals or animal cruelty generally, but it could not criminalize sacrificial religious killings alone. In *McDaniel v. Paty*, Tennessee became cognizant of religion when it singled out religious ministers for exclusion from its constitutional convention. The state of Washington violated Madisonianism in the same way in *Locke v. Davey*. It became impermissibly cognizant of religion when it singled out theology majors from scholarship eligibility and then defined theology as the devotional study of religion. Madisonianism would prohibit all direct burdens on religion because state actions that directly burden religion, by definition, take cognizance of religion.

In summary, the Madisonian approach would adjudicate direct burden free exercise cases as follows:

- Can the state criminalize religious practices as such? (*Lukumi Babalu Aye*) No.
- Can the state use religion as a qualification/nonqualification for public office? (*McDaniel*) No.
- Can the state employ a religiously based classification to disadvantage individuals? (*Davey*) No.

The Washingtonian Approach to Direct Burdens

Washington's approach differs from Madison's in that it looks to the purposes of state action, not whether the state becomes cognizant of religion. It would allow the state to burden religions and individuals' religious practices if those burdens were related to legitimate civic ends. It would not consider

[12] *Church of the Lukumi Babalu Aye v. City of Hialeah*, 508 U.S. 520, 534–36 (1993).

the suppression of a religion or of a religious practice as such, however, to be a legitimate civic purpose.

In *Church of the Lukumi Babalu Aye*, the Washingtonian approach would inquire into the animating purpose of Hialeah's ordinances. Legitimate state interests, such as the prevention of animal cruelty or the maintenance of public sanitation, could be used to justify restrictions on Santeria religious practices. Whereas the Madisonian approach would not allow the state to become cognizant of Santeria as a religion, the Washingtonian approach would allow the criminalization of the religion's practices if such laws were adopted to further a legitimate civic interest unrelated to the suppression of Santeria. The Supreme Court found that the city of Hialeah failed to possess such an interest. Given this finding, the Washingtonian approach would have agreed with the Court and struck down the city's criminal ordinances. However, if the city had demonstrated that its purposes were to protect animals or to protect public morality and decency, the ordinance could have been upheld by the Washingtonian approach.

The constitutionality of minister exclusions from public office, similarly, would depend on the state successfully demonstrating how the exclusion advances a legitimate interest unrelated to the suppression of religion. In *McDaniel v. Paty*, the Tennessee Supreme Court approved of the state's stated purpose of maintaining the separation of church and state. That court found:

Baptists, Methodists and Catholics separately and collectively, far outnumber other religious sects, both separately and collectively. Opening the door to service in the General Assembly by ministers and priests would grant a distinct advantage to ministers and priests of the three mentioned religions, over those of all other sects, because of the far more extensive voter base from which to launch a campaign for office.[13]

The Tennessee Supreme Court approved the minister exclusion because it disadvantaged numerically large religious groups. The Tennessee Supreme Court also found that the state had a legitimate interest in preventing political campaigns by ministers because they "would naturally tend to pit religion against nonreligion."[14] Disenfranchising numerically large religious groups from voting for their preferred candidates because they are potentially politically powerful seems to have no other end beyond hindering religion as such, and therefore is not a legitimate state interest within the Washingtonian approach.

[13] *Paty v. McDaniel*, 547 S.W. 2d 897, 904 (1977).
[14] Ibid.

Other civic purposes, however, might more clearly justify minister exclusions under the Washingtonian approach. Preventing political conflict between religion and irreligion or excluding ministers from office in order not to divert them from their religious ministry could serve as legitimate civic purposes under Washingtonianism. The New York Constitution of 1776, for example, declared,

> And whereas the ministers of the gospel are, by their profession, dedicated to the service of God and the care of souls, and ought not to be diverted from the great duties of their function; therefore, no minister of the gospel, or priest of any denomination whatsoever, shall, at any time hereafter, under any presence or description whatever, be eligible to, or capable of holding, any civil or military office or place within this State.[15]

If religion is needed to develop the moral character necessary for good citizenship, and active religious clergy are needed to maintain religion, the state has a plausible civic interest in not diverting clergy from their religious ministries. Just as the Washingtonian approach would allow direct state aid to religion in order to facilitate the development of the qualities of good citizenship, it would allow direct disabilities on religion for the same purpose.

The same reason could not justify the exclusion of "theology" students from the state scholarship program at issue in *Locke v. Davey*, however. Doing so would not seem to further the end of developing moral character through nurturing religious belief. The purpose Washington State offered in litigation would also be unlikely to pass constitutional scrutiny under the Washingtonian approach. The state excluded "theology" students to comply with its constitution's "Blaine" provisions. The "Blaine" provisions themselves, however, appear to violate Washingtonianism. The Washington State Constitution declares that, "No public money or property shall be appropriated for or applied to any religious worship, exercise, or instruction, or the support of any religious establishment,"[16] and that, "All schools maintained or supported wholly or in part by the public funds shall be forever free of sectarian control."[17] Similar to Tennessee's rationale in *McDaniel v. Paty*, Washington State's Constitution seems to aim directly at maintaining the separation of church and state as an end in itself. Without

---

[15] New York Constitution, §XXXIX, in Francis Newton Thorpe, *Federal and State Constitutions* (Washington, DC: Government Printing Office, 1909), 5:2637.
[16] Washington State Constitution, Article 1, §11.
[17] Washington State Constitution, Article 9, §4.

a civic interest unrelated to the unfavorable treatment of religion, Washingtonianism would not allow the state to impose such disabilities on religion. Furthermore, as discussed in relation to the Establishment Clause, the Washingtonian doctrine would allow and encourage state support of religious education in view of the legitimate civic ends of fostering good citizenship and moral character. Not only would "theology" students be eligible for state scholarships under the Washingtonian doctrine, a Washingtonian approach to church and state would seem likely to encourage state promotion of religious education.

In summary, the Washingtonian approach would answer direct burden free exercise questions as follows:

- Can the state criminalize religious practices as such? (*Lukumi Babalu Aye*) No, unless the state possesses a legitimate interest unrelated to the suppression of religion.
- Can the state use religion as a qualification/nonqualification for public office? (*McDaniel*) No, unless the state possesses a legitimate interest unrelated to the suppression of religion.
- Can the state employ a religiously based classification to disadvantage individuals? (*Davey*) No, unless the state possesses a legitimate interest unrelated to the suppression of religion.

The Jeffersonian Approach to Direct Burdens

For individuals who are not members of the clergy and for nonsectarian institutions, the second prong of the Jeffersonian approach prohibits the state from directly affecting civil rights on account of religious opinions, practices, and worship. The doctrine's first prong, however, allows the state to subject ecclesiastical institutions to specific disabilities, which reflects Jefferson's intention to minimize clerical influence in American society. Jefferson never went so far as to suggest that the state could prevent the advancement of sectarian institutions by criminalizing religious practices as such, but, nonetheless, a consistent application of the first prong of Jefferson's doctrine would not prevent it. No principled difference exists between the imposition of civil disabilities to limit sectarianism and the criminalization of sectarian religious practices to achieve the same purpose – if the state is allowed to do the former, it would possess authority to do the latter. If an inquiry into the Santeria religion found it to be a sectarian institution, the Jeffersonian approach would allow its practices to be outlawed. *Lukumi Babalu Aye* pushes Jeffersonianism's anticlericalism to its logical extreme and reveals the tension within the two prongs of the approach.

Consistent with the doctrine's first prong, the Jeffersonian approach also could uphold Tennessee's exclusion of Reverend McDaniel from the state's constitutional convention. Just as Jefferson himself proposed to exclude ministers from eligibility for election from the state general assembly in his 1783 draft constitution for Virginia, minister exclusions from public offices would be mandated by a Jeffersonian approach to church-state relations, as long as sectarian religious dogmas pose the possibility of holding significant influence in American society.

Depending on how "theology" was defined, the first prong of the Jeffersonian approach also could uphold Washington State's exclusion of theology majors from the "Promise" scholarship program examined in *Locke v. Davey*. During litigation, it was decided that the state's prohibition against theology majors extended to students who pursued degrees that were "devotional in nature or designed to induce religious faith."[18] That definition would not be sufficient to require exclusion under the Jeffersonian approach because Jefferson was not against the encouragement of religious belief per se. Jefferson sought to subvert only those religious beliefs he perceived to be irrational or that supported clerical influence. As defined in litigation, Washington State's prohibition against using "Promise" scholarships for the study of theology would be overly broad and would not be upheld by the Jeffersonian doctrine. In the Court's majority opinion, however, Chief Justice Rehnquist suggested a line of argument that might meet Jeffersonian scrutiny. The chief justice emphasized the state's intention not to fund training for religious professionals and suggested that "majoring in devotional theology is akin to a religious calling as well as an academic training."[19] If Washington State's prohibition was interpreted to prohibit students from using scholarships to train for the ministry or to study sectarian religious beliefs from a devotional perspective, then Jeffersonianism would uphold the restriction. Understood this way, the prohibition would operate similarly to Tennessee's minister exclusion and target the type of religious influence that Jefferson intended to suppress.

A Jeffersonian analysis of *Lukumi Babalu Aye*, *McDaniel*, and *Davey* reveals that the approach would answer free exercise legal questions as follows:

- Can the state criminalize religious practices as such? (*Lukumi Babalu Aye*) Yes.

---

[18] The statute authorizing the scholarship did not define "theology." *Locke v. Davey*, 540 U.S. 712, 716 (2004).
[19] Ibid.

- Can the state use religion as a qualification/nonqualification for public office? (*McDaniel*) Yes.
- Can the state employ a religiously based classification to disadvantage individuals? (*Davey*) Yes, if properly tailored.

INDIRECT BURDENS ON RELIGIOUS EXERCISE

Most Free Exercise Clause jurisprudence has not involved direct burden cases. More typically, the Court has evaluated state actions that do not target religion as such but burden religious exercise in their effects, often the practices of minority religions that lack influence in the democratic political process. Indirect burden cases include statutes and regulations that in their application effectively criminalize or penalize religious exercises, impose obligations of citizenship that lie in tension with religious individuals' perceived religious obligations, or disparately impact religious individuals or religious organizations.

A classic indirect burden case came before the Court in *Reynolds v. United States* (1878), the Court's first significant Free Exercise Clause decision.[20] The case involved a challenge to a federal statute that banned bigamy and polygamy in the U.S. territories. George Reynolds, a practicing member of the Church of Jesus Christ of Latter-Day Saints (often called Mormons), argued that the law prohibited him from and punished him for practicing his religion and, therefore, violated the First Amendment's Free Exercise Clause. The law itself made no mention of Mormonism.

The Church of Jesus Christ of Latter-Day Saints long ago suspended its approval of bigamy and polygamy, but the legal question raised in *Reynolds* remains at the forefront of religious free exercise jurisprudence. More recently, practitioners of the Native American Church brought an indirect burden case to the Supreme Court to defend their religious use of peyote. The church members challenged an Oregon drug law, which classified peyote as an illegal hallucinogenic substance. In *Employment Division v. Smith* (1990), the Supreme Court rejected the Native American Church members' claim for an exemption from the law for the same reason it ruled against George Reynolds: "[A]ny society adopting such a system [of judicially granted exceptions] would be courting anarchy. . . ."[21] by

---

[20] *Reynolds v. United States*, 98 U.S. 145 (1878).

[21] *Employment Division, Oregon Department of Human Resources v. Smith*, 494 U.S. 872, 888 (1990). Accounts of the complicated legal and political history of the case can be found in Garrett Epps, *To An Unknown God: Religious Freedom on Trial* (New York: St. Martin's Press, 2001), and Carolyn N. Long, *Religious Freedom and Indian Rights: The Case of Oregon v. Smith* (Lawrence: University of Kansas Press, 2002).

"permit[ting] every citizen to be come a law unto himself."[22] In both cases, the Court held that a constitutional right to exemptions from generally applicable laws is incompatible with the rule of law and, therefore, not part of the Free Exercise Clause.

A different type of indirect burden arises when the law imposes a civic obligation on individuals that requires them to act contrary to their religious precepts. Around the time of World War II, the Supreme Court decided and then revised its ruling regarding mandatory recitations of the Pledge of Allegiance by public school children. In *Minersville School District v. Gobitis* (1940) and *West Virginia v. Barnette* (1943), Jehovah's Witness children were expelled from public schools for failing to salute and pledge allegiance to the flag.[23] The children's parents believed that the acts violated the Ten Commandments.[24] In *Gobitis*, an eight-to-one majority upheld mandatory flag salutes and pledges of allegiance on the grounds that they fostered the legitimate state interest of patriotism. "The mere possession of religious convictions which contradict the relevant concerns of a political society," the Court stated, "does not relieve the citizen from the discharge of political responsibilities."[25] In a remarkable reversal just three years later, a six-to-three Court invalidated *Gobitis* in *West Virginia v. Barnette* (1943). The *Barnette* Court, over a bitter dissenting opinion by *Gobitis'* author Felix Frankfurter, ruled the Bill of Rights "guards the individual's right to speak his mind," and therefore "no official, high or petty, can prescribe what shall be orthodox in politics, nationalism, religion or other matters of opinion or force citizens to confess by word or act their faith therein." Mandatory flag salutes and pledges of allegiance, the

---

[22] *Reynolds v. United States*, 98 U.S. 145, 167 (1878).

[23] The pledge in both cases was: "I pledge allegiance to the Flag of the United States of America and to the Republic for which it stands; one Nation, indivisible, with liberty and justice for all."

[24] Specifically, Exodus 20:3–5:

> You shall not have other gods besides me. You shall not carve idols for yourselves in the shape of anything in the sky about or on the earth; you shall not bow down before them or worship them. For I, the Lord, your God, am a jealous God, inflicting punishment for their fathers' wickedness on the children of those who hate me, down to the third and fourth generation . . ..

> *The Catholic Bible: Personal Study Edition*, New American Bible translation, ed. Jean Marie Hiesberger (New York: Oxford University Press, 1995), 20–21.

[25] *Minersville School District v. Gobitis*, 310 U.S. 586, 594–95 (1940).

Court found, invade "the sphere of intellect and spirit" that the First Amendment reserves from all official control.[26]

In *Wisconsin v. Yoder* (1972), the Supreme Court evaluated the same type of religious objection in another public school case. After being fined for failing to enroll their high school–aged children in school, Amish parents filed suit to claim an exemption from mandatory school attendance laws. By a six-to-one vote, the Supreme Court granted Amish parents an exemption from the law. The Court said the Amish parents' free exercise interests were more compelling than the state's legitimate interest in the education of children.[27]

A related type of indirect burden controversy can occur when a generally applicable law disparately impacts religious individuals or religious organizations but not in a way that makes their religious practices illegal. Disparate impact cases arise when a generally applicable law that does not target religion directly makes the practice of religion more expensive or less convenient. The Supreme Court decided two significant disparate impact cases in the early 1960s. In *Braunfeld v. Brown* (1961), a six-member majority upheld a Pennsylvania blue law that forbade Sunday retail sales of nonessential items like clothing, furniture, and musical instruments.[28] The law was challenged by Orthodox Jewish store owners who argued that the law interfered with their free exercise of

---

[26] *West Virginia v. Barnette*, 319 U.S. 624, 634, 642 (1943). It should be noted that Justice Jackson's majority opinion explicitly denied that the Court reached its decision on account of the appellee's religious beliefs:

> Nor does the issue as we see it turn on one's possession of particular religious views or the sincerity with which they are held. While religion supplies the motive for enduring the discomforts of making the issue in this case, many citizens who do not share these religious views hold such a compulsory rite to infringe on constitutional liberty of the individual. It is not necessary to inquire whether non-conformists' beliefs will exempt them from the duty to salute unless we first find power to make the salute a legal duty.

West Virginia v. Barnette, 319 U.S. 624, 634–35 (1943). The Court held that the state lacked authority to compel any individual (religious objector or not) to recite the Pledge of Allegiance and salute the flag.

[27] *Wisconsin v. Yoder*, 406 U.S. 205 (1972).
[28] The Pennsylvania statute prohibited the retail sale of clothing and wearing apparel; clothing accessories; furniture; housewares; home, business, or office furnishings; household, business, or office appliances; hardware; tools; paints; building and lumber supply materials; jewelry; silverware; watches; clocks; luggage; musical instruments and recordings; and toys, excluding novelties and souvenirs. The first offense was punishable by a fine not to exceed $100. Second offenses committed within one year after conviction of a first offense were subject to a fine not exceeding $200 or imprisonment of up to thirty days. See *Braunfeld v. Brown*, 366 U.S. 599, 601n.1 (1961).

religion by imposing a serious economic disadvantage on them since they had to close their stores two days a week whereas observant Christians only had to close once a week. The Supreme Court rejected the merchants' claim, finding that the statute "does not make criminal the holding of any religious belief or opinion, nor does it force anyone to embrace any religious belief or to say or believe anything in conflict with his religious tenets," and that it "does not make unlawful any religious practices of appellants."[29]

Two years after *Braunfeld*, the Court considered another Saturday Sabbath case, this one brought forward by a member of the Seventh Day Adventist Church, Adel Sherbert. Sherbert was discharged from her job because she refused to work on Saturdays. Unable to find other employment that would accommodate her religious schedule, she filed a claim for unemployment compensation. After South Carolina state officials denied her claim (on the grounds that she had refused to accept available work when offered), Sherbert filed a lawsuit claiming that the denial of unemployment compensation violated her First Amendment religious free exercise rights. In a six-to-three opinion authored by Justice William Brennan (who had dissented in *Braunfeld*), the Court ruled in favor of Sherbert, holding that a government-imposed choice between practicing one's religion or receiving a governmental benefit "puts the same kind of burden upon the free exercise of religion as would a fine imposed against appellant for her Saturday worship."[30]

The legal questions presented in indirect burden free exercise cases and the Supreme Court's answers to those questions can be summarized as follows:

- Can the state adopt laws that indirectly criminalize religious exercises? (*Reynolds, Smith*) Yes.
- Can the state impose civic obligations that require individuals to act contrary to their religious precepts? (*Gobitis, Barnette, Yoder*) No.[31]
- Can the state adopt laws that indirectly burden religious exercises? (*Braunfeld, Sherbert*) Depends on the Court's balancing of state interests versus religious freedom interests.

---

[29] *Braunfeld v. Brown*, 366 U.S. 599, 603, 605 (1961).
[30] *Sherbert v. Verner*, 374 U.S. 398, 404.
[31] *Barnette* reversed the result reached in *Gobitis*.

The Madisonian Approach to Indirect Burdens

By definition, indirect burden cases do not involve governmental cognizance of religion, and, therefore, all indirect burdens would be presumptively constitutional under the Madisonian approach. The burdensome effects of generally applicable laws such as the antipolygamy statute questioned in *Reynolds* or the drug law challenged in *Smith* would not trigger a Madisonian violation because the statutes did not take explicit account of Mormon marriage practices or Native American Church members' use of drugs. For the same reason, civic obligations like the recitation of the Pledge of Allegiance and salutation of the flag at issue in *Gobitis* and *Barnette* and the mandatory school attendance law in *Yoder* would not violate Madisonianism. Under Madison's rule, the state could also make the practice of particular religions more expensive, as in *Sherbert*, as long as the state action in question does not take cognizance of religion. It would allow a Sunday closing law like the one at issue in *Braunfeld* as long as the law itself does not reference religion.

Not only would Madisonianism allow indirect burdens on religion, it would prohibit all religiously based exemptions from such laws, whether by the judiciary or by ordinary legislation. As we shall discuss in the following section, noncognizance prohibits the state from using religion as a basis to classify citizens, and, therefore, it prevents the state from recognizing religious individuals as such to exempt them from generally applicable statutes.

In summary, the Madisonian approach would adjudicate indirect burden free exercise cases as follows:

- Can the state adopt laws that indirectly criminalize religious exercises? (*Reynolds*, *Smith*) Yes.
- Can the state impose civic obligations that require individuals to act contrary to their religious precepts? (*Gobitis*, *Barnette*, *Yoder*) Yes.
- Can the state adopt laws that indirectly burden religious exercises? (*Braunfeld*, *Sherbert*) Yes.

The Washingtonian Approach to Indirect Burdens

Washingtonianism would not prohibit or grant exemptions from indirect burdens on religious practices as long as the state action burdening religion furthered a legitimate civic interest. Regulation of marriage (*Reynolds*), prohibition of drug use (*Smith*), encouragement of patriotism (*Gobitis* and *Barnette*), education of youth (*Yoder*), establishment of a uniform day of rest (*Braunfeld*), and nonpayment of unemployment compensation to individuals who will not accept work (*Sherbert*) all clearly fall within the traditional police powers of the state and advance nonreligious civic interests. Even if such policies significantly burden or effectively prohibit some individuals' religious exercises, the state would not be obligated to grant legal exemptions to religious individuals under the Washingtonian approach. As discussed in Chapter 2, Washington personally dealt with an indirect burden case in the form of Quaker resistance to military service. His response was charitable but firm. He wrote to the Quakers that his "wish and desire" was that law would accommodate them as extensively as possible; yet he never suggested that they had a right to such accommodations, and his letter explicitly asserted the priority of the state's "essential interests" when they conflicted with the Quakers' religious precepts.[32] As we shall discuss in the next section, the Washingtonian approach would allow legislative and executive accommodations of religion, but it would not require such accommodations as a part of the right to religious freedom.

In summary, the Washingtonian approach would answer indirect burden free exercise questions as follows:

- Can the state adopt laws that indirectly criminalize religious exercises? (*Reynolds, Smith*) Yes.
- Can the state impose civic obligations that require individuals to act contrary to their religious precepts? (*Gobitis, Barnette, Yoder*) Yes.
- Can the state adopt laws that indirectly burden religious exercises? (*Braunfeld, Sherbert*) Yes.

The Jeffersonian Approach to Indirect Burdens

The Supreme Court cited Jefferson when it applied the belief-action dichotomy to uphold George Reynolds' bigamy conviction. The Jeffersonian approach as set forth in Chapter 3, however, would not focus on the distinction between beliefs and actions but rather on the rule that an individual's civil rights (excluding clergy members) cannot be affected on account of religious opinions, religious professions, or religious worship (or the lack thereof). By one's right being "affected," Jefferson meant what he said in the Virginia Statute, that religious opinions "shall in no wise diminish, enlarge, or affect [an individual's] civil capacities." The prohibition against

---

[32] George Washington to the Society of Quakers, October 1789, *Papers of George Washington*, Presidential Series, ed. Dorothy Twohig (Charlottesville: University Press of Virginia, 1987–), 4:266.

"enlarging" an individual's civil capacities would prevent state actors, including the judiciary, from exempting citizens from generally applicable laws on account of their religion. To do so would be to augment a religious individual's civil rights on account of religion because religious citizens would be eligible for a privilege that nonreligious citizens could not equally claim.

A Jeffersonian approach to the Free Exercise Clause, accordingly, would not extend religious exemptions to any of the religious individuals in any of the cases discussed. General prohibitions against bigamy and polygamy at issue in *Reynolds* and drug consumption in *Smith* could be applied against Mormons and Native American Church members, respectively, as could civic obligations such as those involved in *Gobitis*, *Barnette*, and *Yoder*. Jeffersonianism, similarly, would not give relief to religious citizens when generally applicable laws and regulations made the practice of religion more expensive or inconvenient, as in *Braunfeld* and *Sherbert*.

In summary, the Jeffersonian approach would answer indirect burden free exercise questions as follows:

- Can the state adopt laws that indirectly criminalize religious exercises? (*Reynolds*, *Smith*) Yes.
- Can the state impose civic obligations that require individuals to act contrary to their religious precepts? (*Gobitis*, *Barnette*, *Yoder*) Yes.
- Can the state adopt laws that indirectly burden religious exercises? (*Braunfeld*, *Sherbert*) Yes.

STATE IDENTIFICATION OF RELIGION FOR THE PURPOSE OF REGULATION OR EXEMPTION

A third type of free exercise case involves state identification of religion for the purpose of regulation or preferential treatment. Identification cases are similar to direct burden cases insofar as they involve state action that identifies religion as such. Unlike direct burden cases, however, identification cases do not involve state attempts to suppress or to penalize religion. Most identification cases involve legislative attempts to relieve religious individuals or religious groups from the indirect burdens they would otherwise experience on account of generally applicable laws. Other identification cases involve the identification of religion for benign regulation. Because many identification cases involve legislation that seeks to treat religion favorably, they also could fall under the Establishment Clause.

An example of a case of identification for the purpose of regulation was brought before the Court in its first significant incorporated free exercise case,

Cantwell v. Connecticut (1940). *Cantwell* evaluated a Connecticut statute that required, with certain exceptions, persons soliciting "money, services, subscriptions or any valuable thing for any alleged religious, charitable or philanthropic cause" to obtain a certificate of approval from the secretary of the public welfare council. The secretary was authorized to "determine whether such cause is a religious one or is a bona fide object of charity or philanthropy and conforms to reasonable standards of efficiency and integrity."[33] The law, which imposed a type of prior restraint, aimed to prevent fraudulent solicitations. The Supreme Court struck down the statute as a violation of the Free Exercise Clause, ruling that the state could regulate the time, manner, and place of solicitations, but that it could not "condition the solicitation of aid for the perpetuation of religious views or systems upon a license, the grant of which rests in the exercise of a determination by state authority as to what is a religious cause. . . ."[34]

The Connecticut statute struck down in *Cantwell* used religion as a category for an arguably benign regulation. Statutes also can include religion as one of several categories for exemption from generally applicable laws. In *Walz v. Tax Commission of City of New York* (1970), the Court examined a New York State statute that exempted from property taxes:

Real property owned by a corporation or association organized exclusively for the moral or mental improvement of men and women, or for religious, bible, tract, charitable, benevolent, missionary, hospital, infirmary, educational, public playground, scientific, literary, bar association, medical society, library, patriotic, historical or cemetery purposes . . . and used exclusively for carrying out thereupon one or more of such purposes. . . .[35]

---

[33] The law in question stated:

No person shall solicit money, services, subscriptions or any valuable thing for any alleged religious, charitable or philanthropic cause, from other than a member of the organization for whose benefit such person is soliciting or within the county in which such person or organization is located unless such cause shall have been approved by the secretary of the public welfare council. Upon application of any person in behalf of such cause, the secretary shall determine whether such cause is a religious one or is a bona fide object of charity or philanthropy and conforms to reasonable standards of efficiency and integrity, and, if he shall so find, shall approve the same and issue to the authority in charge a certificate to that effect. Such certificate may be revoked at any time. Any person violating any provision of this section shall be fined not more than one hundred dollars or imprisoned not more than thirty days or both. *Cantwell v. Connecticut*, 310 U.S. 296, 301–02 (1940).

[34] Ibid., 301–07.
[35] *Walz v. Tax Commission of the City of New York*, 397 U.S. 664, 667n.1 (1979).

An eight-member Supreme Court majority upheld the exemption. Five justices signed on to Chief Justice Burger's majority opinion, which held that the exemption for religion did not violate the First Amendment since it was granted to all houses of religious worship within a broad class of property owned by nonprofit quasi-public corporations and because it created only a minimal and remote involvement between church and state.[36] A generation later, however, the Court did not look as favorably on a tax exemption extended to religion. In *Texas Monthly, Inc. v. Bullock* (1989), a six-member Court majority struck down a Texas statute that exempted from sales tax "[p]eriodicals that are published or distributed by a religious faith and that consist wholly of writings promulgating the teaching of the faith and books that consist wholly of writings sacred to a religious faith." The Court distinguished *Texas Monthly* from *Walz* by emphasizing that the former provided a tax exemption for religion only, whereas, in the latter, religion was one category among many that was exempt from taxes. The Court found that by making religion the exclusive recipient of a tax exemption, Texas was effectively subsidizing it in violation of the Establishment Clause.[37]

Not all laws that identify religion exclusively for legal privileges have been struck down by the Court. In *Corporation of Presiding Bishop v. Amos* (1987), decided two years before *Texas Monthly*, the Court upheld an amendment to the Civil Rights Act of 1964 that exempted religious organizations from Title VII's prohibition of discrimination in employment on the basis of religion.[38] The *Amos* Court was unanimous in its decision but fractured in its reasoning. Justice White's majority opinion found that the Lemon test allowed as a permissible legislative purpose the alleviation of "significant governmental interference with the ability of religious organizations to define and carry out their religious missions."[39] Justice Brennan, in a concurring opinion, emphasized that it was the nonprofit character of religious activity that made the exemption constitutional.[40] Justice

---

[36] Ibid., 676.
[37] *Texas Monthly, Inc. v. Bullock*, 489 U.S. 1, 14–15 (1989).
[38] Section 702 stated:

> This subchapter [i.e., Title VII of the Civil Rights Act of 1964, 42 U.S.C. 2000 et seq.] shall not apply . . . to a religious corporation, association, educational institution, or society with respect to the employment of individuals of a particular religion to perform work connected with the carrying on by such corporation, association, educational institution, or society of its activities.
>
> *Corporation of Presiding Bishop v. Amos*, 483 U.S. 327, 330n.1 (1987).

[39] Ibid., 335.
[40] Ibid., 340.

O'Connor, who also wrote a concurring opinion, ruled that the exemption could not be considered an "endorsement" of religion.[41]

In the context of military service, the Court has found statutory exemptions for religiously based conscientious objection constitutional. In *Arver v. United States* (1918), the Court dismissed in one sentence the possibility that a military draft law's provision for religiously based exemptions could be unconstitutional. The law in question exempted from draft registration religious ministers and theological students, and it relieved from combat service members of "any well-recognized religious sect or organizations" whose tenets exclude the moral right to engage in war.[42] Regarding these provisions, the Court stated,

And we pass without anything but statement the proposition that an establishment of a religion or an interference with the free exercise thereof repugnant to the First Amendment resulted from the exemption clauses of the act to which we at the outset referred because we think its unsoundness is too apparent to require us to do more.[43]

In *United States v. Seeger* (1965), the Court again upheld religion-based exemptions from military service. *Seeger* involved appeals from individuals whose claims for conscientious objector status had been denied. The 1940 congressional draft law in question exempted from military service persons who by reason of their "religious training and belief" were conscientiously opposed to participation in war in any form. A 1951 amendment defined religious training and belief as meaning "an individual's belief in relation to a Supreme Being involving duties superior to those arising from any human relation, but [not including] essentially political, sociological or philosophical views, or merely personal moral code."[44] The Court upheld the exemption by expanding it to include "whether a given belief that is sincere and meaningful occupies a place in the life of its possessor parallel to that filled by the orthodox belief in God of one who clearly qualifies for the exemption."[45]

[41] Ibid., 348–49.

[42] "An act to authorize the President to increase temporarily the military establishment of the United States," May 18, 1917 (Public No. 12, 65th Congress, c. 15, 40 Stat. 76), in *The Statutes at Large of the United States of America from April, 1917 to March, 1919* (Washington, DC: Government Printing Office, 1919), 40 (part I): 78.

[43] *Arver v. United States*, 245 U.S. 366, 389–90 (1965). The case also decisively affirmed the constitutionality of compulsory military service. *Arver* involved a challenge to a congressional act that allowed the president to conduct a military draft. The Court upheld the statute, citing Congress' Section I, Article 8 powers to declare war and to raise and support armies. See *Arver v. United States*, 245 U.S. 366, 377 (1918).

[44] 50 App. U.S.C.A., §456(j) (1951) cited in *United States v. Seeger*, 380 U.S. 163, 165 (1965).

[45] *United States v. Seeger*, 380 U.S. 163, 166 (1965).

The legal questions presented in free exercise identification cases and the Supreme Court's answers to those questions can be summarized as follows:

- Can the state identify religion as such for the purpose of regulation? (*Cantwell*) No.
- Can the state identify religion as such for the purpose of tax exemption? (*Walz, Texas Monthly*) Depends on the exclusivity of the exemption.
- Can the state identify religion as such for the purpose of benign exemption, including exemption from military service? (*Amos, Arver, Seeger*) Yes.

The Madisonian Approach to Identification Cases

Madisonian noncognizance forbids the state from identifying religion as such and, therefore, it would prohibit the state from using religion-based classifications for purposes of regulation or exemption. The approach would strike down the Connecticut law challenged in *Cantwell* because the law identified religious groups as such to require a certificate of approval to engage in solicitations. Madisonianism would allow the state to regulate solicitations generally, but not to impose specific regulations on religious solicitations. Tax exemptions for religious groups as such also would violate noncognizance. Under Madison's approach, it would make no difference if the tax exemption was extended to religion as one of several groups, as in *Walz*, or if the exemption was extended to religion alone, as in *Texas Monthly*. All tax exemptions that use religion as a basis of qualification would be impermissible.

Not only tax exemptions but all forms of religiously based exemptions would fail the Madisonian doctrine. Because the state could not become cognizant of religion, it could not exempt or prefer religion as such for any purpose, including preferential treatment. Section VII of the 1964 Civil Rights Act (*Amos*), conscientious objector statutes (*Arver, Seeger*), and other such provisions that identify religion in order to exempt it from generally applicable laws would not be allowed. As discussed in Chapter 1, Madison himself deviated from his own principle of noncognizance when he proposed in the First Congress a constitutional amendment for "religiously scrupulous" exemptions from military service. But if we are to follow Madison as a principled thinker, as opposed to his personal actions, then even conscientious objector exemptions cannot be sustained.

While the doctrine of noncognizance would completely curtail governmental attempts to accommodate religion directly, its reach in practice might not be as extensive as it first seems. The Madisonian approach would not prohibit religious individuals or groups from qualifying for exemptions or regulations that were grounded on nonreligious criteria. Churches, for example, might qualify for tax exemptions or regulatory exemptions based on their being nonprofit associations. Just as the state could not extend exemptions to religions on account of religion, noncognizance also would forbid the state from excluding religions from nonreligiously based exemptions. A conscientious objector statute that examined the sincerity and meaningfulness of the individual's objection to participation in war could also pass Madisonian noncognizance as long as it did not require attention to religious beliefs as such. In these ways, the Madisonian approach would allow religious individuals and religious groups to be accommodated by the law for nonreligious reasons.

In summary, the Madisonian approach would adjudicate free exercise identification cases as follows:

- Can the state identify religion as such for the purpose of regulation? (*Cantwell*) No.
- Can the state identify religion as such for the purpose of tax exemption? (*Walz, Texas Monthly*) No.
- Can the state identify religion as such for the purpose of benign exemption, including exemption from military service? (*Amos, Arver, Seeger*) No.

The Washingtonian Approach to Identification Cases

Washingtonianism would differ significantly from Madisonianism on identification cases. Not only would it allow the state to recognize religion, it would hold that preferential treatment of religion is itself a legitimate civic end insofar as religion contributes to the development of moral character and good citizenship. Legislative action that exempts religious individuals from the effects of burdensome laws would be consistent with the "wish and desire" Washington expressed to the Quakers that religion be accommodated as extensively as possible. Tax exemptions for religions alone (*Texas Monthly*) or exemptions that religions might qualify for (*Walz*) would not be constitutionally suspect under the Washingtonian approach. Religiously based exemptions from generally applicable nondiscrimination laws (*Amos*) or from military service (*Arver, Seeger*) also would be allowed, although Washington himself made clear to the Quakers that he viewed citizens who refused to take arms to defend their rights in a less than favorable light.

Aside from a determination that the religions benefited by the state actually did contribute to good citizenship, the Washingtonian approach would place only two other conditions on preferential treatment of religion. All preferential treatment would have to be sufficiently ecumenical in light of the civic purposes being advanced. The state also could not evaluate what constitutes a religion based on a judgment of the religion's theological truthfulness as such a judgment lies beyond the state's legitimate jurisdiction. The state could base its judgment on the sincerity of belief, much like the Court did *Seeger*, but it could not deny a group recognition of religious status on account of a judgment that such a group was a "false" or "improper" religion.

This condition might affect a Washingtonian evaluation of *Cantwell v. Connecticut*. In general, state identification of religion for regulatory purposes would be allowed under the Washingtonian approach as long as the regulation was related to a legitimate civic purpose. The purpose of the Connecticut statute was to prohibit fraudulent solicitations, which clearly qualifies as a legitimate civic interest. The statute, however, empowered a state official to determine whether religious groups that applied for a solicitations certificate were in fact religious. A Washingtonian approach would not allow state officials to make such a judgment based on a consideration of the truth or falsity of a group's religious beliefs. State officials, however, could determine whether a given group's beliefs fall within the realm of religion – for example, by defining religious groups as those that hold beliefs concerning an "ultimate reality" – and state officials could attempt to determine whether a group sincerely held its beliefs. The Connecticut statute in question did not specify how state officials were to determine whether religious groups were in fact religious. To achieve its purpose, it would seem that the state would need only to evaluate the sincerity with which a group held its beliefs. If interpreted in this way, the statute would pass a Washingtonian evaluation.

The Washingtonian approach would answer free exercise identification questions as follows:

- Can the state identify religion as such for the purpose of regulation? (*Cantwell*) Yes.
- Can the state identify religion as such for the purpose of tax exemption? (*Walz, Texas Monthly*) Yes.
- Can the state identify religion as such for the purpose of benign exemption, including exemption from military service? (*Amos, Arver, Seeger*) Yes.

The Jeffersonian Approach to Identification Cases

Jeffersonianism would reach the same results as Madisonianism, although for different reasons. The Jeffersonian approach allows the state to encourage rational, nonsectarian religious beliefs but, as discussed in the context of indirect burden cases, it does not allow legal rights or privileges to be augmented on account of religious opinions. The approach implicitly recognizes a distinction between symbolic state actions and legal privileges. Symbolic actions, such as the inclusion of a nondenominational prayer at a public school graduation, do not affect an individual's civil rights, whereas legal privileges, such as an exemption from an otherwise applicable law, do. Given this distinction, the Jeffersonian approach would strike down the Connecticut law at issue in *Cantwell*, although it would do so for different reasons than the Court. The Jeffersonian approach would not have found it problematic that the statute authorized a state official to determine if religious groups were in fact religious. Instead, it would have struck down the statute because it extended a legal privilege to religious groups on account of their being religious. If a group was determined to be a bona fide religion, then it received the state-sanction privilege of being able to solicit donations. For the same reason, the approach would strike down the legal exemptions at issue in *Walz*, *Texas Monthly*, *Amos*, *Ayer*, and *Seeger*. In each case, the law granted to religious individuals or religious groups special legal status on account of religious beliefs, something that is prohibited under the Jeffersonian approach.

The Jeffersonian approach to free exercise identification cases can be summarized as follows:

- Can the state identify religion as such for the purpose of regulation? (*Cantwell*) No.
- Can the state identify religion as such for the purpose of tax exemption? (*Walz*, *Texas Monthly*) No.
- Can the state identify religion as such for the purpose of benign exemption, including exemption from military service? (*Amos*, *Arver*, *Seeger*) No.

The Founders and the Free Exercise Clause

The tables in this section summarize the jurisprudential results for the Free Exercise Clause cases discussed in this chapter.

For Tables FE 2, FE 3, and FE 4, an "X" in the left-hand column under each case indicates a vote to uphold the state action in question. In *Lukumi*

Babalu Aye, for example, Madison's doctrine would have agreed with the Supreme Court and found the state's attempt to outlaw Santeria animal sacrifice unconstitutional, whereas the Jeffersonian doctrine would have disagreed with the Supreme Court and upheld the state action in question.

Washingtonianism Would Favor Religion the Most, Jeffersonianism the Least

As indicated in Tables FE 1 and FE 6, and similar to the results reached for Establishment Clause cases, Washingtonianism would render decisions favorable to religion more frequently than Madisonianism or Jeffersonianism. Jeffersonianism renders decisions most hostile toward religion – for the cases discussed in this chapter, it would not have decided any case in favor of religion.

What distinguishes Washingtonianism from Madisonianism and Jeffersonianism in free exercise cases is the Washingtonian acceptance of state use of religion for civic purposes. Only Washingtonianism allows the state to identify religion for the purposes of benign regulation and privilege. Madisonianism finds such state identification of religion to be a *prima facie* violation of religious noncognizance. Jeffersonianism prevents free exercise identifications because such actions augment legal rights and privileges on account of religion.

Corporation of Presiding Bishop v. Amos offers a good example to illustrate how Washingtonianism renders free exercise results more favorable to religion than Madisonianism and Jeffersonianism. The case involved the provision of the Civil Rights Act of 1964 that exempted religious institutions from Title VII's prohibition of employment discrimination. The Washingtonian approach would uphold the exemption because the accommodation of religion further legitimates civic purpose (encouraging religion encourages good citizenship). Madisonianism would strike down Title VII's exemption because the law takes cognizance of religion by using it as a basis for exemption qualification. Jeffersonianism would strike down the exemption for a different but related reason. It would find that Title VII grants a legal privilege (exemption from federal nondiscrimination law) to religious institutions on account of religion.

TABLE FE 1. *Free Exercise Clause Results*

	Supreme Court	Madison	Washington	Jefferson
Direct Burdens				
Can the state criminalize religious practices as such? (*Lukumi Babalu Aye*)	No	No	No*	Yes
Can the state use religion as a qualification/nonqualification for public office? (*McDaniel*)	No	No	No*	Yes
Can the state employ a religiously based classification to disadvantage individuals? (*Davey*)	Yes	No	No*	Yes
Indirect Burdens				
Can the state adopt laws that indirectly criminalize religious exercises? (*Reynolds, Smith*)	Yes	Yes	Yes	Yes
Can the state impose civic obligations that require individuals to act contrary to their religious precepts? (*Gobitis, Barnette, Yoder*)	No	Yes	Yes	Yes
Can the state adopt laws that indirectly burden religious exercises? (*Braunfeld, Sherbert*)	Depends	Yes	Yes	Yes
State Identification of Religion for the Purpose of Regulation or Exemption				
Can the state identify religion as such for the purpose of regulation? (*Cantwell*)	No	No	Yes	No
Can the state identify religion as such for the purpose of tax exemption? (*Walz, Texas Monthly*)	Depends	No	Yes	No
Can the state identify religion as such for the purpose of benign exemption, including exemption from military service? (*Amos, Arver, Seeger*)	Yes	No	Yes	No

* Different state interests – namely, interests unrelated to the suppression of religion – would have led the Washingtonian approach to uphold the cases involving direct burdens on religion.

TABLE FE 2. *Direct Burdens on Religious Exercise*

	Lukumi Babalu		McDaniel		Locke	
Supreme Court		X		X	X	
Madison		X		X		X
Washington*		X		X		X
Jefferson	X		X		X	

* Washingtonianism allows direct burdens on religion if the asserted state interest is unrelated to the suppression of religion. Given how the three cases in this table were litigated, however, the Washingtonian approach would not have allowed the challenged burden.

TABLE FE 3. *Indirect Burdens on Religious Exercise*

	Reynolds	Gobitis	Barnette	Yoder	Braunfeld	Sherbert	Smith
Supreme Court	X	X	X	X	X	X	X
Madison	X	X	X	X	X	X	X
Washington	X	X	X	X	X	X	X
Jefferson	X	X	X	X	X	X	X

Although Madisonianism and Jeffersonianism would reach the same result in identification cases, in direct burden cases, Madison's approach would render results more favorable toward religion than Jefferson's. Just as noncognizance prevents the state from identifying religion for the purposes of privilege, it also prevents the state from identifying religion for particular burdens. In *McDaniel v. Paty*, for example, Madisonian noncognizance would prevent the state from identifying religious ministers as ineligible for public office. The first prong of Jeffersonianism, by contrast, allows the state to prevent religious clergy from gaining undue societal influence and, accordingly, allows the state to place particular burdens on religion. Jeffersonianism allows the state to impose particular burdens on religion that Madisonianism prohibits.

The Founders' One Area of Unanimous Agreement: No Right to Religious Exemptions

Although Washingtonianism would favor religion the most, the approach would not always dictate free exercise decisions in favor of religion. Washingtonianism would allow the state to impose indirect burdens on religion, which is a point of agreement among all three of the Founders' approaches. Washingtonianism's concurrence with Jeffersonianism and Madisonianism on this type of case may seem somewhat surprising given its seemingly more favorable disposition toward religion. But just as the Washingtonian

TABLE FE 4. *State Identification of Religion for Regulation or Privilege*

	Cantwell	Walz	Texas Monthly	Amos	Arver	Seeger
Supreme Court		X	X		X	X	X	X
Madison		X	X		X	X	X	X	X
Washington	X	X	X		X	X	X	X
Jefferson		X	X		X	X	X	X	X

TABLE FE 5. *Ratio of Agreement between Founders Free Exercise Clause*

	Madison and Washington	Madison and Jefferson	Washington and Jefferson
Direct Burden	3/3	0/3	0/3
Indirect Burden	7/7	7/7	7/7
Identification for Regulation/Privilege	0/6	6/6	0/6
Ratio of Agreement	10/16	13/16	7/16

approach allows the state to advance religion in order to pursue legitimate civil interests, it also allows the state to encroach on religion in light of legitimate civic interests. Within the realm of legitimate civil interests, Washingtonianism grants state actors wide discretion both to advance and to limit religious exercises. All three of the Founders' approaches agree that when the state acts within its legitimate sphere of responsibility, it possesses no obligation to accommodate the real or perceived burdens imposed on religious individuals or institutions.

Washington Would Allow Legislative Religious Exemptions, Madison and Jefferson Would Not

Washingtonianism departs from Madisonianism and Jeffersonianism, however, on the constitutional propriety of legislative accommodations of religion. While Washington's understanding of the right to religious liberty did not include a right to exemptions from valid laws, he did express his "wish and desire" that religions be accommodated when possible.[46] The Washingtonian approach, accordingly, would allow and encourage legislative

---

[46] George Washington to the Society of Quakers, October 1789, *Papers of George Washington*, Presidential Series, 4:266.

TABLE FE 6. *Ratios of Free Exercise Cases Decided in Favor of Religious Litigants**

	Supreme Court	Madison	Washington	Jefferson
Direct Burden**	2/3	3/3	3/3	0/3
Indirect Burden	3/7	0/7	0/7	0/7
Identification & Privilege***	4/6	0/6	6/6	0/6
Decisions in Favor of Religious Litigants	9/16	3/16	9/16	0/16

   * A vote against the solicitation regulation in *Cantwell v. Connecticut* is interpreted to be a vote against a regulatory privilege for religion and, hence, a decision against religion.

  ** In direct burden and indirect burden cases, a vote against state action is considered a vote in favor of religious litigants.

*** For identification for regulation/privilege cases, a vote in favor of state action is considered a vote in favor of religion. In *Cantwell*, a vote against the Cantwells (and in favor of the state regulation in question) is viewed as a decision in favor of the religious litigants because the solicitation regulation in question benefited religion insofar as it allowed bona fide religious organizations to qualify for otherwise unavailable solicitation licenses.

accommodations for religion, whereas the Madisonian and Jeffersonian approaches would forbid them. As already discussed, this difference appears in cases concerning state identification of religion for the purposes of privilege. The Washingtonian approach would allow the state to exempt religions from complying with generally applicable discrimination law (*Amos*), to extend special tax exemptions for religion (*Walz, Texas Monthly*), and to exempt religious conscientious objectors from compulsory military service (*Arver, Seeger*). Both the Madisonian and Jeffersonian approaches forbid religiously based exemptions. Religious exemptions by definition take cognizance of religion in violation of Madison's approach and extend privileges on account of religion in violation of Jefferson's approach.

Jefferson Would Allow the State to Burden Religion Directly; Washington Would Sometimes; Madison Would Not

The Jeffersonian approach would reach the result that seems to be against religion in every free exercise case discussed in this chapter. In light of the Jeffersonian commitment to overcoming irrational religious influences on American society, the approach would allow the state to impose direct burdens on religion. Perhaps somewhat surprisingly, Washingtonianism, too, would allow the state to impose some direct burdens on religion. In the three direct burden cases discussed, Washingtonianism was found to rule against the state actions in question and in favor of religion. Those results, however, were related to the particular state interests advanced in litigation. The Washingtonian approach would allow the state to impose direct burdens on religion if those burdens could be shown to advance a legitimate civic interest unrelated to the suppression of religion.

Church of the Lukumi Babalu Aye, the case involving city ordinances designed to outlaw Santerian animal sacrifice practices, shows how the Washingtonian approach could allow a direct burden. The Supreme Court found the ordinances to violate the Free Exercise Clause because their aim was the suppression of Santeria. But given the nature of the religious practices in question, other concerns could have been introduced. If the state had demonstrated that its actions were aimed to prevent animal cruelty and/or preserve public sanitation, Washingtonianism could have upheld the laws, even if they only targeted "sacrificial" or "ritualistic" animal sacrifice. *Lukumi Babalu Aye* reveals that Washingtonianism's deference to legitimate civic ends can allow state actions that appear to be "against" religion.

The laws in *McDaniel v. Paty* and *Locke v. Davey* might also be upheld by Washingtonianism, although the arguments for doing so are less persuasive. In the former case, the Tennessee Supreme Court upheld the minister exclusion law on account of the state's objective to minimize the political strength of numerically large religions. That reason would not have passed Washingtonian scrutiny. But if the state asserted that excluding ministers from office was necessary to preserve the dignity and integrity of the religious calling or not to divert ministers from their unique ability to nurture moral character and good citizenship, then the exclusion might have passed Washingtonian scrutiny. In *Locke v. Davey*, the state might have justified its exclusion of theology majors from the state's scholarship program by asserting that individuals who are training for a life in the ministry likely would be more devoted to their congregations if their training were funded by those congregations. Alternatively, the state could have claimed that those students who are willing to make economic sacrifices to train for the ministry might make better ministers. While such justifications may or may not be fully persuasive, they would have linked the law in question to legitimate civic interests from the Washingtonian point of view.

That the Jeffersonian and Washingtonian approaches would allow direct burdens on religion reveals a structural similarity between them and a fundamental difference from Madisonianism. Jeffersonianism and Washingtonianism view religion in a politically utilitarian manner. Both allow direct burdens on religion when such burdens have salutary political effects. Washingtonianism also allows the state to benefit religion directly when that would be politically useful. Jeffersonianism, being more skeptical of religion's political utility, does not allow as much support of religion. Regardless of that particular difference, in their shared emphasis on political utility, the Jeffersonian and Washingtonian approaches are more similar to each other than either is to Madisonianism. Madisonian noncognizance does not allow the state to engage religion in a directly utilitarian manner because it prohibits the state from either imposing direct burdens on religion or extending privileges to religion as such. Rather than structuring the relationship between church and state on the basis of political utility, Madisonianism attempts to sever any sort of direct relationship between church and state and, thereby, to prohibit the state from favoring or disfavoring religion directly to advance state interests. As we shall discuss in the Conclusion, Madison's approach encourages the development of church-state relations around the principles of equality and neutrality in ways that Washingtonianism and Jeffersonianism do not.

7

The Founders v. the Supreme Court

The previous two chapters applied the Founders' legal doctrines to First Amendment religion cases and discussed how the Founders' approaches would adjudicate those cases differently. This chapter compares the Founders' projected decisions with the actual decisions rendered by the Supreme Court. It also compares the decisions the Founders would have rendered with the positions taken by individual Supreme Court justices who have been influential in the development of modern church-state constitutional law. The data collected reveal that the Supreme Court has not consistently adopted any one Founder's approach. The votes of individual Supreme Court justices, however, show high degrees of correlation with individual Founders.

THE FOUNDERS V. THE SUPREME COURT

Table SC 1 illustrates the ratio of cases in which each Founder's approach would accord with the Supreme Court decisions discussed in Chapters 5 and 6.

For the cases discussed in Chapters 5 and 6, the Supreme Court has not rendered decisions that consistently have corresponded to any one of the Founders' approaches. For the different types of cases, the highest frequency of similarity lies between the Court and Madison in cases pertaining to religion in public schools. In six of the seven cases discussed (excluding *Newdow*, which the Supreme Court did not decide on Establishment Clause grounds), the Supreme Court reached the same result as Madisonian noncognizance. Perhaps surprisingly, the Jeffersonian approach would have allowed prayer in public schools on three occasions that the Court did

TABLE SC 1. *Ratio of Agreement between the Founders and the Supreme Court*

	Madison	Washington	Jefferson
Agreement with the Supreme Court Establishment Clause Cases			
Religion in public schools*	6/7	1/7	3/7
Government aid to private religious schools	3/4	3/4	1/4
Religion in the public square**	2.5/5	5.5/7	2.5/7
Ratio of agreement – Establishment Clause	**11.5/16**	**9.5/18**	**6.5/18**
Agreement with the Supreme Court Free Exercise Clause Cases			
Direct burden	2/3	2/3	1/3
Indirect burden	4/7	4/7	4/7
Identification and privilege	2/6	4/6	2/6
Ratio of agreement – Free Exercise Clause	**8/16**	**10/16**	**7/16**
Total ratio of agreement with Supreme Court	**19.5/32**	**19.5/34**	**13.5/34**

* Eight religion in public school cases were discussed in Chapter 5. The Supreme Court did not decide *Elk Grove School District v. Newdow* on Establishment Clause grounds, so it is not counted in this table.

** Seven religion in the public square cases were discussed in Chapter 5. In *Allegheny County v. ACLU*, the Supreme Court evaluated two holiday displays, upholding one and striking down the other. The Court's split decision is signified by a half-vote agreement with each Founder. We determined that Madisonianism did not render clear decisions in two cases, *McCreary* and *Van Orden*, which is why only five cases are used for Madison's ratio.

not – in *Vitale*, *Jaffree*, and *Santa Fe*. In those cases, the type of prayer in question corresponded with Jefferson's own version of demystified Christianity. At times, the Court's own "wall" of separation has been higher than Jefferson's. The Washingtonian approach would have been more lenient than the Court on questions of religion in public schools. It would have allowed religion in public schools in the six cases that the Court did not.

Regarding government aid to private religious school cases and religion in the public square cases discussed in Chapter 5, Washingtonianism most closely approximates the Supreme Court's decisions. In these two categories, the Court upheld the state action in question in eight and one-half of eleven cases (in *Allegheny*, the Court upheld one holiday display but struck down another), whereas the Washingtonian approach would have upheld all eleven state actions. Jeffersonianism, which would have reached results exactly opposite

TABLE SC 2. *Ratio of Agreement between Individual Supreme Court Justices and the Founders*

	Jefferson	Madison	Washington
Black	7/13	8/13	5/13
Frankfurter	7/7	6/7	3/7
Douglas	7/14	8/14	5/14
Brennan	6/16	8/16	4/16
Stewart	2/9	1/9	5/9
White	6/16	6/16	12/16
Burger	2/7	1/7	5/7
Blackmun	5/11	6/11	3/11
Rehnquist	5/18	6/15	17/18
Stevens	13/18	10/16	4/18
O'Connor	8/18	11/15	10/18
Scalia	2/14	7/12	14/14
Kennedy	3/13	8/11	10/13
Souter	8/10	3/8	1/10
Thomas	2/11	6/8	11/11
Ginsburg	7/8	1/6	0/8
Breyer	4/8	3/6	3/8

from Washingtonianism in these cases, would not have permitted any public aid to private religious schools or allowed any state actions placing religion in the public square. The Court would have agreed with Jefferson in only three and one-half of the eleven public aid to religious school and religion in the public square cases discussed. The Madisonian approach would have reached the same result as the Court in a bit more than half (5.5/9) of these cases.

Regarding Free Exercise Clause cases, each Founder's approach would have reached the same result as the Court in about one-half of the cases examined, but no significant patterns of similarity emerge between any of the Founders' positions and the Court's actual jurisprudence. This results primarily from the Court's own inconsistencies.

THE FOUNDERS AND INDIVIDUAL SUPREME COURT JUSTICES

More significant patterns of similarity exist between individual Founders and individual Supreme Court justices. The table above and the tables that follow compare the results of the projected votes of Madison, Washington, and Jefferson with the actual votes of various Supreme Court justices for the thirty-five cases discussed in Chapters 5 and 6. In Table SC 2, the ratio given represents the frequency of agreement between each Founder and the justice for cases in which that justice voted (justices' votes are not projected for cases in which they did not participate). Justice Black, for example, voted in thirteen of the thirty-five cases discussed in Chapters 5 and 6. In seven of those thirteen cases, his vote would have agreed with what we have projected as the Jeffersonian vote. In eight cases, Justice Black would have reached the same result as Madisonianism. In only five cases would Black's vote have corresponded with the Washingtonian vote.

Tables SC 3–SC 8 illustrate in more detailed form the projected results for the Founders' doctrines and the actual votes of individual Supreme Court justices for all the cases discussed in Chapters 5 and 6. Each of the Supreme Court justices selected authored at least five opinions in the thirty-five cases discussed or was a member of the Rehnquist Court (1986–2005). Once again, justices' votes are not projected for cases in which they did not participate. In Tables SC 3–SC 8, an "X" in the left-hand column under each Supreme Court case indicates a vote to uphold the state action challenged in the case.

The votes of some individual Supreme Court justices show high degrees of correlation with individual Founders. As shown in Table SC 2, Justice Felix Frankfurter voted for the result consistent with Jefferson's position in all seven of the sample cases in which he participated. He also had a high degree of correlation with Madisonianism (6/7). The votes of Justice Hugo Black, the author of *Everson* and the justice most responsible for the modern Court's initial turn to the Founders, do not strongly correlate with any one of the Founders.

Of the justices on the Rehnquist Court, Justices Stevens, Souter, and Ginsburg have voting patterns that approximate Jeffersonianism and are most at odds with Washingtonianism. Justice Ginsburg's votes correspond to the Jeffersonian result in seven of eight cases and disagree with Washingtonianism in all eight of the cases in which she participated. Similar patterns of voting exist for Justice Stevens and Justice Souter. They would have agreed with the Jeffersonian result in 13/18 and 8/10 cases, respectively, but reached the Washingtonian result in only 4/18 and 1/10 cases, respectively. Stevens, Souter, and Ginsburg depart from Jeffersonianism, in part, because they would have struck down instances of prayer in public school that Jeffersonianism would have allowed. For example, all three voted against the student-led pre-game football prayer in *Santa Fe*, whereas the Jeffersonian approach would have allowed it. Justice Stevens also would

TABLE SC 3. *Religion in Public Schools, Individual Supreme Court Justices and the Founders*

	Vitale	Schempp	Jaffree	Lee	Santa Fe	Newdow	McCollum	Zorach
Supreme Court	X	X	X	X	X	?	X	X
Madison	X	X	X	X	X	?	X	X
Washington	X	X	X	X	X	X	X	X
Jefferson	X	X	X	X	X	X	X	X
Black	X	X					X	X
Frankfurter							X	X
Douglas	X	X					X	X
Warren	X	X						
Brennan	X	X	X					
Stewart	X	X						
White		X	X	X				
Burger			X					
Blackmun			X	X				
Rehnquist			X	X	X	X		
Stevens			X	X	X			
O'Connor			X	X	X	X		
Scalia				X	X			
Kennedy				X	X			
Souter				X	X			
Thomas				X	X	X		
Ginsburg					X			
Breyer					X			

TABLE SC 4. *Public Aid to Private Religious Schools, Individual Supreme Court Justices and the Founders*

	Everson		Lemon		Mitchell		Zelman	
Supreme Court	X			X	X		X	
Madison	X		X		X		X	
Washington	X		X		X		X	
Jefferson		X		X		X		X
Black	X			X				
Frankfurter		X						
Douglas	X			X				
Warren								
Brennan				X				
Stewart				X				
White				X				
Burger				X				
Blackmun				X				
Rehnquist					X		X	
Stevens						X		X
O'Connor					X		X	
Scalia					X		X	
Kennedy					X		X	
Souter						X		X
Thomas					X		X	
Ginsburg						X		X
Breyer					X			X

have disagreed with Jeffersonianism in *Wallace v. Jaffree* and disallowed the moment of silence for prayer in public schools.[1]

The votes of Justices Rehnquist, Scalia, and Thomas reflect the opposite pattern of agreement and disagreement with Jefferson and Washington. These justices would have agreed with the Jeffersonian result in only 5/18, 2/14, and 2/11 cases, respectively. Justice Rehnquist voted the Washingtonian position in 17/18 cases. For the cases discussed, Justices Scalia and Thomas voted the Washingtonian position in every case in which they participated, 14/14 and 11/11 cases, respectively.

Of the justices on the Rehnquist Court, Justice Kennedy (8/11) and Justice Thomas (6/8) have the highest degree of correlation with Madisonianism, although it should be noted that neither justice has advocated a

---

[1] Justice Souter's other disagreement with Jeffersonianism is in the free exercise direct burden case *Lukumi Babalu Aye*. Souter voted to disallow the burden, whereas Jeffersonianism would allow it.

TABLE SC 5. *Religion in the Public Square, Individual Supreme Court Justices and the Founders*

	Marsh	Rosenberger	Good News Club	Lynch	Allegheny	McCreary	Van Orden
Supreme Court	X	X	X	X	X	?	X
Madison	X	X	X	X	X	?	?
Washington	X	X	X	X	X	X	X
Jefferson	X	X	X	X	X	X	X
Black							
Frankfurter							
Douglas							
Warren							
Brennan	X			X	X		
Stewart							
White	X			X			
Burger	X			X			
Blackmun	X			X	X		
Rehnquist	X	X	X	X	X	X	X
Stevens		X			X	X	X
O'Connor	X	X		X	X	X	X
Scalia		X	X		X	X	X
Kennedy		X	X		X	X	X
Souter			X			X	X
Thomas		X	X			X	X
Ginsburg		X				X	X
Breyer		X	X			X	X

TABLE SC 6. *Direct Burdens on Religious Exercise, Individual Supreme Court Justices and the Founders*

	Lukumi Babalu	McDaniel	Locke	
Supreme Court	X	X	X	
Madison	X	X		X
Washington	X	X		X
Jefferson	X	X	X	
Black				
Frankfurter				
Douglas				
Warren				
Brennan		X		
Stewart		X		
White	X	X		
Burger		X		
Blackmun	X			
Rehnquist		X	X	
Stevens	X	X	X	
O'Connor	X		X	
Scalia	X			X
Kennedy	X		X	
Souter	X		X	
Thomas	X			X
Ginsburg			X	
Breyer			X	

noncognizance interpretation of the religion clauses of the First Amendment. Justice Ginsburg's votes correlate the least (1/6) with Madisonianism. As can be seen in Tables SC 3–SC 8, Justices Black and Brennan show high degrees of correlation with Madison on Establishment Clause cases but not on Free Exercise Clause cases. In our thirty-five case sample, Justice Black voted for the Madisonian position in five of the six establishment cases he heard but only in three of the seven free exercise cases. Justice Brennan's votes, similarly, agreed with the Madisonian result in six of the seven establishment cases but only in two of the nine free exercise cases. Justice O'Connor also tended to reach Madisonian results more in establishment cases (8/10) than in free exercise cases (3/5).

It must be noted that all of the results just described reflect only a similarity in voting outcomes; they do not necessarily indicate that individual justices share the church-state philosophies of Madison, Washington, or Jefferson. As mentioned, neither Justice Kennedy nor Justice Thomas has advocated a noncognizance approach for First Amendment religion

TABLE SC 7. *Indirect Burdens on Religious Exercise, Individual Supreme Court Justices and the Founders*

	Reynolds	Gobitis	Barnette	Yoder	Braunfeld	Sherbert	Smith
Supreme Court	X	X	X	X	X	X	X
Madison	X	X	X	X	X	X	X
Washington	X	X	X	X	X	X	X
Jefferson	X	X	X	X	X	X	X
Black		X	X		X	X	
Frankfurter		X			X		
Douglas		X	X	X	X	X	
Warren							
Brennan				X	X	X	X
Stewart				X	X	X	
White				X		X	X
Burger				X			
Blackmun				X			X
Rehnquist							X
Stevens							X
O'Connor							X
Scalia							X
Kennedy							X
Souter							
Thomas							
Ginsburg							
Breyer							

TABLE SC 8. *State Identification of Religion for Regulation or Privilege, Individual Supreme Court Justices and the Founders*

	Cantwell	Walz	Texas Monthly	Amos	Arver	Seeger
Supreme Court		X		X	X	X
Madison		X		X	X	X
Washington	X	X	X	X	X	X
Jefferson		X		X	X	X
Black	X	X				X
Frankfurter	X					
Douglas	X	X				X
Warren						X
Brennan		X		X	X	X
Stewart		X				X
White		X		X	X	X
Burger		X				
Blackmun				X	X	
Rehnquist			X	X		
Stevens				X	X	
O'Connor				X	X	
Scalia			X	X		
Kennedy			X			
Souter						
Thomas						
Ginsburg						
Breyer						

jurisprudence, despite voting for results that approximate Madisonianism. The Jeffersonian results of Justices Stevens, Souter, and Ginsburg do not mean that their votes were driven by the same anticlericalism that animates Jeffersonianism. Nonetheless, it is notable that those justices whose opinions emphasize the divisive potential of religion show high degrees of correlation with Jefferson. Their interpretations of the First Amendment seem to indicate that they, like Jefferson, perceive religion to pose a danger to liberal democracy. It is also notable and unsurprising that the most conservative justices on the Rehnquist Court – Justices Rehnquist, Scalia, and Thomas – voted in a Washingtonian manner, as that approach allows legislatures to support religion.

Conclusion

The Founders and Church-State Jurisprudence

> A sanction is essential to the idea of law, as coercion is to that of Government.
>
> James Madison, Vices of the Political System of the United States (1787)

> To avoid an arbitrary discretion in the courts, it is indispensable that they should be bound down by strict rules and precedents, which serve to define and point out their duty in every particular case that comes before them. ...
>
> Publius, *Federalist* 78 (1788)

In 1878, the Supreme Court turned to Jefferson to adjudicate its first significant Free Exercise Clause case.[1] Nearly seventy years later, in 1947, the Court turned to Jefferson and Madison to resolve its first significant Establishment Clause case.[2] While not always in the foreground of the Court's deliberations, the Founders have been invoked time and time again to guide church-state jurisprudence, including in 2005, when Jefferson, Madison, and Washington were cited in opinions both for and against the constitutionality of state-sponsored postings of the Ten Commandments.[3] The Court, however, has never gotten the Founders right. Most of the justices who have turned to history – and many of the scholars and litigators who have done the research on which those interpretations are based – have assumed that the Founders shared a uniform understanding of the right to religious liberty and that this understanding should be used to adjudicate the First Amendment's religion clauses. But the leading

---

[1] *Reynolds v. United States*, 98 U.S. 145, 164 (1878).
[2] *Everson v. Board of Education*, 330 U.S. 1, 11–12 (1947).
[3] *McCreary County v. ACLU*, 545 U.S. 844, 877–78, 88n.26, 886–88 (2005); *Van Orden v. Perry*, 545 U.S. 677, 686–87 (2005).

Founders disagreed about the proper separation of church and state. We cannot simply ask, "What would the Founders do?" and then follow their example. Whatever the merits of history-based jurisprudence, the Founders' disagreement means that there is no single church-state position that can claim the exclusive authority of America's founding history and that no one Founder's position can be assumed to reflect the original meanings of the religion clauses.

The Founders' disagreement also means that we should view jurisprudential appeals to any one Founder with a large dose of circumspection, especially if an appeal claims to represent "the views of the Founders." It is easy to pick and choose from the leading Founders to support different church-state jurisprudential results. Want to keep prayer out of public schools? Refer to Madison. Need a quotation to support religion in the public square? Washington's Farewell Address works perfectly. Too often, a single quotation or an example from one Founder is used to imply that the entire founding generation stood for a particular understanding of religious liberty. Wariness of misleading interpretations is also warranted because the Founders tend to be used as judicial trump cards. The frequent use of originalism in church-state jurisprudence has led to a presumption by some that showing that a Founder is on one's side is a compelling legal argument. In most church-state cases, however, if one Founder supports one side, a different Founder supports the opposing side. Because the leading Founders disagreed, simply having a Founder on one's side is an inadequate legal position.

Some will interpret this finding to mean that the Founders are no longer pertinent to contemporary church-state concerns. How the Founders disagreed, however, makes them still worthy of our consideration. Because they disagreed, the Founders advanced arguments to defend their competing positions, and they made those arguments using philosophical reasoning and political considerations that can be as applicable today as they were more than 200 years ago. Understanding the Founders' differences and the reasons why they disagreed can help us think through the proper relationship between church and state today. Disregarding the Founders because they disagreed or because they wrote in a different age unnecessarily overlooks the thoughtfulness of some of America's greatest political thinkers. Even if we cannot simply turn to the Founders in a deferential manner and expect them to resolve our church-state disputes, we still can consult their ideas and arguments and apply them as we see fit.

Toward that end and without suggesting that any one Founder's position represents the original meaning of the First Amendment's religion clauses (the topic of a sequel to this volume), I have attempted to set forth the church-state political philosophies of James Madison, George Washington, and Thomas Jefferson. Part I attempted to explain each Founder's position. Part II attempted to apply those positions to some of the leading Establishment Clause and Free Exercise Clause cases that have come before the Supreme Court. My first aim has been to set the historical record straight so that if and when we consult individual Founders, we do so using a historically accurate record. Ultimately, however, understanding alone is not enough. We must also attempt to evaluate the suitability of the Founders' doctrines for our times. I close, accordingly, with an evaluation of the most and least persuasive elements of each Founder's position. I believe that a modified Madisonian approach captures the strongest elements of all three doctrines, while minimizing the weakest aspects of each. I reverse the order of the book and begin with Jefferson and Washington because the case for Madison can be best made by emphasizing his differences from their approaches. Others may (and certainly will) disagree with my judgments regarding the strengths and weaknesses of each Founder. I welcome that disagreement. My intention is not to end the conversation about which Founder, if any, we should follow. This study will have been successful if it directs that conversation in a manner that is historically accurate and constitutionally helpful.

THE CASE FOR AND AGAINST JEFFERSONIANISM

Grasping Jefferson's position is difficult because many of the political actions he took to establish religious liberty do not correspond to the natural rights philosophy he professed. In his draft of the Virginia Statute, Jefferson wrote that religious opinions were outside the jurisdiction of government and that individuals' civil capacities should not be affected on account of their religious opinions. But, in practice, he sought to use state power to shape Americans' religious opinions and to suppress the clerical political influences he thought dangerous. More so than Madison and Washington, Jefferson directly confronted the dangers that he believed religion posed to individual and political liberty. He thought that a country dedicated to the protection of individual rights and human equality required citizens with corresponding religious beliefs. He aimed, accordingly, to suppress the religious dogmas that priests used to oppress their parishioners and to degrade the religious institutions that used superstition to maintain artificial hierarchies. Jefferson overlooked his philosophical principles of liberty and equality when he thought doing so was necessary to achieve liberty and equality.

Chapter 3 suggested that Jefferson believed society had to progress and become more reasonable before the natural rights of religious freedom could be extended to all – that only after society had been emancipated from irrational theological dogmas could the state secure everyone's right not to be punished on account of religious opinions and not to have one's civil rights affected on account of religious beliefs or practices (or lack thereof). Emphasizing the developmental character of Jefferson's position minimizes the distance between his professed philosophy and his political practice. A candid assessment requires, however, that we acknowledge the inconsistency that lies at the heart of the Jeffersonian project. The second prong of the Jeffersonian doctrine – that the state should not affect an individual's or institution's civil rights on account of (or lack of) religious opinions, religious professions, or religious worship – is premised on the idea of universal natural rights. The first prong of the doctrine – the state should not advance and may curtail the influence of religious clergy, sectarian religious beliefs, and sectarian religious institutions – does not protect those rights for some.

The elements of this contradiction will be seen by some as the doctrine's strength; by others, its fundamental weakness. The first prong's hostility toward irrational theological influences is likely to find favor with those who believe that religion poses intolerable political dangers. The first prong allows the state to impose disabilities on those religions that it believes exercise mental and spiritual tyranny. Cases like *Rosenberger v. University of Virginia* (in which the university excluded evangelical students from using student activity funds) and *McDaniel v. Paty* (in which the state of Tennessee excluded religious ministers from certain political offices) exemplify the types of state discrimination that Jeffersonianism would allow. But this embrace of discrimination also can be considered Jeffersonianism's most alarming feature. The doctrine's first prong eschews the ideal of equal treatment before the law. For those opposed to discrimination on the basis of religion, Jeffersonianism is likely to be viewed as fundamentally unsound.

Jeffersonianism also contains significant methodological problems. The demands of the first prong often contradict the requirements of the second prong, which makes the doctrine exceedingly difficult to apply in a non-discretionary manner. The minister exclusion at issue in *McDaniel v. Paty* offers such an example. The first prong would allow the state to exclude from public office ministers who preach theologically irrational dogmas. Enforcement of the second prong, however, would prohibit such an exclusion. In Chapters 5 and 6, priority was given to the first prong when the two came into conflict because it was asserted that religious clergy still remain dangerous from a Jeffersonian point of view. But this determination, frankly, was made somewhat arbitrarily. How does one render a judgment as to whether religious clergy remain politically dangerous?

The question is not of a legal character and not resolved by the Jeffersonian doctrine itself. Jeffersonianism requires judges to "play Jefferson" and to do what they think Jefferson would do at a given point in society's development. The approach forces judges to make a discretionary judgment about whether irrational theological dogmas should be suppressed (in imitation of Jefferson's political activities) or whether individuals' civil rights should not be affected on account of religion (to follow Jefferson's philosophical principles). At the most basic level, the approach does not embody the rule of law.

If it is determined that religion remains a danger to society and that the first prong of the Jeffersonian doctrine should be applied, another difficulty emerges: Application of the first prong requires judges to distinguish rational from irrational theological dogmas. In Chapter 5, we suggested that Jeffersonianism would allow the state to promote religion that corresponds to Jefferson's own understanding of rational religious belief but suppress religion that reflects irrational theological dogmas. To differentiate what Jefferson considered to be rational (and, hence, constitutional) from irrational (unconstitutional), we consulted Jefferson's own examples of endorsing some and discouraging other religious sentiments. But such examples are, at best, idiosyncratic. Jefferson's theology reflects the currents of natural religion that were popular among leading intellectuals of his time.[4] Jefferson himself never attempted to systematically distinguish rational from irrational religious beliefs. This is not to say that he was necessarily wrong to hold doctrines like the Trinity to be irrational and the idea of a creator god to be rational, but Jefferson did not bother to provide the arguments to sustain the distinction. His few days of work to identify what was "genuine" in the Gospels, which he described to be as difficult as distinguishing diamonds in dunghills, exemplify Jefferson's approach to theology.[5] Whatever its merits, his method was shallowly cavalier and clearly insufficient to form the basis of sound theological or philosophical judgments. To base constitutional interpretations of the First Amendment on it or on Jefferson's understanding of late-eighteenth-century religious rationalism would seem to be outlandish. Dispensing with Jefferson's theology and allowing judges to

---

[4] For a discussion of how Jefferson was influenced by Joseph Priestly in particular, see Paul K. Conkin, "Priestly and Jefferson: Unitarianism as a Religion for a New Revolutionary Age," in *Religion in a Revolutionary Age*, eds. Ronald Hoffman and Peter J. Albert (Charlottesville: The University Press of Virginia, 1994), 290–307.

[5] Thomas Jefferson to Francis Adrian Van der Kemp, April 25, 1816, in *Jefferson's Extracts from the Gospels*, ed. Dickenson W. Adams (Princeton, NJ: Princeton University Press, 1983), 369.

make their own independent judgments about the rationality of theological dogmas would not likely improve matters as such an inquiry extends beyond usual judicial competence. In short, the application of Jeffersonianism's first prong demands more from constitutional law than most judges can deliver.

Jefferson himself seems not to have been overly concerned about treating some types of religion in a discriminatory manner or about the contradictions between his stated principles and actual practices. He may have believed that time and societal progress would overcome the need for state discrimination against religion. With the right system of public education and with an increase of political and intellectual freedom, Jefferson anticipated that belief in irrational religious dogmas would diminish. The problem of imposing public policies at odds with the natural rights of religious freedom (such as excluding ministers from office) would then fade away, and the tension between what was necessary to establish religious freedom and to protect natural rights would correspondingly decrease. But such "progress," if it can be called that, has not materialized. Political liberty has not led most men to adopt Jefferson's religion of rationalism in the way that he expected. The distance between Jeffersonian theory and Jeffersonian practice would still exist today, and that distance creates numerous drawbacks for implementing a Jeffersonian approach to church-state separation.

Jefferson's faith in progress and his uncritical faith in the rationality of his own religious beliefs lie at the heart of what is most unsatisfactory about his approach. Jefferson presumed that his perception of religious truth was the truth about religion. He presumed that, once educated, most people would come to adopt his religious views and his views about religion. One cannot doubt the sincerity of his intention to establish religious freedom, but, taken as a whole, his approach to church and state might more accurately be described as the establishment of the religion of Jeffersonianism.

The preamble of the Virginia Statute contains a striking irony. Jefferson argues against state interference with opinions because every magistrate tends to "make his opinion the rule of judgment, and approve or condemn the sentiments of others only as they shall square with or differ from his own." This describes exactly what Jefferson himself attempted to do. Jefferson sought to use state power to nurture those religious opinions that he thought were reasonable and to suppress those opinions he thought were irrational. The more one has faith in Jefferson's religious opinions and shares his estimation of the dangers that religion poses to individual and political liberty, the more one will find his approach to church-state matters persuasive. But to the extent one doubts Jefferson's religion of rationalism, questions his faith in progress, and is committed to the principle of nondiscrimination in religious matters, one is not likely to become an adherent of, or advocate for, Jeffersonianism.

THE CASE FOR AND AGAINST WASHINGTONIANISM

One finds nothing like Jefferson's attempt to transform the nation's religious opinions in Washington's church-state politics. Washington did not share Jefferson's views of the danger that religion posed to liberal democracy, which helps to explain why he did not hesitate to employ religion for political purposes. Instead of attempting to liberalize religion, Washington tried to harness it to serve civic ends, especially the nurturing of moral character and good citizenship.

For Washington, the right to religious liberty meant that the state could not legitimately coerce individuals to practice a religion they did not believe in or, absent a legitimate nonreligious civic purpose, prevent individuals from practicing their religion. As discussed in Chapters 5 and 6, Washingtonianism would only prevent state actions that, without a legitimate nonreligious civic purpose, directly burden religion. The approach gives wide latitude to legislators to utilize religion to further civic purposes.

Washingtonianism is likely to appeal to those who share Washington's estimation of the beneficial qualities religion offers to republican government. More than Jeffersonianism or Madisonianism, the approach would allow the state to endorse and even fund religion in order to promote civic purposes. Under a Washingtonian construction of the Establishment Clause, voluntary prayer could be included in public schools, taxes could fund religious education, and religion would be allowed and encouraged in the public square. Washingtonianism would not include exemptions from indirectly burdensome laws as part of the right to religious liberty, but it would allow legislative and executive exemptions from such laws. The approach presumes that what is good for religion is usually good for the polity, and, therefore, it allows a cooperative relationship between church and state.

While some will consider the approach's political embrace of religion to be its strength, others might consider this to be the position's most significant weakness. Washingtonianism implicitly encourages and constitutionally requires state actors to view religion in a politically utilitarian manner. Because the approach allows state support of religion only for civic purposes, state actors must define and defend support of religion in nonreligious terms. Legislators could not legitimately adopt a program of funding churches only because it is "good for religion." This requirement can lead the government to support religion in ways that may not be good for religion and to encourage its politicization.

How state support might be bad for religion can be seen in cases pertaining to religion in public schools. As discussed in Chapter 5, Washingtonianism would allow religious instruction programs like the one struck down in *McCollum* and prayers in public schools like the one struck down in *Lee v. Weisman*. In both cases, public school officials oversaw the religious exercises. In *McCollum*, the individuals who taught the religion classes were subject to approval by school officials. In *Lee v. Weisman*, the school principal gave the rabbi who delivered the graduation prayer guidelines to govern the prayer's content. While such oversight may be benign or even useful, as long as the interests of the state and the interests of religion do not perfectly coincide, state control and direction of religion always runs the risk of being harmful to religion. Many religiously devout parents, no doubt, would frown upon the prayers that public school officials would have their children recite.

State support of religion also can infuse ordinary politics with sectarian disagreements. While political disagreement is not necessarily bad, partisan disagreements along religious lines can be especially troublesome. Religious disagreements often are animated by matters of suprarational faith and, as such, are resistant to compromise. Given the history of religious conflict among Christians and among different religions and the fact that religion involves matters of eternal salvation and damnation, it is not unreasonable to conclude that political moderation can become especially hard to reach when political partisanship is infused with sectarian disagreements. To the extent that Washingtonianism allows the state to support religion, it encourages religious citizens to act politically as religious citizens and thereby exposes ordinary politics to the turbulence of religious disagreement.

The politicization of religion can be further exacerbated by state discrimination among religions, which the Washingtonian approach allows. Washingtonianism is different from Justice Rehnquist's nonpreferential interpretation of the Establishment Clause, which would require the state to treat all religions equally. Washingtonianism allows the government to support religion because religion can serve civic ends, which means that religions that fail to further the civic purposes of any given state program do not have to be treated equally to those that do. The Washingtonian approach does not demand state discrimination against any religion and would only allow such discrimination to be based on civic criteria. But the allowance of any state discrimination among religions invites the politicization of religious disagreements and encourages the development of sectarian politics.

Washingtonianism does require public support of religion to be sufficiently ecumenical, and to some extent this would mitigate concerns about sectarian politics. But ecumenicalism itself introduces another potential weakness of the approach. As we discussed in Chapter 2, Washington was aware of the sectarian dangers present with any state support of religion, which is why he always endorsed religion in general, nonsectarian terms. His masterful public pronouncements, which included religion without introducing religious division, remain a model for public officials. Yet this aspect of his church-state politics defies easy translation into a legal doctrine. To integrate Washington's nuanced support of religion into a constitutional doctrine, we included the rule that state support of religion be as ecumenical as possible given the state interest being pursued. But this requirement makes a poor judicial rule. What is sufficiently ecumenical for any given public policy is not easily knowable in an objective, legal sense. If the test of "sufficient ecumenicalism" was not enforced, the approach would lack its check against sectarian politics; but if enforced, the approach is subject to excessive judicial discretion.

This drawback to the Washingtonian approach seems inevitable given the character of who Washington was and the nature of his position. Washington spoke and acted like an executive officer. His church-state politics, like all of his politics, reflect the virtues of prudence and moderation. But these virtues do not translate easily into legal rules that can be straightforwardly applied by judges. Even if Washington offers a model of executive action that should be imitated by presidents and generals, as a judicial doctrine, his position has inherent weaknesses.

THE CASE FOR AND AGAINST MADISONIANISM

More than Jefferson's and Washington's approaches, Madison's church-state doctrine reflects the views of a constitution writer concerned with drafting a principle for others to interpret and execute. In most cases, noncognizance can be applied consistently, straightforwardly, and with a minimum of discretionary judgment. Madisonianism would have judges ask: Does the state action at issue take cognizance of religion as such? It would not require judges to decide the rationality of a theological doctrine from a Jeffersonian point of view or to inquire whether a program was sufficiently ecumenical as required by Washingtonianism. In many instances, the demands of noncognizance are sufficiently knowable that church-state issues likely could be resolved without recourse to litigation. Take, for example, participation by religious groups in state-funded programs. Noncognizance would prevent the state from either including or excluding participation on the basis of religion. Religious groups could participate in government-funded programs as long as they qualified for doing so on the basis of a nonreligious criterion. Any state-funded program that limited participation to religious groups or that funded groups on account of their religious affiliation would be a clear violation of noncognizance. For Free Exercise Clause cases, noncognizance would provide especially clear rules: a categorical prohibition on state actions that directly burden or directly identify religion as such; no prohibition of state actions that indirectly burden religion.

Madisonian noncognizance also would generate constitutional decisions that seem fairer than Jeffersonianism and, compared with Washingtonianism, better protect against religious sectarianism. By removing religion as a cause or object of state action, noncognizance more closely approximates the principle of equality than Jeffersonianism or Washingtonianism. As discussed earlier in this chapter, Jeffersonianism allows the state to treat some citizens differently on account of religion for the purpose of minimizing clerical and irrational theological influences. It would have upheld the minister exclusion for office in *McDaniel v. Paty* and the exclusion of religious groups from eligibility for state-funded subsidies in *Rosenberger v. University of Virginia*. Madisonianism, by contrast, would have prohibited such exclusions because it forbids the state from imposing special disabilities on religion or from excluding religion from programs of general availability. Madisonianism thus erects a higher barrier than Jeffersonianism against state discrimination against religion and, thereby, better realizes the ideal that citizens be treated equally on account of religion or lack thereof.

Madisonianism also furthers equality by imposing a constitutional barrier against state discrimination in favor of religion. By making religion an illegitimate category of political action, noncognizance prohibits the state from extending benefits to religion as such. Politically powerful religious sects are thus prevented from obtaining legislation that would benefit their own sect and from partnering with other sects to obtain legislation that would benefit religion generally, actions that Washingtonianism would likely allow under the rubric of furthering civic interests.

By prohibiting special privileges for religion, Madisonianism also provides an institutional check against sectarian politics that Washingtonianism lacks. Tax exemptions offer a good example of how the two doctrines would lead to different church-state politics. Washingtonianism would not prevent a politically powerful religion from advocating for a tax exemption for itself alone – on the grounds that it especially nurtures good citizenship – or from joining with other religions and advocating for a tax exemption for all religions. Madisonianism, by contrast, would require religions to advocate for a tax exemption by using nonreligious criteria, such as "nonprofit" status. Madison's approach demands that religions define and defend their political interests in nonreligious terms. Similar to Washingtonianism, non-cognizance demands that state actions have a nonreligious purpose or end; but beyond Washingtonianism, Madisonianism does not allow religion to be identified or recognized in law to further those legitimate civic ends. By forcing religions to shed their religious identities when acting politically, Madisonianism imposes a more robust constitutional check against the development of sectarian politics.

Some citizens, no doubt, would criticize Madisonianism for disallowing religion as a category for legitimate political action. Unlike Washingtonianism, noncognizance would prohibit the state from legislating religious exemptions from generally applicable laws and regulations. Religious-based conscientious exemptions from military service, for example, would be unconstitutional. Special tax exemptions for churches also would be prohibited, as would religious exemptions from nondiscrimination legislation, such as the religion exemption from Title VII of the 1964 Civil Rights Act. Even legal exemptions designed to prevent the criminalization of religious behavior or to offset laws that disproportionately impact minority religions, such as exemptions from the drug laws that made the Native American Church's peyote use illegal in *Smith*, would be prohibited. Madisonianism would not prevent religions from qualifying for non-religious-based exemptions, but the approach would not allow religion as such to serve as the basis of qualification for an exemption.

A related criticism is that by prohibiting the state from acknowledging religion, Madisonianism denies religion from receiving the same type of state recognition that other groups receive. As discussed in Chapter 5, noncognizance would prohibit state-sponsored religious displays set up in conjunction with the celebration of holy days. Other culture, ethnic, and identity groups, however, are not subject to the same limitations. Under Madisonianism, state-sponsored celebrations of Black History Month or Gay Pride Week, for example, would be permitted, whereas Christmas trees at a county airport would be prohibited. Strictly applied, noncognizance even would limit the nonlegislative acts of public officials – Madison himself wrote in his "Detached Memoranda" that official presidential proclamations of days of prayer and thanksgiving violated a proper understanding of religious liberty. The prohibition against these types of symbolic state endorsements of religion seems unnecessarily hostile toward religion and to impose a "naked public square" on society. Even though noncognizance promotes equality in many ways, in this sense it subjects religion to unequal treatment.

A further criticism of Madisonianism is that it does not resolve all cases clearly. For most types of cases, noncognizance produces straightforward results that are easy to understand. What constitutes "religion," however, is not always clear; and, in a handful of cases, whether the state has taken cognizance of religion is difficult to determine. Three such cases were described in Chapter 5: *Elk Grove School District v. Newdow*, *McCreary County v. American Civil Liberties Union*, and *Van Orden v. Perry*. In these cases, the state actions in question could be understood in religious terms, nonreligious terms, or both religious and nonreligious terms. Take the Ten Commandments cases, *McCreary County* and *Van Orden*. For obvious reasons, displays of the Ten Commandments can be considered to take cognizance of religion. But particular circumstances in each case make the nature of the challenged displays complicated. In *Van Orden*, the monument in question was donated to the state by a private group and was one of seventeen monuments and twenty-one historical markers on the capitol grounds that commemorated the "people, ideals, and events that compose Texan identity."[6] Given this context, one could consider the monument to be a part of a cultural exhibit akin to a religiously themed painting in an art museum. In *McCreary County*, the county's third display posted the display of the Ten Commandments next to eight other equally sized documents in a (purportedly) educational exhibit depicting the foundations of American government. Whether the display was actually educational, religious, or both is unclear and debatable; but because it is unclear and debatable, so is the display's constitutional status under noncognizance. The same type of problem surfaces with "under God" in the Pledge of Allegiance, the First Amendment issue in *Newdow*. As discussed in Chapter 5, the meaning of "under God" is ambiguous. The words could be interpreted to take cognizance of religion, but they could also be interpreted as being merely political.

The difficulty of specifying what is "religion" in these cases does not make Madisonianism unworkable, but it does reveal that the approach is not self-executing. In some cases, Madisonianism requires contextual judgments, and these judgments will have more to do with the outcome of the

---

[6] H.R. 38, 77th Leg. (Texas 2001), cited in *Van Orden v. Perry*, 545 U.S. 677, 681 (2005).

case than any other determination. What is true for noncognizance is likely
true for any legal doctrine, but it so happens that Madisonianism hits its
limits on two of the most controversial Establishment Clause cases in recent
history.

THE CASE FOR A MODIFIED VERSION OF THE FOUNDERS' APPROACHES: "NO LEGAL PRIVILEGES, NO LEGAL PENALTIES"

None of the Founders' approaches is without its drawbacks. Jeffersonianism's first prong contradicts its second prong. The Jeffersonian approach,
moreover, requires judges to make nonjudicial judgments, and it allows the
state to discriminate against religion. Washingtonianism allows the state to
discriminate in favor of religion and, by so doing, exposes ordinary politics
to religious sectarianism and religion to politicization. The Washingtonian
approach also includes the requirement of sufficient ecumenicalism, which
makes for a poor judicial rule. Madisonianism does not allow religion to
receive recognition equal to other groups and it does not resolve all cases
clearly. Yet each approach also has advantages. I would contend that a
modified version of Madisonianism can retain what is most advantageous
in all three approaches while minimizing the weaknesses of each.

We can call this modified approach "No legal privileges, no legal penalties." As its name suggests, the doctrine would prohibit the state from
extending legal privileges and legal penalties to religion as such. It is similar
to the Madisonian approach insofar as it would prohibit religion from being
used as a category for most state action. Unlike Madisonianism, however,
"no legal privileges, no legal penalties" would allow the state to become
cognizant of religion in symbolic ways. It would allow the state to set up
religious displays in the town square to celebrate holidays and allow public
officials to endorse religion in noncoercive ways. Postings of the Ten Commandments, prayers at public school graduations, and "under God" in the
Pledge of Allegiance would not amount to constitutional violations. The
state could not affect an individual's civil rights or privileges on account
of religion – participation in a graduation prayer, for example, would have
to remain voluntary, meaning nonparticipation could not be punished. But
so long as the state did not affect an individual's rights or legal privileges on
account of religion, state recognition of religion would be permissible.

"No legal privileges, no legal penalties" would more easily resolve the
types of cases that noncognizance fails to adjudicate decisively. For noncoercive symbolic speech and display cases, judges would not have to ask the
difficult question of whether such speech was religious. Instead, judges

would ask the preliminary question of whether an individual was privileged or punished in a nonsymbolic way – for example, by being expelled from school for not reciting "under God" in the Pledge. If no such penalty was imposed, no possibility of a constitutional violation would exist. "No legal privileges, no legal penalties" would not overcome the Madisonian difficulty of identifying religion as such, but it would reduce the likelihood of that difficulty affecting constitutional decision-making because symbolic recognition of religion would no longer raise constitutional concerns.

"No legal privileges, no legal penalties" also would better approximate equality than Madisonianism. Given modern identity politics and the pervasive impact of public education on American culture, Madison's prohibition against state recognition of religion can appear to single out religious persons or groups for unfavorable treatment, as was mentioned previously. Take the promotion of culture and identity that lies at the heart of state promotion of "diversity." If the state promotes Black History Month (officially the month of February), Asian/Pacific Islander Heritage Month (officially the month of April), and Gay Pride Week (usually in June) but cannot take cognizance of religious celebrations such as Christmas, religion seems subject to unequal treatment. In a more libertarian age when the state was not involved in the promotion of culture and identity, noncognizance would not have the same impact. But given modern identity politics, the prohibition against state recognition seems unnecessarily hostile toward religion. "No legal privileges, no legal penalties" would allow religion to receive the same type of symbolic state acknowledgment that other identity and cultural groups receive.

"No legal privileges, no legal penalties" also would incorporate some of the strongest aspects of Washingtonianism while minimizing its shortcomings. To the extent that "no legal privileges, no legal penalties" allows the state to acknowledge religion in symbolic ways, it allows promotion of the religiously based moral character that Washington thought essential to republican citizenship. But by prohibiting the state from extending legal privileges or imposing penalties on religion, the approach would retain Madisonianism's powerful checks against the development of sectarian politics and the politicization of religion. "No legal privileges, no legal penalties" provides the state a way to endorse religion while, at the same time, retaining an institutional check against the development of political divisions along religious lines. More clearly than the Washingtonian call for sufficient ecumenicalism, the approach provides an institutional mechanism for balancing the advantages and disadvantages of governmental support of religion.

"No legal privileges, no legal penalties" also captures what is best in Jefferson's approach. We have called the approach a modification of Madisonianism, but it also could be called a modification of Jeffersonianism. "No legal privileges, no legal penalties" is the same as the second prong of the Jeffersonian doctrine. The approach captures Jefferson's natural rights philosophy, that the state should not affect individuals' rights on account of religion, but eschews Jefferson's anticlericalism. Consistent with the second prong of Jefferson's doctrine, "no legal privileges, no legal penalties" would prevent politically powerful religious groups from legislating special privileges for their own members and from saddling nonmembers with particular burdens. At the same time, by not allowing the state to discriminate against some types of religion or religious individuals, it would avoid the contradictions and hostility toward religion that are reflected in Jefferson's politics.

It must be acknowledged that Madison himself would likely object to "no legal privileges, no legal penalties" because it fails to respect the boundaries he articulated in the "Memorial and Remonstrance." As was discussed in Chapter 1, Madison derives his doctrine of state noncognizance of religion directly from the "unalienable right" of every person to exercise religion as his conscience dictates. It is arguable, however, that Madison's social contract theory in the "Memorial" is partially mistaken, and that noncognizance is *not* a necessary inference from the inalienable right to religious freedom. Madison argues that within the social contract, individuals retain the right to discharge religious obligations as they see fit. This right, however, only would seem to restrict the state from prescribing religious obligations and from punishing individuals for exercising their religion as such. State action that merely acknowledges religion (without imposing legal privileges or punishments) would not seem to interfere with the right to exercise religion according to conscience. To speak more generally, noncognizance imposes an unnecessarily wide barrier because it fails to distinguish government action that restricts freedom from state action that influences the ways individuals exercise their freedom. It fails to recognize the difference between punishing nonattendance at Christmas religious services (restriction of religious freedom) from making Christmas day an official government holiday (recognition of religion).

Madison's overreaching in the "Memorial," if we can call it that, is somewhat surprising given that he himself drew an essential connection between law and sanctions in his essay "Vices of the Political System of the United States." There Madison wrote, "A sanction is essential to the idea of law, as coercion is to that of Government."[7] Governmental actions that fall short of coercion and that do not grant privileges or impose penalties do not qualify as "law" in the precise Madisonian sense of the term. Such actions, accordingly, do not trespass the limits on law required to respect man's inalienable right to religious freedom.

This minimal defense of "no legal privileges, no legal penalties" is not meant to be exhaustive, but rather to show how constitutional jurisprudence can be informed by the Founders without blindly or erroneously following them. The approach does not reflect everything in the Founders' church-state positions – a point of this study is to explain why no legal doctrine could. I believe that it does, however, account for what is best in Madison's, Washington's, and Jefferson's different doctrines.

As I have tried to demonstrate, those differences mean that we cannot simply adopt "the Founding view" to guide our church-state constitutional politics. Rather, the Founders can serve as a rich source of ideas and understandings about religious freedom and the proper separation of church and state. They may not be able to govern us directly or provide us with a uniform constitutional doctrine, but we can consult the Founders to help us govern ourselves more thoughtfully, to separate church and state more intelligently, and to better protect religious freedom.

---

[7] James Madison, "Vices of the Political System of the United States," April 1787, in *The Mind of the Founder: Sources of the Political Thought of James Madison*, ed. Marvin Meyers, rev. edition (Hanover, NH: Brandeis University Press, 1981), 59.

Appendix A

"Memorial and Remonstrance against Religious Assessments" by James Madison, 1785

To the Honorable the General Assembly of the Commonwealth of Virginia
A Memorial and Remonstrance

We the subscribers, citizens of the said Commonwealth, having taken into serious consideration, a Bill printed by order of the last Session of General Assembly, entitled "A Bill establishing a provision for Teachers of the Christian Religion," and conceiving that the same if finally armed with the sanctions of a law, will be a dangerous abuse of power, are bound as faithful members of a free State to remonstrate against it, and to declare the reasons by which we are determined. We remonstrate against the said Bill,

1. Because we hold it for a fundamental and undeniable truth, "that Religion or the duty which we owe to our Creator and the manner of discharging it, can be directed only by reason and conviction, not by force or violence" [Virginia Declaration of Rights, art. 16]. The Religion then of every man must be left to the conviction and conscience of every man; and it is the right of every man to exercise it as these may dictate. This right is in its nature an unalienable right. It is unalienable, because the opinions of men, depending only on the evidence contemplated by their own minds cannot follow the dictates of other men: It is unalienable also, because what is here a right towards men, is a duty towards the Creator. It is the duty of every man to render to the Creator such homage and such only as he believes to be acceptable to him. This duty is precedent, both in order of time and in degree of obligation, to the claims of Civil Society. Before any man can be considered as a member of Civil Society, he must be considered as a subject of the Governour of the Universe: And if a member of Civil Society, who enters into any subordinate Association, must always do it with a reservation of his

duty to the General Authority; much more must every man who becomes a member of any particular Civil Society, do it with a saving of his allegiance to the Universal Sovereign. We maintain therefore that in matters of Religion, no mans [sic] right is abridged by the institution of Civil Society and that Religion is wholly exempt from its cognizance. True it is, that no other rule exists, by which any question which may divide a Society, can be ultimately determined, but the will of the majority; but it is also true that the majority may trespass on the rights of the minority.

2. Because if Religion be exempt from the authority of the Society at large, still less can it be subject to that of the Legislative Body. The latter are but the creatures and vicegerents of the former. Their jurisdiction is both derivative and limited: it is limited with regard to the co-ordinate departments, more necessarily it is limited with regard to the constituents. The preservation of a free Government requires not merely, that the metes and bounds which separate each department of power be invariably maintained; but more especially that neither of them be suffered to overleap the great Barrier which defends the rights of the people. The Rulers who are guilty of such an encroachment, exceed the commission from which they derive their authority, and are Tyrants. The People who submit to it are governed by laws made neither by themselves nor by an authority derived from them, and are slaves.

3. Because it is proper to take alarm at the first experiment on our liberties. We hold this prudent jealousy to be the first duty of Citizens, and one of the noblest characteristics of the late Revolution. The free men of America did not wait till usurped power had strengthened itself by exercise, and entangled the question in precedents. They saw all the consequences in the principle, and they avoided the consequences by denying the principle. We revere this lesson too much soon to forget it. Who does not see that the same authority which can establish Christianity, in exclusion of all other Religions, may establish with the same ease any particular sect of Christians, in exclusion of all other Sects? That the same authority which can force a citizen to contribute three pence only of his property for the support of any one establishment, may force him to conform to any other establishment in all cases whatsoever?

4. Because the Bill violates that equality which ought to be the basis of every law, and which is more indispensible, in proportion as the validity or expediency of any law is more liable to be impeached. If "all men are by nature equally free and independent" [Virginia Declaration of Rights, art. 1], all men are to be considered as entering into Society on equal conditions; as relinquishing no more, and therefore retaining no less, one than another,

of their natural rights. Above all are they to be considered as retaining an "*equal* title to the free exercise of Religion according to the dictates of Conscience" [Virginia Declaration of Rights, art. 16]. Whilst we assert for ourselves a freedom to embrace, to profess and to observe the Religion which we believe to be of divine origin, we cannot deny an equal freedom to those whose minds have not yet yielded to the evidence which has convinced us. If this freedom be abused, it is an offence against God, not against man: To God, therefore, not to man, must an account of it be rendered. As the Bill violates equality by subjecting some to peculiar burdens, so it violates the same principle, by granting to others peculiar exemptions. Are the Quakers and Menonists the only sects who think a compulsive support of their Religions unnecessary and unwarrantable? Can their piety alone be entrusted with the care of public worship? Ought their Religions to be endowed above all others with extraordinary privileges by which proselytes may be enticed from all others? We think too favorably of the justice and good sense of these denominations to believe that they either covet preeminences over their fellow citizens or that they will be seduced by them from the common opposition to the measure.

5. Because the Bill implies either that the Civil Magistrate is a competent Judge of Religious Truth; or that he may employ Religion as an engine of Civil policy. The first is an arrogant pretension falsified by the contradictory opinions of Rulers in all ages, and throughout the world: the second an unhallowed perversion of the means of salvation.

6. Because the establishment proposed by the Bill is not requisite for the support of the Christian Religion. To say that it is, is a contradiction to the Christian Religion itself, for every page of it disavows a dependence on the powers of this world: it is a contradiction to fact; for it is known that this Religion both existed and flourished, not only without the support of human laws, but in spite of every opposition from them, and not only during the period of miraculous aid, but long after it had been left to its own evidence and the ordinary care of Providence. Nay, it is a contradiction in terms; for a Religion not invented by human policy, must have pre-existed and been supported, before it was established by human policy. It is moreover to weaken in those who profess this Religion a pious confidence in its innate excellence and the patronage of its Author; and to foster in those who still reject it, a suspicion that its friends are too conscious of its fallacies to trust it to its own merits.

7. Because experience witnesseth that ecclesiastical establishments, instead of maintaining the purity and efficacy of Religion, have had a contrary operation. During almost fifteen centuries has the legal establishment

of Christianity been on trial. What have been its fruits? More or less in all places, pride and indolence in the Clergy, ignorance and servility in the laity, in both, superstition, bigotry and persecution. Enquire of the Teachers of Christianity for the ages in which it appeared in its greatest lustre; those of every sect, point to the ages prior to its incorporation with Civil policy. Propose a restoration of this primitive State in which its Teachers depended on the voluntary rewards of their flocks, many of them predict its downfall. On which Side ought their testimony to have greatest weight, when for or when against their interest?

8. Because the establishment in question is not necessary for the support of Civil Government. If it be urged as necessary for the support of Civil Government only as it is a means of supporting Religion, and it be not necessary for the latter purpose, it cannot be necessary for the former. If Religion be not within the cognizance of Civil Government how can its legal establishment be necessary to Civil Government? What influence in fact have ecclesiastical establishments had on Civil Society? In some instances they have been seen to erect a spiritual tyranny on the ruins of the Civil authority; in many instances they have been seen upholding the thrones of political tyranny: in no instance have they been seen the guardians of the liberties of the people. Rulers who wished to subvert the public liberty, may have found an established Clergy convenient auxiliaries. A just Government instituted to secure & perpetuate it needs them not. Such a Government will be best supported by protecting every Citizen in the enjoyment of his Religion with the same equal hand which protects his person and his property; by neither invading the equal rights of any Sect, nor suffering any Sect to invade those of another.

9. Because the proposed establishment is a departure from that generous policy, which, offering an Asylum to the persecuted and oppressed of every Nation and Religion, promised a lustre to our country, and an accession to the number of its citizens. What a melancholy mark is the Bill of sudden degeneracy? Instead of holding forth an Asylum to the persecuted, it is itself a signal of persecution. It degrades from the equal rank of Citizens all those whose opinions in Religion do not bend to those of the Legislative authority. Distant as it may be in its present form from the Inquisition, it differs from it only in degree. The one is the first step, the other the last in the career of intolerance. The magnanimous sufferer under this cruel scourge in foreign Regions, must view the Bill as a Beacon on our Coast, warning him to seek some other haven, where liberty and philanthrophy in their due extent, may offer a more certain repose from his Troubles.

10. Because it will have a like tendency to banish our Citizens. The allurements presented by other situations are every day thinning their

number. To superadd a fresh motive to emigration by revoking the liberty which they now enjoy, would be the same species of folly which has dishonoured and depopulated flourishing kingdoms.

11. Because it will destroy that moderation and harmony which the forbearance of our laws to intermeddle with Religion has produced among its several sects. Torrents of blood have been spilt in the old world, by vain attempts of the secular arm, to extinguish Religious discord, by proscribing all difference in Religious opinion. Time has at length revealed the true remedy. Every relaxation of narrow and rigorous policy, wherever it has been tried, has been found to assuage the disease. The American Theatre has exhibited proofs that equal and compleat liberty, if it does not wholly eradicate it, sufficiently destroys its malignant influence on the health and prosperity of the State. If with the salutary effects of this system under our own eyes, we begin to contract the bounds of Religious freedom, we know no name that will too severely reproach our folly. At least let warning be taken at the first fruits of the threatened innovation. The very appearance of the Bill has transformed "that Christian forbearance, love and charity" [Virginia Declaration of Rights, art. 16], which of late mutually prevailed, into animosities and jealousies, which may not soon be appeased. What mischiefs may not be dreaded, should this enemy to the public quiet be armed with the force of a law?

12. Because the policy of the Bill is adverse to the diffusion of the light of Christianity. The first wish of those who enjoy this precious gift ought to be that it may be imparted to the whole race of mankind. Compare the number of those who have as yet received it with the number still remaining under the dominion of false Religions; and how small is the former! Does the policy of the Bill tend to lessen the disproportion? No; it at once discourages those who are strangers to the light of revelation from coming into the Region of it; and countenances by example the nations who continue in darkness, in shutting out those who might convey it to them. Instead of Levelling as far as possible, every obstacle to the victorious progress of Truth, the Bill with an ignoble and unchristian timidity would circumscribe it with a wall of defence against the encroachments of error.

13. Because attempts to enforce by legal sanctions, acts obnoxious to so great a proportion of Citizens, tend to enervate the laws in general, and to slacken the bands of Society. If it be difficult to execute any law which is not generally deemed necessary or salutary, what must be the case, where it is deemed invalid and dangerous? And what may be the effect of so striking an example of impotency in the Government, on its general authority?

14. Because a measure of such singular magnitude and delicacy ought not to be imposed, without the clearest evidence that it is called for by a majority of citizens, and no satisfactory method is yet proposed by which the voice of the majority in this case may be determined, or its influence secured. "The people of the respective counties are indeed requested to signify their opinion respecting the adoption of the Bill to the next Session of Assembly." But the representation must be made equal, before the voice either of the Representatives or of the Counties will be that of the people. Our hope is that neither of the former will, after due consideration, espouse the dangerous principle of the Bill. Should the event disappoint us, it will still leave us in full confidence, that a fair appeal to the latter will reverse the sentence against our liberties.

15. Because finally, "the equal right of every citizen to the free exercise of his Religion according to the dictates of conscience" is held by the same tenure with all our other rights. If we recur to its origin, it is equally the gift of nature; if we weigh its importance, it cannot be less dear to us; if we consult the "Declaration of those rights which pertain to the good people of Virginia, as the basis and foundation of Government," it is enumerated with equal solemnity, or rather studied emphasis. Either then, we must say, that the Will of the Legislature is the only measure of their authority; and that in the plenitude of this authority, they may sweep away all our fundamental rights; or, that they are bound to leave this particular right untouched and sacred: Either we must say, that they may controul the freedom of the press, may abolish the Trial by Jury, may swallow up the Executive and Judiciary Powers of the State; nay that they may despoil us of our very right of suffrage, and erect themselves into an independent and hereditary Assembly or, we must say, that they have no authority to enact into law the Bill under consideration. We the Subscribers say, that the General Assembly of this Commonwealth have no such authority: And that no effort may be omitted on our part against so dangerous an usurpation, we oppose to it, this remonstrance; earnestly praying, as we are in duty bound, that the Supreme Lawgiver of the Universe, by illuminating those to whom it is addressed, may on the one hand, turn their Councils from every act which would affront his holy prerogative, or violate the trust committed to them: and on the other, guide them into every measure which may be worthy of his blessing, may redound to their own praise, and may establish more firmly the liberties, the prosperity and the happiness of the Commonwealth.

Source: *The Founders' Constitution*, eds. Philip B. Kurland and Ralph Lerner (Chicago: University of Chicago Press, 1987), 5:82–84.

Appendix B

A Bill "Establishing a Provision for Teachers of the Christian Religion" by Patrick Henry, 1784

Whereas the general diffusion of Christian knowledge hath a natural tendency to correct the morals of men, restrain their vices, and preserve the peace of society, which cannot be effected without a competent provision for learned teachers, who may be thereby enabled to devote their time and attention to the duty of instructing such citizens, as from their circumstances and want of education, cannot otherwise attain such knowledge; and it is judged that such provision may be made by the Legislature, without counteracting the liberal principle heretofore adopted and intended to be preserved by abolishing all distinctions of preeminence amongst the different societies or communities of Christians;

Be it therefore enacted by the General Assembly, That for the support of Christian teachers, _____ per centum on the amount, or _____ in the pound on the amount, or _____ in the pound on the sum payable for tax on the property within this Commonwealth, is hereby assessed, and shall be paid by every person chargeable with the said tax at the time the same shall become due; and the Sheriffs of the several Counties shall have power to levy and collect the same in the same manner and under the like restrictions and limitations, as are or may be prescribed by the laws for raising the revenues of this State.

And be it enacted, That for every sum so paid, the Sheriff or Collector shall give a receipt, expressing therein to what society of Christians the person from whom he may receive the same shall direct the money to be paid, keeping a distinct account thereof in his books. The Sheriff of every County, shall, on or before the _____ day of _____ in every year, return to the Court, upon oath, two alphabetical lists of the payments to him made, distinguishing in columns opposite to the names of the persons who shall have paid the same, the society to which the money so paid was by them appropriated; and one column for the names where no appropriation shall be made. One of which lists, after being recorded in a book to be kept for that purpose, shall be filed by the Clerk in his office, the other shall by the Sheriff be fixed up in the Court-house, there to remain for the inspection of all concerned. And the Sheriff, after deducting five per centum for the collection, shall forthwith pay to such person or persons as shall be appointed to receive the same by the Vestry, Elders, or Directors, however denominated of each such society, the sum so stated to be due to that society; or in default thereof, upon the motion of such person or persons to the next or any succeeding Court, execution shall be awarded for the same against the Sheriff and his security, his and their executors or administrators; provided that ten days previous notice be given of such motion. And upon every such execution, the Officer serving the same shall proceed to immediate sale of the estate taken, and shall not accept of security for payment at the end of three months, nor to have the goods forthcoming at the day of sale, for his better direction wherein, the Clerk shall endorse upon every such execution that no security of any kind shall be taken.

And be it further enacted, That the money to be raised by virtue of this act, shall be by the Vestries, Elders, or Directors of each religious society, appropriated to a provision for a Minister or Teacher of the Gospel of their denomination, or the providing places of divine worship, and to none other use whatsoever; except in the denominations of Quakers and Menonists, who may receive what is collected from their members, and place it in their general fund, to be disposed of in a manner which they shall think best calculated to promote their particular mode of worship.

And be it enacted, That all sums which at the time of payment to the Sheriff or Collector may not be appropriated by the person paying the same, shall be accounted for with the Court in manner as by this Act is directed; and after deducting for his collection, the Sheriff shall pay the amount thereof (upon account certified by the Court to the Auditors of Public Accounts, and by them to the Treasurer) into the public Treasury, to be disposed of under the direction of the General Assembly, for the encouragement of seminaries of learning within the Counties whence such sums shall arise, and to no other use or purpose whatsoever.

Source: Thomas E. Buckley, S.J., *Church and State in Revolutionary Virginia, 1776–1787* (Charlottesville: University Press of Virginia, 1977), 188–89.

Appendix C

A Bill for Establishing Religious Freedom in Virginia by Thomas Jefferson, 1777

Well aware that the opinions and belief of men depend not on their own will, but follow involuntarily the evidence proposed to their minds; that Almighty God hath created the mind free, *and manifested his supreme will that free it shall remain by making it altogether insusceptible of restraint;* that all attempts to influence it by temporal punishments, or burthens, or by civil incapacitations, tend only to beget habits of hypocrisy and meanness, and are a departure from the plan of the holy author of our religion, who being lord both of body and mind, yet chose not to propagate it by coercions on either, as was in his Almighty power to do, *but to extend it by its influence on reason alone;* that the impious presumption of legislators and rulers, civil as well as ecclesiastical, who, being themselves but fallible and uninspired men, have assumed dominion over the faith of others, setting up their own opinions and modes of thinking as the only true and infallible, and as such endeavoring to impose them on others, hath established and maintained false religions over the greatest part of the world and through all time: That to compel a man to furnish contributions of money for the propagation of opinions which he disbelieves *and abhors,* is sinful and tyrannical; that even the forcing him to support this or that teacher of his own religious persuasion, is depriving him of the comfortable liberty of giving his contributions to the particular pastor whose morals he would make his pattern, and whose powers he feels most persuasive to righteousness; and is withdrawing from the ministry those temporary [temporal] rewards, which proceeding from an approbation of their personal conduct, are an additional incitement to earnest and unremitting labours for the instruction of mankind; that our civil rights have no dependance on our religious opinions, any more than [on] our opinions in physics or geometry; that therefore the proscribing any citizen as unworthy of the public confidence by laying upon him an incapacity of being called to offices of trust and emolument, unless he profess or renounce this or that religious opinion, is depriving him injuriously of those privileges and advantages to which, in common with his fellow citizens, he has a natural right; that it tends also[1] to corrupt the principles of that *very* religion it is meant to encourage, by bribing, with a monopoly of worldly honours and emoluments, those who will externally profess and conform to it; that though indeed these are criminal who do not withstand such temptation, yet neither are those innocent who lay the bait in their way; *that the opinions of men are not the object of civil government, nor under its jurisdiction;* that to suffer the civil magistrate to intrude his powers into the field of opinion and to restrain the profession or propagation of principles on supposition of their ill tendency is a dangerous falacy, which at once destroys all religious liberty, because he being of course judge of that tendency will make his opinions the rule of judgment, and approve or condemn the sentiments of others only as they shall square with or differ from his own; that it is time enough for the rightful purposes of civil government for its officers to interfere when principles break out into overt acts against peace and good order; and finally, that truth is great and will prevail if left to herself; that she is the proper and sufficient antagonist to error, and has nothing to fear from the conflict unless by human interposition disarmed of her natural weapons, free argument and debate; errors ceasing to be dangerous when it is permitted freely to contradict them.

We the General Assembly of Virginia do enact[2] that no man shall be compelled to frequent or support any religious worship, place, or ministry whatsoever, nor shall be enforced, restrained, molested, or burthened in his body or goods, nor shall otherwise suffer, on account of his religious opinions or belief; but that all men shall be free to profess, and by argument to maintain, their opinions in matters of religion, and that the same shall in no wise diminish, enlarge, or affect their civil capacities.

And though we well know that this Assembly, elected by the people for the ordinary purposes of legislation only, have no power to restrain the acts of succeeding Assemblies, constituted with powers equal to our own, and that therefore to declare this act [to be] irrevocable would be of no effect in

---

[1] The Act replaced "also" with "only." See Dreisbach, *Thomas Jefferson and the Wall of Separation Between Church and State*, 243n.3.

[2] The Act started with the paragraph: "Be it enacted by the General Assembly. . . ." Ibid., 243n.4.

law; yet we are free to declare, and do declare, that the rights hereby asserted are of the natural rights of mankind, and that if any act shall be hereafter passed to repeal the present or to narrow its operation, such act will be an infringement of natural right.

The italicized words were deleted during the October 1785 session of the Virginia General Assembly. According to Merrill D. Peterson, Jefferson initially drafted the bill sometime in 1777.[3] In 1779, the bill was debated in, but not adopted by, the Virginia House of Delegates. The bill was amended and then adopted by the Virginia General Assembly on January 16, 1786.

Source: Daniel L. Dreisbach, *Thomas Jefferson and the Wall of Separation between Church and State* (New York: New York University Press, 2002), 133–35.

[3] *The Portable Thomas Jefferson*, ed. Merrill D. Peterson (New York: Viking Penguin, 1975), 251.

Index